Smart Contracts and Comparative Law

Andrea Stazi

Smart Contracts and Comparative Law

A Western Perspective

Springer

IUSTITIAM COLIMUS
G. Giappichelli Editore

Andrea Stazi
Law
European University of Rome
Rome, Italy

National University of Singapore
Singapore, Singapore

ISBN 978-3-030-83239-1 ISBN 978-3-030-83240-7 (eBook)
https://doi.org/10.1007/978-3-030-83240-7

This Springer imprint is published by the registered company Springer Nature Switzerland AG.
The registered company address is: Gewerbestrasse 11, 6330 Cham, Switzerland

To Katerina and Giorgio, my beloved gifts

Contents

Chapter 1
Introduction: Contract Automation and "Smart Contracts" in Comparative Law

The incessant development and ubiquitous diffusion of information and communication technologies give rise to phenomena of considerable socio-economic and therefore legal significance.

Among these, contractual relationships are strongly affected by technological evolution, which provides new tools for negotiating, concluding, and executing contracts, with specific operating dynamics and unprecedented legal issues.

In this perspective, from a legal point of view, the contract-technology combination represents a topical issue for a comparative analysis, which provides the interpreter with an overall view of different local responses to common developments and problems deriving from the use of technology in contracts.

Technology creates new opportunities for socio-economic relations, commercial exchange and overcoming national borders, allowing to conclude and execute agreements more quickly regardless of the distance between the contracting parties. On the other hand, technology tests the legal institution of contract making it necessary to adapt it to immediate, transnational, automatic uses and to the legal issues deriving from them.

Furthermore, technology emerges as a tool for regulating the interests of the parties, sometimes considered an alternative to the contract and/or judicial intervention. The adage "code is law" proposed in doctrine since the nineties of the last century finds new strength today, with the development of technologies that seem to make possible the realization of that hypothesis.

In consideration of these developments, this book aims to analyze the evolution of the relationship between technology and contract, with particular regard to the profile of contractual automation as the *fil rouge* of the path, starting from the contract concluded automatically until today's "smart contracts" built on distributed ledger—blockchain technologies.

Contracts are essentially social institutions, not produced by a central authority but the results of the free and decentralized exercise of individual autonomy. In this context, the automatic execution of smart contracts, with the relative trend towards a reduced use of the legal system, is in line with the general phenomenon of the

A. Stazi, *Smart Contracts and Comparative Law*,
https://doi.org/10.1007/978-3-030-83240-7_1

increase in rules and private institutions which is giving rise to a gradual loss of relevance of state law.

Nowadays in trade practice, in addition to the now widespread standardization of the conditions drafted by one of the contracting parties, with the specific protections dictated in the various legal systems for the weak contracting parties, there is an increasing practice of "modularization" of the contractual texts, which are increasingly based on modules that legal advisors or contracting parties themselves assemble and customize according to their specific needs.

On these phenomena scholars highlight, on the one hand, the tendency towards the reception of the Anglo-Saxon model of the "self-sufficient" contract, also in virtue of the widespread use of the English language; on the other hand, the increasingly central role played by technology, which contributes to the global diffusion of contractual models through technological means.

This diffusion gives rise in practice to "techno-legal transplants", about which the need for a comparative approach aimed at identifying the regulation applicable to increasingly delocalized and automated cases and the coordination of the same is increasingly evident.

As regards the reaction of the legal systems to such phenomena, in the various legal systems today there seem to be forms of reaction to the same and to the relative disruption of the consolidated schemes which oscillate between the conscious acceptance, the unaware one, the adaptation of the practice and domestic law, and the refusal.

In this perspective, the renewed strength of the references to a leading role for the "techno-regulation" with respect to the legal system, together with the growing relevance of the computer scientists as editors of the code from which the techno-legal rules would derive, are screened under the lens of the comparative lawyer, in order to check their effective usefulness and efficacy, which seem existing when considered as an aid *secundum* or *praeter legem*, but not *contra legem* or *sine lege*.

Thus, the elements, pathologies, and classical remedies of contract law are reviewed and adapted with regard to the features and operational profiles of smart contracts. Through a comparative law approach, essentially from a Western perspective but including considerations of law & economics and legal process, the peculiarities of the elements, pathologies, and remedies in the context of smart contracts are examined, to identify the solutions through which the latter can be integrated and protected in the legal framework.

Chapter 2
Contract and Technology from Automatic to Telematic Contracts

2.1 *Liaisons dangereuses* Between Contract and Technology in a Comparative Perspective

The relationship between contract and technology and its implications for contract law are not a recent phenomenon. Bargaining has always been influenced at different levels using new techniques and advanced contracts with the development of modern forms of communication.[1]

Over a century has passed since the German doctrine, primarily with Auwers,[2] and a few years later the Italian doctrine, with Cicu and Scialoja,[3] began the exploration of the then futuristic relationships between automatic devices, private relations, and contractual stipulation.

Such authors traced the first steps of the subsequent long and still articulated path of analysis of the impact of the so-called automatic with respect to the *modus*

[1] See, for example: Monateri (2000), p. 530, who recalls that according to Roman law the *stipulatio* required that formalities be put in place, and they were carried out using technologies: a pair of scales and a piece of copper, a formula to pronounce and certain gestures to perform. Symbols, procedures, and technical objects imitated or replaced consent, then as today. See also: Landels (1978), p. 203, who recalls how almost 2000 years ago a Greek engineer and mathematician described a coin-operated vending machine to be inserted at the entrance of a temple which, in exchange for a piece of five drachmas, dispensed a small amount of water for ritual washing of the face and hands.

[2] See: Auwers (1891); Guenther (1892); Schels (1897); Schiller (1898); Ertel (1898); Neumond (1899).

[3] Cicu (1901); Scialoja (1902), pp. 150 ff. More recently, see among others: Gambino (1997); Delfini (2002); Sica and Stanzione (2002). In recent European doctrine, see: Schulze and Staudenmayer (2016); Grundmann and Hacker (2018).

A. Stazi, *Smart Contracts and Comparative Law*,
https://doi.org/10.1007/978-3-030-83240-7_2

operandi, and therefore to the taxonomy and evolution of the institution of the contract, its elements, and related events.[4]

The massive emergence of technology in the field of contracts and contract law has been interpreted primarily in terms of reducing transaction costs, since technology is instrumental in the formation of agreements more quickly, regardless of the distance between the contracting parties.[5]

The development of digital technology and telematics[6] has led to the emergence of new contractual typologies based on economic behaviors that go beyond weighting, to satisfy needs through exchanges characterized by ever greater speed, or often immediacy, and effectiveness.[7]

On the other hand, existing or adopted solutions have often been considered inadequate with respect to the real impact that the latest technologies have on the contract as a pillar of individual autonomy and on consensus as the fundamental core of the same.[8]

---

[4]With reference to the regulation of cyberspace and the so-called *lex informatica* proposed in the US doctrine as an extension of *lex mercatoria* to cyberspace, see among others: Marrella and Yoo (2007); Lessig (1999a); Reidenberg (1998); Johnson and Post (1996); Reed (2000). *Lex informatica* is seen as a natural extension of the *lex mercatoria* to cyberspace, a set of complementary tools for the regulation of online transactions through the establishment of technical standards, in addition to contractual rules. Like *lex mercatoria*, *lex informatica* is ultimately based on self-regulation. It is a system of customary rules or standards and technical standards developed by online users for internal use by members of the community. The system operates on a transnational level, regardless of national borders and laws; in this regard, see especially: Reidenberg (1996). Specifically about contracts, see: Easterbrook (1996), who said that approving special legislation for electronic bargaining would be like adopting an improbable "horse law"; Moringiello and Reynolds (2013), who found that the courts recognized that the legal problems posed by new technologies were no different from those presented in the previous century and, therefore, rejected attempts to change the traditional contract law. *Contra*: Lessig (1999b); Matwyshyn (2013); and in part, with a law & economics approach: Katz (2004), arguing that changes in the level of application of the law would be justified by the different way in which transaction costs emerge in electronic contexts compared to traditional ones. For the resilience of contract law, see e.g.: Kidd and Daugthrey Jr (2000); Sommer (2000).

[5]In this regard, see among others: Granieri (2017); Kalemi and Ndreka (2012); Want (2010).

[6]The term telematics derives from the Greek adverb "tele-" which means distant and from the suffix "-ema" which means functional element that gives shape to something. Thélème was also the imaginary abbey with which Gargantua, a character conceived by Francois Rabelais, French humanist of the sixteenth century, foreshadowed a world of complete freedom. Unlike all the others, it was an abbey without walls and external barriers: everyone could enter it, well received, someone could be lost. The concept of telematics, therefore, indicates a set of IT services offered and used, in real time, through a telecommunication network, which may act as communication tools between the parties. On the subject, one may also see: Gambino et al. (2019), pp. 2 ff.

[7]In this regard, see, *ex multis*: Kryczka (2005); Sammarco (2006), p. 73.

[8]See, among others: Granieri (2017), p. 2; Farnsworth (2006), pp. 900–901, who underlines that "the eminent position of contracts is also due to their central role for the ordering of market relations, especially in the heyday of liberalism, and to the symbolic importance of private agreements for the ideology of individual autonomy."

Contracts are primarily social institutions. As such, they are generally not a product of authority at the central level, but the result of the free exercise of individual autonomy at a decentralized level, which is accompanied by the liability provided for by the legal system.[9]

With this in mind, the consent of the parties is the mechanism that establishes their binding commitment and contract law has developed mainly by focusing on it, both as a meeting of wills at a given time and in space and as a promise based on a consideration.[10]

On a broader level, it is worth remembering that technology is a means that allows humanity to achieve certain goals.[11] In this light, technology is in principle the result of decentralized individual choices to solve problems, a feature that makes technology very close to contracts.

On the other hand, both contracts and technology are subject and exposed to the risk of centralization, since as decentralized private orders they can be controlled by a more restricted set of individuals and institutions, or become instruments of exercising substantially unilateral bargaining power of a part on the other.[12]

Thus, because of the use of IT and telematics for the conclusion of contracts, the parties bear an unprecedented risk factor—no longer, as in the past, dependent on the nature of the business or the reliability of the contracting parties—- but rather intimately connected to the means of concluding the contract.

The relation between technology and contract then requires a regulation, beyond the technical rules, capable of governing the relation between the appearance generated by the symbolic language of telematics and the substance of the economic relationship that is intended to be managed through the contract.[13]

In the broad debate on the matter, a point of reference can be identified in the fact that both the philosophers of science[14] and the legal scholars[15] agree in considering the notions of self-responsibility and protection of entrustment as guiding principles in the construction of the rules applicable to online relationships.

---

[9] See, e.g.: Sacco and De Nova (2016), pp. 15 ff. and 701, who emphasized that: "the law regulates the autonomy of the subject, and regulates it by using tools of autonomy and responsibility for its use." Regarding the authoritarian theory of the contract, see: Monateri (2017a).

[10] See again: Sacco and De Nova (2016), p. 335, who specify that the bilateral declaration of consent is not always necessary for the conclusion of the contract, in general the consent of the only party that undertakes is requested, and as for the party that buys, it is sufficient that it does not refuse; Granieri (2017), pp. 3–4.

[11] Thus, see: Arthur (2009), p. 27.

[12] Consider, for example, the unilateral arrangement of terms and conditions in standardized contracts and the systems for managing digital rights. See again: Granieri (2017), p. 4.

[13] See: Gemma (2007).

[14] See among others: Jonas (1979).

[15] See, e.g.: Sacco and De Nova (2016), p. 127, according to whom as a general rule the responsibility of who appears to be the sender, combined with the legitimate expectation of the recipient, guarantee the integrity of the contractual case.

The process of depersonalization of relationships, and the consequent objectification of the contract, already matured with mass bargaining, have their fulfillment in telematic negotiation, even more when it operates through electronic agents, that is, automatic programs which conclude contracts between machines based on preventive instructions but without individual control.[16]

This book analyzes those forms of bargaining, gradually from automatic to telematics, up to today's smart contracts, which have increasingly been responsible for the evolution of the model of a progressive formation of contractual consent.

In such a model, the perplexities due to a lesser reflection on the purchase have been overcome through a reduction in transaction costs and a greater possibility of information regarding the subject of the exchange.[17]

The ambition of nation states to regulate trade has long clashed with its extraterritorial vocation. In this sense, technology has been instrumental in facilitating transnational communication, and online bargaining is one of the most significant challenges for the authority of the states.

Digital technologies, in fact, allow exchanges without geographical limits and can be used to relocate negotiating activities, also in relation to applicable law and jurisdiction. Furthermore, national laws may even be harmful to electronic bargaining, as regulatory fragmentation can increase transaction costs and limit the benefits of technology to commerce.[18]

In this perspective, it is possible to understand the regulatory efforts of the states and, first, the initiatives of model laws that the United Nations Commission for International Commercial Law has undertaken in the last decades. Among them, the controversial issue of the place of conclusion of the contract is of particular importance.

Therefore, Art. 15 of the UNCITRAL Model Law on electronic commerce,[19] and the so-called EC Regulation Rome I on the law applicable to contractual obligations,[20] identify the solution in the address of the proposer. In the case of contracts concluded between consumers and professionals, on the other hand, the Rome I

[16]The use of an electronic agent, which, through complex processing mechanisms, leads to the determination of an artificial, predetermined negotiating will, even if, with the technological evolution, potentially increasingly differentiated from that of the user—introduces a path alternative beyond the control of the party in the traditional production process and manifestation of the will to negotiate. In this case, the results of the bargaining are not always predictable upstream, and it cannot be excluded that the electronic agent will complete the contracts at least in part unwanted or beyond the expectations of the user of the program.

[17]See, e.g.: Gambino (1997); Id. (1999).

[18]Granieri (2017), p. 5.

[19]UNCITRAL Model Law of Electronic Commerce, adopted on 12 June 1996, available at: http://www.uncitral.org/uncitral/en/uncitral_texts/electronic_commerce/1996Model.html, Art. 15, according to which "unless otherwise agreed between the originator and the addressee, a data message is deemed to be sent to the place where the originator has its place of business, and is deemed to be received at the place where the addressee has its place of business."

[20]Regulation (EC) no. 593/2008 of the European Parliament and of the Council of 17 June 2008 on the law applicable to contractual obligations (Rome I) (OJ 4.7.2008 L 177/1).

Regulation provides for the application of the law of the place of residence or activity of the consumer "by any means," so including electronic means.[21]

Moreover, the issue relating to the place of conclusion of the contract is not a decisive factor in the choice of the law applicable to the relationship between parties from different countries.

Pursuant to the 1980 Rome International Convention on the law applicable to contractual obligations,[22] and today to the Rome I Regulation,[23] the alternative resides or in the preventive agreement of the contracting parties on the applicable national law, or, in the absence of choice, the criterion of the "closest connection" has been provided, to be determined based on the characteristic performance and the usual location.[24]

Another consequence, sometimes overlooked, of these first considerations is that the interaction between technology and contract and its implications for contract law are necessarily influenced by the approaches adopted by legislators, jurisprudence, doctrine, etc. of the different legal systems.

Therefore, with respect to the analysis of the many unceasingly emerging issues in the relation between technological evolution and the institution of the contract, by virtue of three main considerations, it is necessary to adopt an approach inspired by the comparative method.

First, the Internet and therefore the contracts that are put in place through it are—at least potentially—transnational in nature, and so they require a vision that goes beyond the state borders. As already mentioned, the instruments of international private law aimed at resolving the conflict between specific rules and national legal

[21] Jurisdictional issues are dealt with in Regulation (EC) no. 44/2001 of the Council of 22 December 2000 on jurisdiction and the recognition and enforcement of judgments in civil and commercial matters (OJ 16.1.2001 L 12/1), replaced by Regulation (EU) 1215/2012 of European Parliament and of the Council of 12 December 2012 on jurisdiction and the recognition and enforcement of judgments in civil and commercial matters (OJ 21.12.2012 L 351/1). Also, Art. 17, par. 1, lett. a), of Regulation 1215/2012, corresponding to Article 15 (1) (c) of regulation 44/2001, refers to "any means." On the other hand, the relocation of contracts through digital technologies can also be a way to escape bans and trade in illicit objects. This is the case of counterfeit goods, or the black market of illegal drugs, etc. which uses the so-called deep web, such as the Silk Road platform closed by the FBI in 2013.

[22] Rome Convention of 19 June 1980 on contractual obligations, which entered into force on 1 April 1991.

[23] Regulation (EC) no. 593/2008 of the European Parliament and of the Council of 17 June 2008 on the law applicable to contractual obligations (Rome I), OJ L 177, 4.7.2008. The Rome I Regulation has been transposed into the European Union the Rome Convention, an international convention adopted by the Member States of the then European Community. See: Ferrari and Leible (2009); Garcimartìn Alférez (2017).

[24] Rome I Regulation, Art. 4, par. 1–4 (Rome Convention, Articles 3–4), according to which the contract is governed by the law chosen by the parties. The choice must be expressed or be reasonably certain by the provisions of the contract or by the circumstances, and in the absence of a choice, the country is presumed to be the country in which the party providing the characteristic performance usually resides or, if it is a company, a legal person or an association, the place where the headquarters or organization is located. See: Volker (2011); Tang (2008).

systems can in any case be used to identify the applicable law.[25] In this way, incidentally,[26] the recurrent hypotheses of the existence of a peculiar "cybernetic law" in which "code is law" can also be set aside.[27]

On the other hand, this makes clear at the same time the need, also in substantial terms, for a common regulation[28] and/or national rules that are clearly identifiable and accepted. They should be based on the specifically applicable principles,[29] with a view to preserve the function of protection of the law that only the options of the *lex mercatoria* or the computer code obviously cannot guarantee.

In addition, the comparative method allows, on the one hand, a broader reflection on the scope of the individual rules that affect the subject on several sides; on the other, to fully consider the relevance on further disciplines in addition to the law: computer science, sociology, linguistics, economics, etc.[30]

Finally, the rules of electronic commerce have traditionally developed in a series of institutes which derive their legal nature more from the spontaneous, or necessary, adhesion of the users of the telematic network, than from their own legal constraint, although over time increasing options for co-regulation or direct regulation are being developed in different legal systems.[31]

Technology and contract, therefore, represent a binomial that requires a comparative analysis, which provides a view of the different answers to the questions posed by the use of technology in negotiation.

In contract law, the civil law and common law systems still appear to be the most relevant ones in terms of principles, rules, and cases. A comparative study on the subject, then, must start from the lines drawn by these systems.[32]

2.2 Taxonomy from Automatic to Telematic Contracts

The classification of contracts represents the hermeneutic operation which, beyond the terminological formalisms, is aimed at offering the interpreter as much as possible the detailed systematic nature of the broad contractual phenomenology.

[25] See also the Uniform Commercial Code of the United States, which allows the parties to choose the applicable law within the limits of its relationship with the contract.

[26] Referring wider to the next chapters.

[27] In this sense, see e.g.: Burnstein (1996); Rubin et al. (1995).

[28] See e.g.: Bonell (2006); Lambert (1900).

[29] Consider the case of the principles applicable in contracts with consumers, expressly protected by the Rome Convention with regard to the choice of applicable law.

[30] In this regard, see *ex multis*: Michaels (2016); Spamann (2015); Reitz (1998); one may also see: Stazi (2015), pp. 258 ff.

[31] See, among others: Winn (2010).

[32] In the same perspective, see: Granieri (2017), pp. 1 ff.

This can be done by grouping together existing and recurring models in practice in legal categories that may contain common principles and elements, and identify the regulation applicable to the chosen model.[33]

According to scholars who pointed out the relevance of economic analysis of contract law, the contract, due to the numerous interests that flow into it, can no longer be traced back to a mere legal framework, rather having to be related to an economic operation, understood as the set of both the interests pursued and the negotiation activities carried out by the parties.[34]

The economic operation allows, in such a dynamic vision of the act of private autonomy, to reveal the intertwining of the underlying interests, which regulation provides at the same time a hermeneutic tool useful both for identifying the prevailing contractual type and for assessing the merit of the protection of the agreements adopted between the parties.[35]

This reconstruction led, therefore, to the definition of contractual categories—always of a legal nature but with the "qualifying contribution" of the economic operation criterion—such as those of the banking, financial, insurance, IT contracts, or, subjectively, of business contracts, consumer contracts, etc.[36]

As far as it is relevant here, contracts concluded using automatic devices first emerged. In them, a professional contracting party prepares equipment that allows the customer to insert payment means into the machine, or to make a payment through it. This operation makes it possible to appropriate goods or a legitimizing title, or to enjoy a service.[37]

The evolution of information technology and the digitalization of socio-economic relations,[38] then, have contributed to the development of increasingly articulated and complex contractual relationships, which have forced interpreters to deepen the issue of the relation between automation and contract and of the legal classification of electronic contracts.[39]

---

[33] See, among others: Mouzas and Furmston (2013); Monateri (2017b).

[34] See for example: Shavell (2003); Brousseau and Glachant (2002); Mattei and Pardolesi (1991); Kronman and Posner (1979).

[35] See, specifically: Lambertiere (1983).

[36] See, e.g.: Hermalin et al. (2007).

[37] The tenderer prepares the appliance, the execution of the services and the implementation of her and the client's rights, and the client performs her performance and implements her right. There are no declarations, but other facts: implementations and preparations of the same. The exclusion of individual negotiation and bargaining, the fixing of the price and the unchangeability of the proposal, however, do not contradict the essential characteristics of the contract and agreement. see: Sacco and De Nova (2016), p. 333; Cicu (1901); Auwers (1891).

[38] With regard to which one may see: Stazi (2019b); Gambino and Stazi (2020), pp. XI ff.

[39] See among others: Brownsword (2020); Mik (2020); Kirillova et al. (2020); Wilkinson (2020); Gambino and Stazi (2021).

Thus, in recent years, new categories have been suggested, such as telematic, digital, or cybernetic contracts.[40] Such categories actually do not identify a unitary type of negotiation, but a heterogeneous range of models, held together by specific common denominators—subjective qualification of the contracting parties, methods of conclusion of the contract, provision of services, or enjoyment of the assets—but they do not come to outline a specific regulatory framework for those new contracts.

Telematic contracts, which are characterized by the use of the electronic means to put distant parts in contact, in particular, are an interesting category with concrete regulatory impact. With reference to them, therefore, the analysis focused on their different characteristics and operational profiles, and identified specific subcategories.

A first general distinction is between telematic contracts in a broad sense, characterized by the provision of a service electronically, and those in the strict sense, in which the bargain is formed thanks to the electronic impulses exchanged between the terminals connected to distance.[41]

A key classification of telematic contracts is based on the subjective profile, distinguishing the business-to-business contracts relating to the negotiations between professional operators, the business to consumer for relationships between professional operators and consumers, and consumer-to-consumer relationships between private entities outside their professional activities.[42]

However, this classification was linked to statutory schemes that the new commercial techniques have overcome. The provisions aimed at protecting the "weak part" in the regulation of electronic commercial relations are, in fact, not anchored merely to the subjective condition of the part itself, consumer or professional, but they are based on the objective conditions in which the parties place themselves in such relationships.[43]

Another reconstruction, of French origin, proposes a subdivision of the telematic contracts into three heterogeneous classes. The first one is characterized by the conclusion of the agreement outside the system and the execution of the contract through the terminals. In the second, the conclusion of an agreement through the IT medium and its execution happens outside the telematic network. In the third case, both the conclusion and the execution take place online, e.g., for the circulation of rights relating to intangible assets and IT services.[44]

---

[40] That is, concluded and possibly modified through electronic agents. Regarding these categories, see e.g.: Kirillova et al. (2020); Stazi (2019a, b), pp. 11 ff.; Finocchiaro (2003).

[41] French doctrine lists electronic contracts and "*conclus et exécutés par la télématique (par exemple, procédures de réservation électronique); – conclus para la télématique mais exécutés en dehors de cette technique (par exemple procédures de commande par terminal); – conclus en dehors de la télématique mais exécutés par elle (par exemple contrats d'accès aux banques de données)*": Linant De Bellefonds and Hollande (1988), p. 141.

[42] In a comparative perspective, see e.g.: Pappas (2020); Tang (2015); Wang (2014).

[43] One may see also: Stazi (2012); Stazi and Mula (2012).

[44] In this perspective, see: Le Tourneau (2006).

On the procedures for concluding electronic contracts functional to electronic commerce, two main options for expressing consent are identified: (a) contracts where consent is expressed with a "click", the so-called point and click on an offer contained in a website or more recently in an app on mobile devices;[45] (b) contracts in which consent is expressed by email.[46]

In the context of contracts concluded via access to a website or app, according to a part of the doctrine, the completion of the agreement and therefore the *Idealtypus* of the electronic contract, consists in completing a form including the typing of the card numbers, the buyer's credit, the receipt of which by the offeror is communicated to the oblate by an acknowledgment of receipt.[47]

In the contract concluded by email, on the other hand, by virtue of the completion of the agreement through an effective dialogue with mutual communication, the principle of receptivity is followed, tempered by the principle of effective knowledge.[48]

2.3 Legal Issues and Regulation of Online Exchanges

The characteristic common to all forms of regulatory intervention in the field of electronic negotiation at national and international level was the idea that there were legal obstacles at national level that would have prevented the full exploitation of the opportunities offered by electronic bargaining, especially in transactions involving foreign subjects.

The need to occasionally solve some aspects and to facilitate the use of technology for bargaining explains why in most cases the legal systems have adopted

---

[45] The term "app" is an abbreviated form of "application", which in practice is used especially with regard to mobile apps for mobile phones, tablets, etc. Most of the applications are found in real virtual stores called app stores. The contracts concluded through the app appear similar to the hypothesis of the contract concluded through access to the website, since also in this case it is a form of communication one to many and not one to one as in the contracts via email.

[46] These typologies can be framed in the inter-absent relationships. However, they have at least an unusual aspect with respect to them, in that the parties do not follow the normal logical-chronological sequence between the moment of processing the communication and that of sending the reply, or at least this sequence is strongly compressed. So, while in the contact *de visu* the assignment that follows an announcement can be easily corrected, according to canons of reasonableness, in telematics the screen of the program does not allow to easily identify neither the professional quality of the offeror nor the legal binding nature of the commitment undertaken; see: Sasso (2016).

[47] In this perspective, the spending of the credit card manifests the willingness to legally bind the purchaser, and has real efficacy involving the conclusion of the contract for the beginning of execution, according to a unilateral contract scheme; see: Gambino (1997), pp. 138 ff.

[48] Provided, e.g., in the civil law systems at Art. 1335 of the Italian Civil Code and in the common law systems in the so-called mailbox rule; in this regard, see *Amplius*, below in the following paragraph.

fragmented solutions rather than holistic approaches. The existing rules were changed, or new rules were introduced, only to the extent that it was necessary to facilitate trading online.[49]

At the same time, the telematic sphere has been widely considered by private and public actors as naturally predisposed to essentially self-regulation or co-regulation interventions, inspired by a previous scheme renamed "the new *lex mercatoria*".[50]

On the regulations applicable to online exchanges, first, the mechanisms of international private law, aimed at resolving the conflict between rules of different legal systems, such as the Rome Convention, are also to be considered operating in this context.[51]

Furthermore, the opportunity to pursue the greatest possible uniformity to facilitate the dissemination and transnational management of these relations, in identifying the applicable law, leads to a reflection on the scope of the different rules that affect the matter, with particular regard to that common core that from Western contractual systems turns to international rules on telematic contracts.[52]

On cases governed by rules of international conventions, it is possible to trace principles already rooted in the rules of individual states. So, for example, the Vienna Convention on international contracts between businesses[53] provides the obligation to repay the undue payment,[54] the right of retention by the purchaser,[55] the prohibition to act against *factum proprium*,[56] and the duty to limit the damage.[57]

In the case of *vacatio* with respect to a conventional rule, a reference to national laws is made through the options to: (a) deduce the general principles converging on

[49] See: Granieri (2017), p. 5; Savirimuthu (2005), p. 116.

[50] Starting from the standards for electronic communications, from the domain names of the Internet, etc. See, among others: Reidenberg (1998), pp. 553 ff. The different opinions on the intensity of deregulation in cyberspace go as far as anarchy, as argued by one of the leading Internet experts; see: Barlow (1996). Of particular interest are the so-called open-source communities, as a new private order but interdependent with public legislation; see: Marrella and Yoo (2007). See also, regarding online contracts between consumers: Guadamuz Gonzàlez (2003).

[51] See among others: Ruhl (2020).

[52] As an alternative to the *lex mercatoria*, Rubino Sammartano (1987) considers the application of the common core of the laws relating to the two parts.

[53] United Nations Convention on Contracts for the International Sale of Goods, Vienna, 11 April 1980.

[54] As an obligation to pay for goods received in excess in the absence of "refuse to take delivery of the excess quantity" (Art. 52.2 CISG).

[55] Specifically "to retain them (the goods) until he has been reimbursed his reasonable expenses by the seller" (Art. 86.1 CISG).

[56] See the references to the "observance of good faith" in the interpretation of the Convention (Art. 7.1) and to the "reliance" pursuant to Art. 16.2 and 29.2 of the Convention itself. In doctrine, also for application uncertainties, see: Bonell (1987).

[57] On this point, see Articles 74–77 CISG.

the matter in question from the relevant national laws; (b) integrate the content of the *lex mercatoria* with uniform material laws.[58]

Then, there is the hypothesis of the general principles of private international law, or of the so-called uses accepted in the practice of exchanges, as a rule deduced from the elaborations of legal operators, to which relevance has been given in arbitration decisions in cases of regulatory gap of the international legal system.[59]

Moreover, the widespread choice of the parts of the *lex contractus* shows the tendency not to recall non-exclusive principles, which operate rather in an integrative function, where the decision-making body itself assesses their application to the present case more equitably.[60]

Although in recent years there has been growing worldwide interest in the regulation and facilitation of online contractual relationships, the main actors remain the common law and civil law systems, primarily the United States and the European Union, which have followed different approaches in the regulation but with solutions to specific problems that sometimes coincide (for example regarding the formation of contracts or the validity of digital signatures).

The different systems, however, have been influenced to some extent by the action of international organizations and agencies.[61]

Internationally, one of the first signs of regulatory activism came from the United Nation Commission on International Trade Law—UNCITRAL, which in 1996 adopted a Model Law on electronic commerce.[62] The Model Law of 1996, with the subsequent amendment of 1998, was the first case in which a legislative text adopted the principles of non-discrimination, technological neutrality, and functional equivalence, which subsequently inspired many countries.[63]

A further Model Law on electronic signatures was adopted in 2001 to allow and facilitate the use of the electronic signature by introducing equivalence criteria between it and the manual one.[64]

---

[58] Regarding the first see: Lando (1985). *Contra*: Mustill (1987). For the second, see: Gaillard (1995). *Contra*: Goldman (1987), believing that only non-state rules should be part of the *lex mercatoria*.

[59] See, among others: Bonell (2009).

[60] See e.g.: Gambino (1997), pp. 94 ff.

[61] In this regard, see: Granieri (2017), pp. 6–7.

[62] UNCITRAL Model Law on Electronic Commerce, cit. In this regard, see e.g.: Hermann (1999).

[63] A complete list of the countries that have implemented the Model Law and the subsequent Convention can be found in: UNCITRAL, Promoting confidence in electronic commerce: legal issues on international use of electronic authentication and signature methods, Wien, 2009, p. 38. In particular, the work of UNCITRAL formed the basis for United States legislation; see: Poggi (2000) p. 238; Winn and Haubold (2002), p. 578.

[64] UNCITRAL Model Law on Electronic Signatures, adopted on 5 July 2001, available at: http://www.uncitral.org/uncitral/en/uncitral_texts/electronic_commerce/2001Model_signatures.html.

Subsequently, the Model Law of 1996 and its principles represented the reference point for the Convention on the use of electronic communications in international contracts, adopted by the United Nations General Assembly in 2005.[65]

The strategy of the editors of the UNCITRAL legislation was that of an approach based on technological neutrality, providing only legislative criteria to establish a generic functional equivalence between traditional manual and electronic signatures.

In this way, a change in the technological paradigm would not have made the regulation obsolete. These first legal sources at international level represented a guide for states to adapt their internal laws, with a view to achieving a certain level of uniformity regarding cross-border transactions.[66]

2.4 The Regulatory Framework in the European Union

The European Union and the United States have followed original, and only partially convergent, approaches which have also been influenced by the institutional peculiarities of each legal system. The most obvious difference in the regulatory approaches of the European Union and the United States lies in the aims of the regulation, which in the EU is inspired by the goal of creating an internal market.[67]

The European institutions believed that the transactional opportunities offered by the use of technology in cross-border exchanges could be instrumental to this objective, but to this end, at the same time, it was necessary to support private autonomy.[68]

Furthermore, since the internal market is an area where consumers are expected to receive a high level of protection in commercial transactions,[69] the European

[65] United Nations Convention on the Use of Electronic Communications in International Contracts, adopted on 23 November 2005 and entered into force on 1 March 2013, available at: https://www.uncitral.org/pdf/english/texts/electcom/06-57452_Ebook.pdf. In this regard, see: Boss and Kilian (2008); Martin (2008). The Convention was deemed necessary to overcome a gap in the Convention on the international sale of goods, so that it could also be applied to electronic transactions; its Article 13 referred to "writing" including telegram and telex, but not other more advanced tools. See: Hill (2003); Smith (2007).

[66] In this sense, see again: Granieri (2017), p. 7.

[67] See, among others: Poggi (2000) p. 248.

[68] See: Winn and Bix (2006); Kierkegaard (2007). According to Winn and Haubold (2002), pp. 568 f., the legislative or self-regulatory approach inspired by *laissez faire* in the United States and the more rigorous regulatory approach of the European Union are also partly due to the different approach to innovation, enthusiastic in the United States and more ambivalent in the European Union.

[69] See Art. 114, point 3, of the Treaty on the Functioning of the European Union. This provision is also considered the legal basis for the adoption of the Common European Sales Law, although some Member States have raised concerns about its adequacy.

regulation about online contracts is largely focused, although not exhausted, on consumer protection.[70]

Consumer transactions are separate from those between businesses, while in both cases there must be consistency with the goal of market integration and with fundamental rights, such as the protection of personal data, etc.

In such a context—even institutional with various Directorates General of the European Commission and other institutions competent on the various aspects—the regulatory approach remains fragmented, with the absence of a general framework in national legislation and with a multiplication of sources at the expense of the unitary category of the contract.[71]

In the United States, common law has shown flexibility in addressing issues arising from digital technologies, including those caused by consumer inexperience and vulnerability.[72]

The solutions adopted according to this approach, on the other hand, in some cases—such as on the protection of privacy—have not been considered sufficient by the European Union for the services and/or relationships involving European consumers.[73]

European e-contract legislation is made up of five specific directives and a set of rules contained in other directives or regulations. The first is the so-called E-commerce Directive.[74] The second is the Electronic signature Directive.[75] There are also two other recent Directives on contracts for the supply of digital content or services and on certain aspects of contracts for the sale of goods.[76]

---

[70] European contract law is partial in many aspects and has led to the fact that national laws have lost their unitary character in contract matters. In this regard, see: Kotz (2017); Rutgers and Sirena (2015).

[71] See: Winn and Bix (2006); p. 181; Martin (2008), p. 500. Regarding the relevance of the process of formation and application of the rules in comparative law, see: Hart Jr. and Sacks (1994); Hart Jr. and Wechsler (2009); Rubin (1996); one may also refer to: Stazi (2015), pp. 263 ff.

[72] In this sense, see: Moringiello and Reynolds (2013), pp. 455–456.

[73] Leading to the reform of the US-EU Safe Harbor Privacy Principles in favor of the new EU-US Privacy Shield; regarding which see e.g.: Castets-Renard (2018); Schwartz and Peifer (2017).

[74] Directive 2000/31/EC of the European Parliament and of the Council of 8 June 2000 relating to certain legal aspects of information society services, in particular electronic commerce, in the internal market (the 'Electronic Commerce Directive'), OJ 17.7.2000 L 178/1. The Directive is currently under review through the Proposal for a Regulation of the European Parliament and of the Council on a Single Market for Digital Services (Digital Services Act) and amending Directive 2000/31/EC, COM/2020/825 final.

[75] Directive 1999/93/EC of the European Parliament and of the Council of 13 December 1999 concerning a Community framework for electronic signatures, OJ 19.1.2000 L 13/12.

[76] Respectively: Directive (EU) 2019/770 of the European Parliament and of the Council of 20 May 2019 on certain aspects of contracts for the supply of digital content and digital services, and Directive (EU) 2019/771 of the European Parliament and of the Council, of 20 May 2019, relating to certain aspects of contracts for the sale of goods, which amends regulation (EU) 2017/2394 and directive 2009/22/EC, and which repeals directive 1999/44/EC, both in OJ 22.5.2019 L 136.

The rest of the framework includes existing regulations applicable also to electronic trading, including in particular the Directive on contracts negotiated away from business[77] premises, the Unfair Contract Terms Directive,[78] and the Directive on distance contracts.[79]

To consolidate the acquis least referred to, then, Directive 2011/83/EU on consumer rights[80], first, aimed at the objective of high consumer protection and the functioning of the internal market, but it also introduced an extension of the deadline for withdrawal, the possibility of exercising the withdrawal through a standard form, and the applicability of the withdrawal to online auctions.[81]

Lastly, Directive 2019/2161, so-called Omnibus, pursued the objective to strengthen consumer protection through increased transparency measures, extension of consumer rights and increased powers of enforcement (also updating among others the Unfair Contract Terms Directive and Directive 2011/83/EU). The E-commerce Directive 2000/31/EC had a wider scope than the regulation of telematic contracts. It aimed to remove obstacles and created the internal market for information society services. This formula included, but does not exhausted, electronic bargaining.[82]

---

[77] Council Directive 85/577/EEC of 20 December 1985 for the protection of consumers in the event of contracts negotiated away from business premises, OJ 31.12.1985, L 372/31.

[78] Council Directive 93/13/EEC of 5 April 1993 concerning unfair terms in contracts concluded with consumers, OJ 21.4.1993, L 95/29. For an overview and on the impact of the directive on the harmonization of the regulation of consumer contracts and on online contracts, see among others: Maxeiner (2003), p. 131; Winn and Bix (2006), pp. 184 ff.

[79] Directive 97/7/EC of the European Parliament and of the Council of 20 May 1997 concerning the protection of consumers in respect of distance contracts, OJ 4.6.1999, L 144/19. In distance contracts, the seller surprises the consumer with a commercial proposal that the latter does not have the time to carefully evaluate and compare with others on the market. To this situation of information imbalance and insufficient attention to the negotiating object, the legislator intended to set a limit by recognizing the consumer's right to be informed with more details, preventive and contextual to the stipulation, as well as a right to repentance, or *ius poenitendi*, consisting of the right to unilaterally withdraw from the contract entered into. In the cases of e-commerce, in addition to the surprise factor mentioned above, there are also the difficulties arising from the lack of familiarity of the user with the use of technological tools. For this reason, other specific and peculiar electronic commerce are added to the information burdens of distance contracts, in this case to protect the user—weaker party.

[80] Directive 2011/83/EU of the European Parliament and of the Council of 25 October 2011 on consumer rights, amending Council Directive 93/13/EEC and Directive 1999/44/EC of the European Parliament and of the Council and which repeals Council Directive 85/577/EEC and Directive 97/7/EC of the European Parliament and of the Council, OJ 22.11.2011 L 304/64.

[81] In this regard, see: Finocchiaro (2003).

[82] Directive cited, Art. 1. An information society service is any service normally provided for remuneration, remotely, electronically, by electronic equipment for processing and storing data, and at the individual request of a recipient of a service. See: directive 2000/31/EC, art. 2, lett. a) and recital 17; EU Directive 2015/1535 of the European Parliament and of the Council of 9 September 2015, which provides for an information procedure in the field of technical regulations and rules relating to information society services, Art. 1, par. 1, lett. b).

Contract law in Europe remains a sectoral discipline, which is based on national contract laws.[83] Articles 9–11 of the Directive refer to the conclusion of the contract, providing for the general requirement that Member States must ensure that their systems allow for the conclusion of contracts by electronic means.[84]

Since the Internet makes it particularly easy to conceal one's identity, and to guarantee the awareness of the contractual negotiation, the EU legislator has introduced multiple information obligations for the providers of information society services, to be fulfilled in a clear, complete, and unambiguous way, regardless of whether the recipient acts for professional or non-professional purposes.[85]

The information must be provided before the order is sent by the recipient,[86] and the provisions do not apply when contracts are concluded exclusively through the exchange of emails or equivalent individual communications.[87]

On the clauses and general conditions of the contract unilaterally prepared and proposed to the recipient, Art. 10, paragraph 3 of the Directive is limited to providing that they must be made available in a way that allows them to be memorized and reproduced.

The requirement can be considered fulfilled with the activation of a hypertext link that introduces a screen where the conditions are represented, or with the insertion of the same in a screen prior to the provision of consent.[88] The European Court of Justice has deemed it sufficient, so that electronic communication can offer the same guarantees, even evidentiary, that it is possible to save and print the information before the conclusion of the contract, regardless of whether the contracting party actually takes care of the conservation of the contract.[89]

---

[83] And, in this sense, it adopts an approach similar to that of the United States with the UETA and the E-Sign, on which reference is made below in the following paragraph.

[84] See among others: Winn and Haubold (2002), p. 574.

[85] In this regard, see: Finocchiaro (2003); Riefa (2009), pp. 35 ff.; Melison (2009).

[86] The European legislator uses the term "order", technical with respect to contract law. Its possible meaning is both the offer and the invitation to negotiate, and the final choice has been left to national legislation. Regarding the possible confusion caused by the use of terminology, justified by the need to reconcile civil law and common law, in the absence of a sort of common vocabulary, see: Riefa (2009), p. 30.

[87] See Articles 10.4 and 11.3. Since the Directive does not provide for a specific sanction for violation of the information duties pursuant to Art. 10, it is left to the contract law of the Member States to assess whether an agreement has been formed on the basis of the information actually made available by the service provider; see: Hillman (2006), p. 854, argued that a possible side effect of mandatory disclosure is not the increase in the cost to sellers, which is marginal and would be passed on to consumers, but the application of terms that would otherwise have been deemed unreasonable under the doctrine of the procedural unconscionability, because they are made accessible to consumers *ex ante* and cannot be considered surprising.

[88] This does not apply to bargaining via email, where specific individual communication will be required.

[89] EU Court of Justice, Jaouad El Majdoub c. CarsOnTheWeb.Deutschland GmbH, 21 May 2015, case no. C-322/14.

The "point and click" can also be considered suitable in approving the unfair clauses, where the contracting party proceeds in advance with her own identification that allows the unequivocal attribution of the negotiating behavior to the same. On abusive clauses towards consumers, then, the online offer actually acts according to predetermined algorithms upstream, so the notion of negotiation, as an activity aimed at defining the content of a clause, must be reduced to a selection operation among the options provided.[90]

Regarding the subsequent obligation of the provider to send the recipient of the service a receipt of the order provided for in Art. 11 of the Directive, it is not an element of the process of formation of the electronic contract, which on the contrary must be understood, at that time, already completed. Rather, it fulfills the function of summarizing the content in a synthetic way to the user, regardless of the subjective quality of consumer or professional,[91] the terms of the deal.[92]

The compliance with the disclosure obligations set out in the Directive is not only a tool to increase the certainty of online exchanges, but it also produces effects on the proceduralization of the agreement.

Thus, for the agreement to be considered valid, it will be necessary that the information burdens required by the directive have been fulfilled. This, in accordance with the principle of accountability, which provides the duty to account for the actions taken by the subject and her ability to certify compliance with the regulatory provisions.[93]

To identify the most adequate rules for correct information of users by service providers, according to the different product areas of activity, as well as with a view to increasing users' confidence in electronic commerce, Art. 16 of the Directive formulates the invitation to business, professional, and consumer associations or organizations to promote the adoption of codes of conduct.

With this invitation, in a space that tends to be free and governed mainly by technical and self-regulatory rules, the so-called *netiquette*, the EU legislator seems to acknowledge the limited usefulness of state regulatory interventions, structurally linked to the territory, and therefore ineffective towards a phenomenon by nature "a-territorial" and, consequently, "a-jurisdictional".

---

[90] See e.g.: Gemma (2007), pp. 276 ff.

[91] Except, only in contracts between professionals, that they have expressly waived it.

[92] This provision in fact makes sense only for the so-called indirect e-commerce, in which the execution of the contract is deferred. On the contrary, in the direct e-commerce the order confirmation is simultaneous with the execution of the provider's obligation.

[93] As regards negotiation fairness, then, the recent adoption of Regulation (EU) 2019/1150 of the European Parliament and of the Council of 20 June 2019 on promoting fairness and transparency for business users of online intermediation services, is also relevant. The Regulation, in fact, places operators who provide them with specific transparency obligations on distribution channels and related affiliate programs, as well as on ownership, control of intellectual property rights and the parameters that determine positioning (see below for further details).

The result is a model based on a duplication of regulatory sources, in which state legislation offers the general framework and the network operators insert detailed rules according to a self-regulation or co-regulation procedure.[94]

Directive 1999/93 on electronic signatures, then, is aimed at allowing contracting parties to use e-signature for the conclusion of contracts. On the effects side, a distinction is introduced between electronic signature and advanced electronic signature.[95]

The Directive does not concern aspects relating to the conclusion and validity of contracts or other legal obligations in cases where formal requirements exist, nor does it affect rules and limits relating to the use of documents prescribed by national or EU legislation.[96]

With reference to the subjective sphere of professional-consumer relationships, Directive 2019/770 on contracts for the supply of digital content or services, and Directive 2019/771 on certain aspects of the sale of goods, were recently adopted.[97]

Directive 2019/770 is aimed at harmonizing, in particular, the rules relating to the conformity of the digital content or digital service[98] to the contract,[99] to the possible modification of the same in the duration contracts,[100] and to the remedies that can be found in the event of a lack of conformity or failure to supply with the relative operating methods.

Directive 2019/771 establishes common provisions on sales contracts concluded between sellers and consumers. The rules concern, on the one hand, the compliance

---

[94] On the role of self-regulation and related issues relating to the need to obtain the adhesion of the interested parties, to the powers reserved to the self-regulatory bodies, as well as to the nature of the same, see: Winn (2010); Gambino et al. (2019), pp. 151 ff.

[95] Regarding that distinction, unknown to United States legislation, see: Winn and Haubold (2002), p. 587; Kierkegaard (2007), pp. 45–46; Troiano (2005).

[96] Art. 1.2. On the regulation of electronic signatures, see below at Sect. 2.2.

[97] Cited, which must be implemented by 2021 and applied from 1 January 2022. For a first comment, see: Morais Carvalho (2019); see also, on the initial proposal: Sein (2017).

[98] Defined respectively, the digital content as the data produced and supplied in digital format, and the digital service as: (a) a service that allows the consumer to create, transform, store data, or access it in digital format; or (b) a service that allows the sharing of data in digital format uploaded or created by the consumer and other users of this service or any other interaction with such data (Directive 2019/770, Art. 2, n. 2).

[99] The Directive applies to any contract in which the economic operator provides or undertakes to provide a digital content or service to the consumer and the consumer pays a price or undertakes to pay a price. Furthermore, it also applies in the event that the economic operator provides or undertakes to provide digital content or service to the consumer and the latter provides or undertakes to provide personal data to the economic operator. This, except in the case where the personal data provided by the consumer are processed exclusively by the economic operator for the purpose of providing the digital content or digital service or to allow the fulfillment of legal obligations (Directive 2019/770, Art. 3, par. 1). Regarding the transfer of personal data, see among others: Drexl et al. (2016); Drexl (2016); one may also see: Stazi (2019a, b).

[100] Option provided for in cases where the contract provides that the digital content or service is provided or made accessible to the consumer for a certain period, with the right of withdrawal of the consumer if this entails significant negligible consequences (Directive 2019/770, Art. 19).

with the contract of movable property, including those which incorporate or are interconnected with digital content or services;[101] on the other, remedies in the event of lack of conformity, methods of exercising these remedies, and commercial guarantees.

The rationale of these Directives is to make it easier for businesses to supply digital content or services or to offer mobile goods also linked to them in the various EU Member States, and at the same time to make consumers benefit from a high level of protection also with respect to contractual relationships that concern digital content or services, or goods connected to them.[102]

Directive 2019/2161, so-called Omnibus, also aimed at strengthening consumer rights through: (1) increased transparency measures on online marketplaces regard in ranking, reviews and personalized prices, (2) extension of consumer rights to free digital services such as social media or cloud, and (3) enhanced enforcement measures, with compensation and other individual remedies for consumers and more effective penalties for cross-border infringement. Another legislation recently adopted at European level is the EU Regulation 2019/1150[103] aimed at promoting fairness and transparency for business users of online intermediation services.[104] In this perspective, the Regulation dictates a set of provisions intended to ensure that commercial users of such services and users of company websites that are related to search engines have adequate transparency, fairness, and effective appeal options.[105]

For these purposes, in particular, information obligations are dictated concerning, among other things, the terms and conditions of the service, the hypotheses of different treatment reserved for the products or services offered, the parameters that determine their positioning, limitation, suspension or termination of the supply,

---

[101] Specifically, any tangible movable property even if it incorporates or is interconnected with a digital content or service in such a way that the lack of said content or service would prevent the performance of the functions of the asset ("goods with digital elements"; Directive 2019/771, Art. 2, no. 5). Therefore, the Directive also applies to digital content or services incorporated or interconnected with goods and which are supplied with the good pursuant to the sales contract, regardless of whether said digital content or services are provided by the seller or by third parties (Art. 3, par. 3).

[102] See e.g.: Morais Carvalho (2019); Gambino et al. (2019), pp. 168–169.

[103] Regulation (EU) 2019/1150 of the European Parliament and of the Council of 20 June 2019 on promoting fairness and transparency for business users of online intermediation services, OJ 11.7.2019 L 186.

[104] Defined as those services which simultaneously satisfy the following requirements: (a) are information society services; (b) allow commercial users to offer goods or services to consumers, with the aim of facilitating the initiation of direct transactions between these commercial users and consumers regardless of where they are concluded; (c) they are provided to commercial users who offer goods and services to consumers on the basis of contractual relationships between the provider of these services and the commercial users themselves (Regulation 2019/1150, Art. 2, n. 2).

[105] For a first comment on the proposal, see: Twigg-Flesner (2018).

and access by the supplier or third parties to personal data or other data provided by commercial users or consumers.[106]

Finally, a further attempt at intervention by the European Union is the proposed regulation for a Common European Sales Law.[107] To some extent, the CESL adoption model resembles that adopted by the United States with UCITA, in the sense that it moves from similar premises.[108]

The European Commission's choice is to make CESL an optional tool, which will not replace national laws, but will add to existing options available to contracting parties to regulate their contracts.[109] If the CESL is converted into legislation, Europe will have a harmonized body of contract law which will also be applicable to telematic contracts.[110]

2.5 The Regulatory Framework in the United States

The minimalist approach of the United States in the regulation of electronic contracts, based on the UNCITRAL Model Electronic Commerce Act, has produced a uniform model law and federal legislation. The Uniform Electronic Transaction Act,

---

[106] See: Regulation 2019/1150, Articles 3–9. Regarding contractual discrimination, see for all: Zeno-Zencovich (2020). In such a perspective, see also the Proposal for a Regulation of the European Parliament and of the Council on a Single Market for Digital Services (Digital Services Act) and amending Directive 2000/31/EC, COM/2020/825 final.

[107] Proposal for a Regulation of the European Parliament and of the Council relating to a common European law of the sale, COM/2011/0635 final. In this regard, see: Dannemann and Vogenauer (2013); Adar and Sirena (2013); Pongelli (2013); Lando (2011); Aubert de Vincelles (2011); Kryczka (2005).

[108] In the EUROPE 2020 program: A European strategy for smart, sustainable and inclusive growth, COM (2010) 2020 final, available at: https://eur-lex.europa.eu/legal-content/it/TXT/?uri=CELEX:52010DC2020, the European Commission has expressed the need to adapt European and national legislations to the digital age to promote the circulation of content with a high level of trust for consumers and businesses. The Commission took the opportunity of CESL to introduce a framework of certain contracts relating to the purchase of digital content in a set of rules aimed at regulating the sales of goods.

[109] The European Parliament approved the draft on 26 February 2014, with changes to the original Commission proposal, which was first introduced in 2011. The proposal was expected to be approved by the European Council for adoption by regulation, but it has been opposed by the resistance from some national parliaments, including the German, the Belgian, the Austrian and the British, as it was considered inconsistent with the subsidiarity principle or lacking a legal basis. Consumer and business associations have also voiced strong criticism of the proposed regulation, at least in its current form. The same is true of the legal doctrine, with that of the United States in particular criticizing the proposal as an attempt to over-regulate the European institutions. See: Ancel et al. (2011); Caruso (2013).

[110] This legal solution has been adopted by the Commission to achieve the highest level of harmonization, on the one hand, without relying on implementation by the Member States, on the other, without replacing national contract laws. Furthermore, Member States could make the regulation applicable also to entirely national transactions. See: Rühl (2012).

or UETA, was adopted in 1999 as a uniform law aimed at eliminating any doubt that contracts concluded by electronic means could satisfy the written provisions of the Statute of Frauds.[111]

The UETA was soon followed by the Electronic Signatures in Global and National Commerce Act, or E-Sign,[112] a federal law that adopted the most significant provisions of the UETA. Both have no general contract law ambitions, remain sectoral, and leave issues relating to conclusion in contract law.[113]

According to both the UETA and the E-Sign, the legal effect or enforceability of a document or signature cannot be denied only because it is in electronic form. Furthermore, a contract cannot be denied such effects only because an electronic document was used in its establishment.

If a regulation requires a written registration or signature, an electronic registration or signature meets these requirements. Such basic provisions have met with the favor of many states as they aim to facilitate the use of technology in transactions, without altering the fundamental structure of contract law at national level.[114]

A more structured and complete approach has been proposed in the Uniform Computer Information Transaction Act, or UCITA, aimed at providing complete regulation to contracts relating to the information society and to validate certain standard terms in IT licenses such as click-wrap contracts.[115]

The basic assumption was that some characteristics of the digital economy are so radical as to require a substantial rewriting of contract law in the United States, starting from Article 2 of the Uniform Commercial Code, which deals with the sale of goods, in a new economic scenario in which exchanges mainly concern the provision of access services.[116]

The UCITA project[117] had been carried out by the Uniform Law Commission and completed in 1999, but the American Law Institute had abandoned the project before its approval and later proposed the Principles of the Law of Software Contract.[118]

---

[111] Uniform Electronic Transactions Act, § 1–21, 7A ULA 211 (1999); regarding which see: Nimmer (1996), pp. 227 ff.; Winn and Haubold (2002), p. 581.

[112] Electronic Signatures in Global and National Commerce Act, 15 USC §§ 7001–7031 (2006), regarding which see: Wittie and Winn (2000); Hays (2001); Balloon (2001).

[113] See: Moringiello and Reynolds (2013), p. 460; Kierkegaard (2007), p. 13.

[114] This also explains why the UETA does not include a checklist of the information to be provided *ex ante* to the consumer similar to that envisaged at European level. The institutional constraint to respect contract law at the state level explains the peculiar pre-emption mechanism that regulates the relationship between the E-Sign and the incompatible UETA provisions. If States have laws incompatible with E-Sign, it would precede those laws, establishing national uniformity based on federal law, while if States instead adopt the uniform version of the UETA, this will prevail over the E-Sign. See again: Winn and Haubold (2002), p. 579.

[115] See: Maxeiner (2003), pp. 131 ff.; Chow and Kinstlick (2001); Nimmer (2000).

[116] In this perspective, see: Nimmer (2000), pp. 232–233. Regarding the "age of access", see: Rifkin (2001).

[117] Started as an expansion of the Uniform Commercial Code, with the addition of Article 2B.

[118] Software contracts: as adopted and promulgated by the American Law Institute at Washington, DC, 19 May 2009, St. Paul, 2010. For a comment see: Hillman and O'Rourke (2010).

UCITA has been adopted by only two states, Maryland and Virginia, while at least four—Iowa, North Carolina, West Virginia, and Vermont—have adopted anti-UCITA laws to prevent contracting parties operating in those states from opting for the application of this legislation through connection to a state in which it is in force.[119] The criticisms were widespread and it was questioned by many that the final text reflected the consolidated practices of the sector.[120]

Thus, as highlighted by some scholars,[121] when a change in the common law essentially involved formalities, the legislation was quickly passed and its adoption was successful, solving the problems created by the promulgation of numerous laws based on a variety of cryptographic standards and specific technologies, which did not facilitate interstate transactions.

Conversely, as in the case of UCITA, common law resisted when the changes concerned the formation and essential characteristics of the contracts.

References

Adar Y, Sirena P (2013) Principles vs. rules in European contract law: from the PECL to the CESL, and beyond. Eur Rev Contract Law 9:1–37

Ancel P et al (2011) De quelques conditions de succès d'un instrument optionnel droit européen des contrats. Revue des contrats:1313–1342

Arthur WB (2009) The nature of technology. Free Press, New York

Aubert de Vincelles C (2011) Premier regard sur la proposition d'un droit commun européen de la vente. JCP 2011:1376 ff.

Auwers W (1891) Des Rechtsschutz der automatischen wage nach gemeinem Recht. W. Fr. Kästner, Göttingen

Balloon AM (2001) From wax seals to hypertext: electronic signatures, contract formation, and a new model for consumer protection in internet transactions. Emory Law J 50:905–937

Barlow JP (1996) A declaration of independence of cyberspace. www.eff.org/~barlow/Declaration-final.html

Bonell MJ (1987) In: Bianca CM, Bonell MJ (eds) Commentary on the international sales law. The 1980 Vienna Sales Convention, Giuffrè, Milan, pp 81 ff.

Bonell MJ (2006) Un codice Internazionale del Diritto dei Contratti. I principi Unidroit dei contratti commerciali internazionali, 2nd edn. Giuffrè, Milan

Bonell MJ (2009) An international restatement of contract law: the Unidroit principles of international commercial contracts, 3rd edn. Transnational Publishers, Ardsley

Boss AH, Kilian W (2008) The United Nation Convention on the use of electronic communications in international contracts. An in-depth guide and sourcebook. Wolters Kluwer, Alpeen aan den Rijn

Brousseau E, Glachant JM (2002) The economics of contracts: theories and applications. Cambridge University Press, Cambridge

[119] In this regard, see: Winn and Bix (2006), p. 180.

[120] See among others: Lemley (1997); Moringiello and Reynolds (2013), pp. 464 ff.

[121] See: Winn and Haubold (2002), p. 570; Moringiello and Reynolds (2013), p. 457.

Brownsword R (2020) Automated transactions and the law of contract. When codes are not congruent. In: Furmston M (ed) The future of the law of contract. Routledge, Abingdon, pp 94 ff.
Burnstein MR (1996) Conflicts of the net: choice of law in transnational cyberspace. Vanderbilt J Transnatl Law 29:75–116
Caruso D (2013) The baby and the bath water: the American critique of European contract law. Am J Comp Law 61:479–506
Castets-Renard C (2018) Privacy shield: toward a strong personal data protection between the US and the EU? Revue des Juristes de Sciences Po 14:109–122
Chow SY, Kinstlick RF (eds) 2001) Uniform Computer Information Transactions Act. A broad perspective. PLI, New York
Cicu A (1901) Gli automi nel diritto privato. Società Editrice Libraria, Milan
Dannemann G, Vogenauer S (eds) (2013) The common European sales law in context: interactions with English and German Law. Oxford University Press, Oxford
Delfini F (2002) Contratto telematico e commercio elettronico. Giuffrè, Milan
Drexl J (2016) Designing competitive markets for industrial data – between propertisation and access. Max Planck Institute for Innovation & Competition Research Paper No. 16-13. https://ssrn.com/abstract=2862975
Drexl J, Hilty RM et al (2016) Data ownership and access to data – position statement of the Max Planck Institute for Innovation & Competition of 16 August 2016 on the Current European Debate. Max Planck Institute for Innovation & Competition Research Paper No. 16-10. http://ssrn.com/abstract=2833165
Easterbrook FH (1996) Cyberspace and the law of the horse. Univ Chic Leg Forum 207:216 ff.
Ertel P (1898) Der Automatenmissbrauch und seine Charakterisierung als Delikt. Druck von Wilhelm Pilz, Berlin
Farnsworth EA (2006) Comparative contract law. In: Reimann M, Zimmermann R (eds) The Oxford handbook of comparative law. Oxford University Press, Oxford, pp 900 ff.
Ferrari F, Leible S (eds) 2009) Rome I Regulation. The law applicable to contractual obligations in Europe. Sellier, Munich
Finocchiaro G (2003) The conclusion of the electronic contract through "software agents": a false legal problem? Brief considerations. Comput Law Secur Rev 19:20–24
Gaillard E (1995) Trente ans de lex mercatoria. Pour une application sélective de la méthode des principes généraux du droit. Clunet, 5–30
Gambino AM (1997) L'accordo telematico. Giuffrè, Milan
Gambino AM (1999) Il contratto telematico. In: Bigiavi W (ed) Giurisprudenza sistematica di diritto civile e commerciale, vol 2. Utet, Turin, pp 1460 ff.
Gambino AM, Stazi A (2020) La circolazione dei dati. Titolarità, strumenti negoziali, diritti e tutele. Pacini, Rome
Gambino AM, Stazi A (2021) Contract automation from telematic agreements to smart contracts. Italian Law J 7:97–115
Gambino AM, Stazi A, Mula D (2019) Diritto dell'informatica e della comunicazione, 3rd edn. Giappichelli, Turin
Garcimartìn Alférez F (2017) Rome Convention and Rome I Regulation (contractual obligations). In: Basedow J et al (eds) Encyclopedia of private international law. Edward Elgar, Cheltenham, pp 1554 ff.
Gemma A (2007) L'accordo telematico. In: Clarizia R (ed) I contratti informatici, in Trattato dei contratti, directed by Rescigno P, Gabrielli E. Utet, Turin, pp 237–280
Goldman B (1987) The applicable law: general principles of law – the lex mercatoria. In: Lew J (ed) Contemporary problems in international arbitration. Springer, Dordrecht, pp 113–125

Granieri M (2017) Technological contracts. In: Monateri PG (ed) Comparative contract law. Edward Elgar, Cheltenham, pp 408–450. https://papers.ssrn.com/sol3/papers.cfm?abstract_id=2666191, pp 1 ff
Grundmann S, Hacker P (2018) The digital dimension as a challenge to European contract law. The architecture. In: Grundmann S (ed) European contract law in the digital age. Intersentia, Cambridge, pp 3 ff.
Guadamuz Gonzàlez A (2003) Ebay law: the legal implications of the C2C electronic commerce model. Comput Law Secur Rep 19:468–473
Guenther F (1892) Das Automatenrecht. W. Fr. Kästner, Göttingen (repr. 2010, Kessinger, Whitefish)
Hart HM Jr, Wechsler H (2009) In: Fallon RH Jr et al (eds) The Federal Courts and the Federal System, 6th edn. Foundation Press, New York
Hart HM Jr, Sacks AM (1994) In: Eskridge WN Jr, Frickey PP (eds) The legal process. Basic problems in the making and application of law. Foundation Press, New York
Hays MJ (2001) The E-Sign Act of 2000: the triumph of function over form in American contract law. Notre Dame Law Rev 76:1183–1213
Hermalin BE, Katz AW, Craswell R (2007) The law and economics of contracts. In: Polinski AM, Shavell S (eds) Handbook of law and economics. Elsevier, Amsterdam, pp 3–138
Hermann G (1999) Establishing a legal framework for electronic commerce: the work of the United Nations Commission on International Trade Law (UNCITRAL). World Trade Arbitr Mater 11: 45 ff.
Hill JE (2003) The future of electronic contracts in international sales: gaps and natural remedies under the United Nations Convention on contracts for the International Sale of Goods. Northwest J Technol Intellect Prop 2:1–34
Hillman RA (2006) Online boilerplate: would mandatory website disclosure of E-Standard terms backfire? Mich Law Rev 104:837–856
Hillman RA, O'Rourke MA (2010) Principles of the law of software contracts: some highlights. Tulane Law Rev 84:1519 ff.
Johnson DR, Post D (1996) Law and borders-the rise of law in cyberspace. Stanf Law Rev 48: 1367–1402
Jonas H (1979) Das Prinzip Verntwortund, Versuch einer Ethik fur die technologiesche Zivilisation. Suhrkamp, Frankfurt
Kalemi E, Ndreka D (2012) The impact of information technology in electronic contracting. Acad J Interdiscip Stud:225–235
Katz AW (2004) Vertragsrecht im Zeitalter des Internets: Eine ökonomische Perspektive. In: Schäfer HB, Ott C (eds) Eine Ökonomische Analyze des Sozialschutzprinzips im Zivilrecht. Mohr Siebeck, Tubinga, pp 433–473
Kidd DN, Daugthrey WH Jr (2000) Adapting contract law to accommodate electronic contracts: overview and suggestions. Rutgers Comput Technol Law J 26:215–276
Kierkegaard SM (2007) E-Contract formation: US and EU perspectives. Shider J Law Commerce Technol 3:12 ff.
Kirillova EA et al (2020) Legal status, classification, and features of electronic contracts. Revista Inclusiones 7:325–336
Kotz H (2017) European contract law, 2nd edn. Oxford University Press, Oxford
Kronman AT, Posner RA (1979) The economics of contract law. Little Brown, Boston
Kryczka K (2005) Electronic contracts and the harmonization of contract laws in Europe – an action required, a mission impossible? Eur Rev Priv Law 13:149–170
Lambert E (1900) Une réforme nécessaire des études de droit civil, in Revue internationale de l'enseignement, 218–233
Lambertiere I (1983) Les contrats informatique. Litec, Paris
Landels JG (1978) Engineering in the ancient world. University of California Press, Berkeley
Lando O (1985) The lex mercatoria in International Commercial Arbitration. ICLQ 34:747–768

Lando O (2011) Comments and questions relating to the European Commission's proposal for a regulation on a common European sales law. Eur Rev Priv Law 6:717–728
Le Tourneau P (2006) Contrats informatiques et électroniques, 4th edn. Dalloz-Sirey, Paris
Lemley MA (1997) Beyond preemption: the law and policy of intellectual property licensing. Calif Law Rev 87:111–172
Lessig L (1999a) Code and other laws of cyberspace. Basic Books, New York
Lessig L (1999b) The law of the horse: what cyberlaw might teach. Harv Law Rev 113:501–549
Linant De Bellefonds X, Hollande A (1988) Contrats informatiques et télématiques. Delmas, Paris
Marrella F, Yoo CS (2007) Is open source software the new Lex Mercatoria? Vanderbilt J Int Law 47:807–838
Martin CH (2008) The electronic contracts convention, the CISG, and new sources of E-Commerce law. Tulane J Int Comp Law 16:467–503
Mattei U, Pardolesi R (1991) Law and economics in civil law countries: a comparative approach. Int Rev Law Econ 11:265–275
Matwyshyn AM (2013) The law of the zebra. Berkeley Technol Law J 28:155–225
Maxeiner JR (2003) Standard-terms contracting in the global electronic age: European alternative. Yale J Int Law 28:109–182
Melison D (2009) Arrêt Bundesverband c. DIV: l'identification du numéro de téléphone par les prestataires de service de la société de l'information. Revue européenne de droit de la consommation, 582–594
Michaels R (2016) Transnationalizing comparative law. Maastricht J Eur Comp Law 23:352–358
Mik E (2020) The resilience of contract law in light of technological change. In: Furmston M (ed) The future of the law of contract. Routledge, Abingdon, pp 112 ff.
Monateri PG (2000) Black Gaius. A quest for the multicultural origins of the "Western Legal Tradition". Hastings Int Comp Law Rev 51:479–555
Monateri PG (2017a) The authoritarian theory of contract. In: Id (ed) Comparative contract law. Edward Elgar, Cheltenham, pp 47–66
Monateri PG (2017b) Comparative contract law. Edward Elgar, Cheltenham
Morais Carvalho J (2019) Sale of goods and supply of digital content and digital services – overview of directives 2019/770 and 2019/771. J Eur Consumer Mark Law 8:194–201
Moringiello JM, Reynolds WL (2013) From Lord Coke to internet privacy: the past, present and future of the law of electronic contracting. Maryland Law Rev 72:452–500
Mouzas S, Furmston M (2013) A proposed taxonomy of contracts. J Contract Law 30:1–11
Mustill MJ (1987) The new Lex mercatoria: the first twenty-five years. In: Boos M, Brownlie I (eds) Liber Amicorum for Lord Wilberforce. Clarendon, Oxford, pp 149–183
Neumond H (1899) Der Automat. Ein Beitrag zur Lehre über die Vertragsofferte. In: Archiv für die civilistische Praxis. Mohr Siebeck, Heidelberg, p 166 ff.
Nimmer RT (1996) Electronic contracting: legal issues. Marshall J Comput Inf Law 14:211–246
Nimmer RT (2000) The UCITA revolution. The new E-Commerce model for software and database licensing. PLI, New York
Pappas CW (2020) Comparative U.S. & (and) EU approaches to E-Commerce regulation: jurisdiction, electronic contracts, electronic signatures and taxation. Denver J Int Law Policy 31: 325–348
Poggi CT (2000) Electronic commerce legislation: an analysis of European and American approaches to contract formation. Vanderbilt J Int Law 41:224–277
Pongelli G (2013) The proposal for a regulation on a Common European Sales Law (CESL) and its gradual evolution. Comp Law Rev 4:1–26
Reed C (2000) Internet law: texts and materials. Butterworths, London
Reidenberg JR (1996) Governing networks and rule-making in cyberspace. Emory Law J 45:911–929
Reidenberg JR (1998) Lex Informatica: the formulation of information policy rules through technology. Tex Law Rev 76:553–594
Reitz JC (1998) How to do comparative law. Am J Comp Law 46:617–636

Riefa C (2009) The reform of electronic consumer contracts in Europe: towards an effective legal framework? Lex Electronica 14:1–44

Rifkin J (2001) The age of access: the new culture of hypercapitalism, where all of life is a paid-for experience. TarcherPerigee, New York

Rubin E (1996) The new legal process, the synthesis of discourse, and the microanalysis of institutions. Harv Law Rev 109:1393–1438

Rubin MR et al (1995) US and international law aspects of the internet: fitting square pegs into round holes. Int J Law Inf Technol 3:117–143

Rubino Sammartano M (1987) Le "tronc commun" des lois nationales en présence (Réflections sur le droit applicable par arbitre international). Revue de l'arbitrage, 133 ff.

Rühl G (2012) The common European Sales Law: 28th Regime, 2nd Regime, or 1st Regime? Maastricht European Private Law Institute Working Paper No. 2012/5. https://papers.ssrn.com/sol3/papers.cfm?abstract_id=2025879

Ruhl G (2020) Smart (legal) contracts, or: which (contract) law for smart contracts? In: Cappiello B, Carullo G (eds) Blockchain, law and governance. Springer, Berlin, pp 159–180

Rutgers J, Sirena P (eds) (2015) Rules and principles in European contract law. Intersentia, Cambridge

Sacco R, De Nova G (2016) Il contratto, 4th edn. Utet, Turin

Sammarco P (2006) I nuovi contratti dell'informatica. Sistema e prassi. In: Galgano F (ed) Trattato di diritto commerciale e diritto pubblico dell'economia. Cedam, Padua

Sasso L (2016) Certain comparative notes on electronic contract formation. J Higher Sch Econ, 204–219

Savirimuthu J (2005) Online contract formation: taking technological infrastructure seriously. Univ Ottawa Law Technol J 2:105–143

Schels K (1897) Der strafrechtliche Schutz des Automaten. Jur. Diss. Erlangen, Munich

Schiller F (1898) Rechtsverhältnisse des Automaten. Zürcher Diss, Zurich

Schulze R, Staudenmayer D (2016) Digital revolution – challenges for contract law. In: Id (ed) Digital revolution: challenges for contract law in practice. Hart/Nomos, Baden-Baden, p 19 ff

Schwartz PM, Peifer KN (2017) Transatlantic privacy. Georgetown Law J 106:115–179

Scialoja A (1902) L'offerta a persona indeterminata ed il contratto concluso mediante automatico. Tipografia S. Lapi, Città di Castello

Sein K (2017) What rules should apply to smart consumer goods? Goods with embedded digital content in the borderland between the digital content directive and "Normal" contract law. JIPITEC 8:96–110

Shavell S (2003) Economic analysis of contract law. NBER Working Paper 9696. https://papers.ssrn.com/sol3/papers.cfm?abstract_id=382040

Sica S, Stanzione P (eds) (2002) Commercio elettronico e categorie civilistiche. Giuffrè, Milan

Smith SE (2007) The United Nations Convention on the Use of Electronic Communication in International Contracts (CUECIC): why it should be adopted and how it will affect international E-Contracting. SMU Sci Technol Law Rev 11:133–162

Sommer JH (2000) Against cyberlaw. Berkeley Technol Law J 15:1145–1232

Spamann H (2015) Empirical comparative law. Annu Rev Law Soc Sci 11:131–153

Stazi A (2012) Digital copyright and consumer/user protection: moving toward a new framework? Queen Mary J Intellect Prop 2:158–174

Stazi A (2015) Biotechnological innovations and patenting of the living. Legal issues and bioethical profiles in the US and European models. Edward Elgar, Cheltenham

Stazi A (2019a) Automazione contrattuale e "contratti intelligenti". Gli smart contracts nel diritto comparato. Giappichelli, Turin

Stazi A (2019b) Data circulation and legal safeguards: a European perspective. Comp Law Rev 10:89–113

Stazi A, Mula D (2012) Intellectual property and consumer law. In: Ramalho A, Angelopoulos C (eds) Crossroads of intellectual property: intersection of intellectual property and other fields of law. Nova Science, New York, pp 1–47

Tang Z (2008) Law applicable in the absence of choice: the new Article 4 of the Rome I Regulation. Mod Law Rev 71:785–800

Tang ZS (2015) Electronic consumer contracts in the conflict of laws, 2nd edn. Bloomsbury, London

Troiano O (2005) Die elektronische Signatur: Angleichung und Diversifizierung der Vorschriften auf Eg-ebene, im italienischen und de deutschen Recht. Zeitschrift für Europäisches Privatrecht 13:43–70

Twigg-Flesner C (2018) The EU's proposals for regulating B2B relationships on online platforms – transparency, fairness and beyond. J Eur Consumer Mark Law 7:222–233

Volker B (2011) Rome I Regulation a – mostly – unified private international law of contractual relationships within – most – of the European Union. J Law Commerce 29:233–272

Wang FF (2014) Law of electronic commercial transactions: contemporary issues in the EU, US and China, 2nd edn. Routledge, London

Want FF (2010) Law of electronic commercial transactions: contemporary issues in the EU, US, and China. Routledge, London

Wilkinson S (2020) Six levels of contract automation: evolution to digitalised smart (and legal) contracts. https://papers.ssrn.com/sol3/papers.cfm?abstract_id=3748266

Winn JK (2010) Electronic commerce law: direct regulation, co-regulation and self-regulation. Cahiers du CRID. https://papers.ssrn.com/sol3/papers.cfm?abstract_id=1634832

Winn JK, Bix BH (2006) Symposium: cyberpersons, propertization, and contract in the information culture: diverging perspectives on electronic contracting in the U.S. and EU. Cleveland State Law Rev 54:175–189

Winn JK, Haubold J (2002) Electronic promises: contract law reform and E-Commerce in a comparative perspective. Eur Law Rev 27:567–588

Wittie RA, Winn JK (2000) Electronic signatures under the Federal E-SIGN Legislation and the UETA. Bus Lawyer 11:293–340

Zeno-Zencovich V (2020) "Smart contracts", "granular norms" and non discrimination. In: Busch C, De Franceschi A (eds) Algorithmic regulation and personalized law. CH Beck/Hart/Nomos, Munich/Oxford/Baden-Baden, pp 264–278

Chapter 3
Peculiarities and Regulation of Electronic Bargaining

3.1 Formation of the Electronic Contract

The topic of the contract formation, which plays a central role in the dogmatic reconstruction of the system, has returned to be widely addressed in the debate on the subject with the increase in online negotiations, after classical studies and analyses on the mass contracting of consumption civilization.[1]

Attention is focused on the origin of the obligation, also in relation to time and place, and on the possibility and limits for private individuals to agree, model, and/or modify both the content and the contract formation techniques.[2]

Telematic bargaining is characterized by the absence of a traditional dialogue through words and gestures.[3] However, even in the digital scenario and in electronic bargaining, the acts are wanted, and in any case, there are behaviors that show conclusive profiles.

Thus, the agreement is still an essential element of the contract which is formed according to the different techniques developed by the law, albeit through innovative technologies and dynamics and with peculiar characteristics and limits.[4]

In configuring a contract as an act of autonomy, it is not necessary for the content of the negotiating regulation to be defined by both contracting parties. The dialogue procedure through the exchange of proposals and acceptance does not necessarily imply an effective negotiation, but a voluntary acceptance by both parties.[5]

---

[1] See, among others: Lew (1998); Mouly (1990); Murray Jr (1988).

[2] See e.g.: Moringiello and Ottaviani (2016); Wijayasriwardena (2016).

[3] These peculiarities led some legal scholars to deny the same configurability of online agreements, believing that in this context there is rather only a binary combination of unilateral acts that converge on the object of negotiation; see e.g.: Irti (1998).

[4] See e.g.: Goldman (2019); Kim (2012).

[5] See, among others: Smits (2017), pp. 41 ff.; Wijayasriwardena (2016); Ghirardelli (2015).

A. Stazi, *Smart Contracts and Comparative Law*,
https://doi.org/10.1007/978-3-030-83240-7_3

Agreement and dialogue do not constitute a monad. The Principles of European Contract Law, or PECL, reaffirm the centrality of the agreement even in the absence of dialogue.

The PECL identify the contract with sufficient agreement, thus marking a clear break with the principle of completeness of consent on all elements of the contract.[6]

On the one hand, technology has been considered a solution to the problem of the formation of contracts with a view to facilitating the exchange of promises, reducing the time delay due to distance, limiting communication risks, automating responses, and reducing transaction costs.[7]

On the other, the trade-off between the use of technology and consent is increasingly evident, and the bottom line is that their very presence is inversely related. In fact, consensual contracts have been increasingly replaced by formalities-based agreements.[8]

Therefore, the interpreter must assess the meaning of the tenderer's communications on a case-by-case basis, starting from the moment the purchase is solicited, and inspired by the usual criteria of good faith and correctness.

Furthermore, in a system that from the beginning was based especially on spontaneous adherence to certain rules of good conduct, the so-called *netiquette*,[9] it was found that such "needed" courtesy generates constraints, which, although not legally punishable, are still socially penalized.[10]

Legal systems have responded to the problem of forming contracts between distant parties in different ways, and the two main solutions—the dispatch or mailbox rule, and the receipt rule—have given rise to a debate that has never been exhausted.[11]

Several technical solutions have appeared in the history of the contract for the formation of agreements when the parties are not in the same place at the same time. Some of these solutions have been completely replaced over time, others have been added recently, still others are under development.

Whenever new technology emerged, the question arose as to whether pre-existing contractual law rules could meet trade needs and ensure an adequate level of certainty in commercial practice.[12]

The dispatch rule, according to which the contract is intended to be perfected at the time of sending the acceptance by the oblate, has been the solution adopted in the

---

[6] See: European Union (2002), Arts. 2:101 and 2:103. In the same sense, Art. 2:204 states that: "Any form of statement or conduct by the offeree is an acceptance if it indicates assent to the offer," and Art. 2:211 states that: "The rules in this section apply with appropriate adaptations even though the process of conclusion of a contract cannot be analysed into offer and acceptance."

[7] See: Granieri (2017); Moringiello and Reynolds (2013), p. 461; Savirimuthu (2005), p. 110.

[8] In this sense, see: Nimmer (1996), p. 214; Reed (2000), p. 175; Winn and Bix (2006), p. 176; Moringiello and Reynolds (2013), p. 453.

[9] Term composed of *net* (network) + *etiquette* ("label").

[10] On this point, see: Hardy (1993); Burnstein (1996).

[11] See, among others: Schlesinger and Bonassies (1968); Macneil (1964).

[12] In this regard, see e.g.: Gambino and Stazi (2021); Holmes (2010); Rawls (2009), pp. 205 ff.

common law system.[13] The leading case on the matter is a decision of the British High Court on the Mondial Shipping case,[14] which identified the moment of consent in the act of sending the declaration by the accepting subject.[15]

Civil law countries have preferred the receipt rule, according to which a contract is formed when the offeror receives the recipient's acceptance, following a logic close to that of contextual bargaining in person.[16]

---

[13]The rule was established in Adams v. Lindsell (1818) 106 ER 250, and later accepted in the United States: Mactier's Admr's v. Frith, 6 Wend. 103 (NY 1830). In legal doctrine, see: LeRoy Miller and Jentz (2010); Nimmer (1996), pp. 222 ff.; Rawls (2009), pp. 205 ff.; Farnsworth (2006), p. 916; Maniruzzaman (2001), p. 487.

[14]Mondial Shipping & Chartering BV v. Astarte Shipping Ltd., [1995] CLC 1011.

[15]The case assessed the rituality of the declarations of legal relevance made by email communications, as well as the operation of the same where concerning the withdrawal from its contractual obligation, manifested by sending an electronic communication within the deadline. The Court opted for the applicability of the rules relating to inter absent contracts, based on the so-called shipping principle, or dispatch rule, which identifies the moment of consent in the act of sending the declaration by the oblate, i.e., the accepting subject. Having to establish the time to which the withdrawal dated, considering that it had to be activated not before a certain term and that the relative declaration had been sent a few minutes before the same term, but coinciding with the non-working weekend, the Court ended up stating the full operation of the withdrawal declaration, in light of the fact that it would have become known only on the first following business day.

[16]See Art. 11 of Directive 2000/31/EC and, e.g., Arts. 1326–1335 of the Italian Civil Code, while in France, the Civil Code does not provide for a solution and the French courts have generally decided these questions on a case-by-case basis. Bell et al. (1998), p. 312, however, note that there seems to be a preference among the French courts for acceptance at the time and place of dispatch. According to the actual notice rule, then, a contract is formed when the offeror acquires knowledge of the acceptance. Anyway, the jurisdictions that adopt the actual notice rule mitigate it by presuming that the offeror acquires knowledge of the acceptance when it reaches her address unless the offerer proves that acquiring knowledge of the acceptance was impossible for reasons not dependent on her fault; see: Finocchiaro and Bomprezzi (2020), p. 119.

In Italy, Art. 1335 of the Civil Code establishes a presumption of knowledge *iuris tantum* with respect to the declaration sent to the address of the recipient, therefore at the time of the knowledge or knowability of the communication by the latter; presumption, therefore, that can be won by proof against the recipient that it was, without fault, in the impossibility of having news of the communication.

In Germany, the contract is concluded when the acceptance reaches the offeror. This rule can be inferred from § 130(1) BGB, according to which any declaration of intention—being it an offer, a revocation of an offer, an acceptance, or another declaration—directed to an absent person becomes effective when it reaches that person. See: Kötz (2012), para. 99; Flume (1979), p. 657; Beale et al. (2019), p. 257. Zweigert and Kötz (1998), p. 362 state that every declaration of will is effective as soon as it comes into the "sphere of influence" of the addressee. They take the old school example of a bird-lover that chooses not to empty the letterbox in his garden for fear of affrighting the tomtits within. In that case, the declaration is treated as having arrived. The concept of reaching (*zugehen*) is well explained in the *Delivery to a housemaid* case, although it concerns an offer. In that case, the Reichsgericht stated that an offer becomes effective when the letter or the telegram containing it has been delivered at the offeree's house, regardless of whether the offeree has been informed of the offer. See RG, 25 October 1917 RGZ 91, 60 (Delivery to a housemaid).

International trade legislation has shown a preference for the receipt rule,[17] while over time the dispatch rule has lost relevance, also because of the spread of digital technologies.[18]

Comparative studies have dealt extensively with the issue of evaluating one option over the other and the ability of each solution to adapt to online bargaining.[19]

In the telematic context in some cases, such as in email or instant messaging, there is such a short interval between sending and delivery that the offer and acceptance are separated by a negligible fraction of time and the revocation is almost impossible.

This explains the rationale of the European Union legislator in extending the application to electronic bargaining of the *jus poenitendi* already foreseen in the distance contracts directive.[20] If there is no time to weigh an agreement, some time is given to change your mind and dissolve the agreement.

Also in the United States, the Restatement of Contracts subjects "substantially instantaneous" bidirectional communications to the same principle that applies to acceptances where the parties are present with each other.[21]

The dispatch and receipt rules are only different solutions to allocate the risk of communication between the parties. In common law, it was stated that a rule based on the actual receipt of the acceptance by the tenderer would have given rise to the risk that a withdrawal of the acceptance could arrive before it was received.[22]

To regulate this situation, common law has evolved in such a way that all contractual communications—offers, revocations, refusals—are effective upon receipt, except acceptance.[23] The dispatch rule is also instrumental in favoring a

[17] Regarding the complex interaction between the provisions adopted in the Convention on contracts for the international sale of goods and the Convention on the use of electronic communications in international contracts, see: Martin (2008), pp. 484 ff.

[18] Rawls (2009), pp. 207 ff.; Mik (2009), p. 8. UCITA denies the application of the dispatch rule for electronic messages; see: Kierkegaard (2007), p. 37. Watnick (2004), p. 197, believes that since there is no clear default rule for electronically sent acceptance times, the dispatch rule should be maintained for electronic acceptances of contracts not covered by UCITA.

[19] Moringiello (2005) highlighted how in practice consumers perceive transactions on paper as different from electronic transactions.

[20] See Articles 9 ff. Directive 2011/83/EU, which has extended the provisions of Directive 97/7/EC.

[21] Restatement (Second) of Contracts § 64 (1981). In doctrine, see: Rawls (2009), pp. 210 ff.; Fasciano (1997): Mik (2009), pp. 16 ff., according to whom the dispatch rule is still suitable for the use of email in the formation of the contract.

[22] Macneil (1964), p. 953, regarding the time that passes from the offer and acceptance, notes that it is not surprising that the Anglo-American courts have kept it as short as possible by adopting the dispatch rule. Indeed, it can be said that one of the main functions of this rule is to reduce the duration of the offeror's right of revocation. Furthermore, not only does the rule itself shorten the revocation period, but it also removes an element of uncertainty from the contractual relationship. By comparing the risks, the offeror is already exposed to the possibility that his offer is never received by the counterparty; see: Rawls (2009), pp. 212 ff.

[23] See: Fasciano (1997), p. 222.

faster conclusion of the contract, to the point that a contract is in any case concluded if the tenderer has not yet received acceptance.[24]

Since with technological evolution the withdrawal of acceptance is less and less practicable, and it would not make sense to maintain a difference in treatment between the different ways of forming the contract, the receipt rule has become prevalent in many legal systems.[25]

In the European Union, Article 11 of the E-commerce Directive requires that the service provider acknowledges receipt of the recipient's order without undue delay and by electronic means.[26]

The order and the acknowledgement of receipt are considered received when the parties to whom they are addressed are able to access them, a rule that also applies to the exchange of email or equivalent individual communications.

The Directive is therefore based on a sort of reinforced receipt rule for a harmonized solution at European level.[27]

In addition, as an additional protection for users, the Directive introduces a differentiating element with overseas solutions, requiring the service provider to make available to the recipient appropriate, effective, and accessible means[28] that allow identification and correction of insertion errors before placing the order.[29]

In common law systems, the binding nature of the offer has traditionally been opposed to the use of the invitation to treat, which is rather a mere promotional message.[30]

In line with this orientation is the Vienna Convention, also applicable to international sales, which in Art. 14.2 provides that: "(a) proposal other than one addressed to one or more specific persons is to be considered merely as an invitation to make offers, unless the contrary is clearly indicated by the person making the proposal."[31]

---

[24] In this regard, see: Macneil (1964), p. 954; Mik (2009), p. 9. "Receiving" an acceptance does not necessarily correspond to the recipient's actual knowledge. In electronic bargaining, it has been argued that receipt of acceptance occurs when it has entered the information processing system designated for such messages by the tenderer; see: Rawls (2009), p. 211.

[25] In this regard, see again: Rawls (2009), pp. 204 ff.

[26] On this point, see: Kierkegaard (2007), p. 28; Ramberg (2001), pp. 439 ff.

[27] Winn and Haubold (2002), p. 575, recognize a possible interference with the national provisions, mentioning § 130.1 of the German BGB regarding the moment in which the contractual declaration is considered as received. Neither the UETA nor the E-Sign take a position on the applicability of the rule of the dispatch or of the receipt for the formation of the contract. Rawls (2009), pp. 209 ff., proposes the adoption of the receipt rule for all contracts in the United States, however formed, to ensure consistency in the decisions on the subject at national and international level.

[28] For example, a home screen, or a pop-up window, or an intermediate review image.

[29] This step is only procedural and does not change the solutions adopted by national laws for the formation of contracts; see: Granieri (2017), p. 19.

[30] This, in the reductive perception that "the merchant might find himself involved in any number of contractual obligations ... which he would be quite unable to carry out his stock ... being necessarily limited;" see: Owsia (1994), p. 406; *contra*: Atiyah (1989), p. 65.

[31] Therefore, the intention to bind to the offer must be explicitly expressed, since the presence of the essential elements of the contractual proposal is not considered a sufficient requirement. In

On the other hand, considering its peculiar stipulatory mechanisms, the electronic offer takes on characteristics that are likely to influence what appears to the other party.

In fact, a "click" on the digitized goods on the screen could mean a request for information on the pre-contractual phase, an invitation to offer, a purchase request, a request to send the goods, or an acceptance of the offer. Through hypertext navigation, then, one can easily switch from the advertisement to the actual offer of an online contract.[32]

The method followed by the common law courts consisted in the case-by-case assessment between invitation to offer and offer binding, with strong relevance of the context in which the business takes place,[33] and of the existence of an intention to be obliged.[34]

In civil law, instead, for example the French system bases the analysis on the principle of completeness of the offer, which is traced back to the figure of the unilateral declaration of will, *déclaration unilatérale de voluntée*, and must also include, in addition to the expression of the intention to contract, the essential contractual elements.[35]

So, for example, the sending of catalogs and price lists and the display of the goods in the shop window with the relative price are generally considered to be offers made to the public, which, once accepted by the customer, cannot change in the conditions.[36] The offeror can refuse to fulfill only because of a serious and legitimate reason, such as the exhaustion of the goods.[37]

---

substantial compliance with the common law principle, it is also Art. 2.2 of the UNIDROIT Principles of International Commercial Contracts of 1994, according to which: "A proposal for concluding a contract constitutes an offer if it is sufficiently defined and indicates the intention of the offeror to be bound in case of acceptance."

[32] In this regard, see e.g.: European Commission, Communication from the Commission to the European Parliament, the Council, the European Economic and Social Committee and the Committee of the Regions, A comprehensive approach to stimulating cross-border e-Commerce for Europe's citizens and businesses, COM/2016/0320 final; one may also see: Stazi (2004), pp. 16 ff.

[33] See: US District Court, Southern District of New York, September 9, 1996; Memorandum, Attorney General, State of Minnesota, County of Ramsey, Second Judicial District, C6-95-7227, December 1996, pp. 6 f.

[34] Which can be inferred through "an inquiry whether the facts show some performance was promised in positive terms in return for something requested;" see Williston (1957), p. 65. See also, among others: Peel (2015), pp. 2 ff.; Smith (2006), pp. 35 ff.

[35] Weill and Terré (1986), p. 142, define the offer as "*une declaration unilatérale de volunté adresée par une personne à une autre, et par laquelle l'offrant proposed à autrui la conclusion d'un contract.*" According to Ghestin (1988), p. 219: "*On peut* a priori *définir l'offre* ... *comme une manifestation de volunté unilatérale par laquelle une personne fait connaître son intention de contracter et les conditions essentielles du contrat.*" The *invitation*, the French expression of the invitation to treat, distinguishes between the non-binding offer subsystems the *invitation to faire des offres* and the offer *avec réserves* or *sans engagement*; see: Planiol and Ripert (1953), pp. 145 ff.

[36] In this regard, see e.g.: Weill and Terré (1986), p. 220.

[37] The problem of the scarcity of the goods available to the seller is resolved here with the application of the "first come, first served" principle, since "*est de la nature des choses que l'offre*

The level of information required in the content of the offer, then, changes depending on the *nature du contrat.*[38]

In the Italian system, regarding online electronic catalogs in which goods or services are offered for direct purchase, a type of offer to the public pursuant to Art. 1336 of the Civil Code is configured provided that the website: (a) is open to any user or, in any case, to a number of users so vast as to make the sending of the offer independent of the person; (b) contains all the essential elements of the contractual proposal.[39]

If there is a mere invitation to offer, instead, the applicable rules will be, on one hand, those on advertising communications, with particular reference to the principles of non-deception, truth, correctness, and completeness; on the other hand, the regulation of pre-contractual liability in Art. 1337 of the Italian Civil Code.[40]

In the German system, a declaration is not qualified as an offer but rather as an invitation to make offers if the offeror prevents his or her offer from having binding force by using express phrases, such as "*freibleibend*" or "*ohne Obligo*" ("without engagement").[41] However, if the addressee agrees to the invitation, and the proposer remains silent, the jurisprudence usually considers such a declaration as an acceptance.[42]

Thus, beyond the formal solutions provided individually by the legal systems, the comparative perspective shows that the most interesting question is that relating to the role of consent as a mechanism of formation of the contract.

---

au public soit réservée aux premiers acceptants dans les limites des quantités offertes;" see: Ghestin (1988), p. 266.

[38] See e.g.: Cass. civ., 3e, 27 June 1973, which ruled that in a hypothesis of *bail* (lease), the offer must mention "*la chose louée, le montant du loyer, et la date possible d'entrée en jouissance.*"

[39] Examples of offers to the public can be found in the products of a supermarket that have exhibited the sale price, in the products offered in teleshopping, etc. According to Art. 1336, par. 2, the revocation of the offer to the public in the same forms as the offer or in another equivalent is also effective for those who have not heard of it. It is not necessary, therefore, that anyone who has heard of the offer must then know of the revocation in order for it to be also effective against her. It is sufficient that the offer and revocation are carried out in the same forms.

[40] Pursuant to Art. 13, par. 3 of Legislative Decree no. 70/2003, consistent with Art. 11, par. 2 of Directive 2000/31/EC, then, both the order and the communication of receipt of the same are considered received when the parties to whom they are addressed have the possibility to access them. This equation between the accessibility of the declaration and the actual receipt of the same, therefore, overlaps the presumption of knowledge foreseen in general for the conclusion of the contract through proposal and acceptance between contracting parties placed at a distance, similarly to what happens in communication via email. In this regard, one may see e.g.: Stazi (2004), pp. 167 ff.

[41] According to § 145 BGB, the offeror is bound by his or her offer and cannot withdraw it.

[42] For example, in the Aeroplane Charter case (BGH, 8 March 1984, NJW 1984, 1885) the Federal Court of Justice has declared that the use of the words "without engagement" does not necessarily prevent a communication from constituting an effective offer. Indeed, according to the principle of good faith, the proposer should have expressly rejected the offer. On the contrary, her silence should count as acceptance. See: Beale et al. (2019), p. 362.

In the digital context, in fact, the relevance of the human factor is reduced to the point that there is a tendency to replace the complexity of the will with formality, and the "humanistic model" of contractual behavior is put aside in favor of prevailing needs for speed and efficiency of transactions.[43]

3.2 Manifestation of Consent and Imputation of the Effects

Other crucial issues of online bargaining are those of the modalities for the expression of consent and the imputation of the negotiation declarations and the effects of the contract.

The peculiar nature of the medium and the consequent depersonalization of the negotiating activity require careful reflection on the methods of expression of consent and on the techniques of imputation of the effects.

There are, in fact, three main areas regarding the imputation of the effects of the electronic contract. The first, as mentioned above, is that of the electronic signature. The second is the area of click-wrap or browse-wrap contracts. The third is that of bargaining through electronic agents.

Electronic signature means the logical connection between computer data aimed at identifying a subject with authorized information systems.[44]

---

[43] In this regard, see: Granieri (2017), pp. 19 ff., who notes that in mass market transactions the practice of standard terms has provoked discussions on consensus which are now superseded by the so-called "Rolling contracts", which continue until someone decides to terminate them, rather than until a certain date (such contracts are generally known for example in the practice of insurance relationships); Nimmer (1996), p. 212; Radin (2000), who distinguishes between "contract as consent" and "contract as product". For a discussion of the reconstruction of individual will in contract theory and the adoption of a subjective consensus theory linked to liberalism, see: Weitzenboek (2001), p. 218.

[44] Along with the traditional criterion in representing the material authorship of a document, US pragmatism has outlined from common experience other ways of identifying the subject to whom to attribute a text. From a unique and unrepeatable element such as handwriting, summed up in the expression "something you are", the list of criteria useful for the identification of the subject to which to attribute legal facts has been expanded to that of knowledge of a secret element that activates a presumption about the lawfulness of its use—criterion of "something you know". The criterion of possession of an element that allows identification, as a key, according to the principle of something you have, has also been adopted. These criteria inform the so-called electronic signature technique. On the subject, see e.g., Smedinghoff (2008); one may also see: Gambino et al. (2019), pp. 34 ff.

On this issue, the e-IDAS Regulation intervened at European level,[45] aimed at making interoperable the online identification tools used in the Member States to strengthen the security of transactions and exchanges in the EU internal market.[46]

In the United States, as mentioned, similar provisions have been dictated in the UETA and especially in the E-Sign.

At the international level, there are no shared rules aimed at guaranteeing the recognition and/or interoperability of the systems. Therefore, the UNCITRAL Working Group on E-commerce drafted a Model Law that defines shared minimum requirements for international authentication in compliance with national provisions.[47]

Electronic signatures have been the subject of intervention by the EU legislator through the e-IDAS Regulation, which provides the conditions for mutual recognition in the field of electronic identification, as well as the common rules for electronic signatures, web authentication, and related trust services for electronic transactions.[48]

The e-IDAS Regulation defines three types of electronic signatures, namely, the simple, advanced, and qualified electronic signature. According to the Regulation, then:

1. "Electronic signature" means data in electronic form which is attached to or logically associated with other data in electronic form, and which is used by the signatory to sign.[49]

---

[45] Regulation (EU) No. 910/2014 of the European Parliament and of the Council of 23 July 2014 on electronic identification and trust services for electronic transactions in the internal market and repealing Directive 1999/93/EC, OJ L 257, 28.8.2014. In the abbreviation "e-IDAS", where "e" stands for "electronic", "ID" for "identification", "A" for "authentication", and "S" for "signature". See e.g.: Dumortier (2016).

[46] Based on the principle of technological neutrality, the Regulation does not require the adoption of a single identification system but provides that Member States notify the Commission of the system adopted, which respects warranty and safety conditions.

[47] See: UNCITRAL, Model Law on Electronic Signatures, adopted on 5 July 2001; see also: Uncitral (2009).

[48] The European Regulation defines the electronic signature as a set of "data in electronic form, included or connected by logical association to other electronic data and used by the signatory to sign." This definition enhances the declarative function of the electronic signature that is used by the signatory to express his adhesion to the content of the signed electronic document.

[49] See: Regulation (EU) n. 910/2014, Art. 3 (10). The technical characteristics or the security level of this type of signature were not predefined and could consist of a password, or an autographed signature digitized by a scanner. An example of a simple electronic signature is given by the use of user ID and password that allow a subject to access a service. It is interesting to note that in the definition of simple electronic signature provided for in Art. 3 of the Regulation, the emphasis is placed no longer on the identification function, given on the assumption, but on the declarative function, as an instrument used precisely "to sign"; on this point, see: Dumortier (2016), pp. 18 ff. Certificates for electronic signatures are electronic certificates aimed at linking the validation data of an electronic signature to a natural person, confirming at least the name or pseudonym of that person; see Art. 3 (14). These certificates are distinguished from qualified certificates which, unlike

The technical characteristics or the security level of this type of signature were not predefined and it could consist of a password, or an autographed signature digitized by scanner. An example of a simple electronic signature is given by the use of user ID and password that allow a subject to access a service.

2. "Advanced electronic signature" means an electronic signature which is: (a) uniquely linked to and capable to identify the signatory; (b) created using electronic signature creation data that the signatory can, with a high level of confidence, use under her sole control; (c) linked to the data signed therewith in such a way that any subsequent change in the data is detectable.[50]

   An example of an advanced electronic signature is the so-called graphometric signature, which consists of an autograph signature affixed with a nib, on an electronic tablet, giving very high certainty as to the traceability of that signature to a particular individual.

3. "Qualified electronic signature" means an advanced electronic signature that is created by a qualified electronic signature creation device, and which is based on a qualified certificate for electronic signatures.[51]

   The qualified signatures, once affixed to the document, allow the recipient to impute the same unequivocally to the sender, also allowing to ensure the integrity of the document.

A particular type of advanced electronic signature is the so-called digital signature, which is based on a qualified certificate and on a system of cryptographic keys, one public and one private, related to each other, which allows the holder through the public key, respectively, to make it manifest and to verify the origin and integrity of an electronic document or a set of electronic documents.[52]

The digital signature is characterized by the use of two different techniques: one first represented by a mathematical function, named Hash, and a second one based on an asymmetric cryptographic technique. The cryptographic key that constitutes

---

the first, can only be issued by a qualified trust service provider in compliance with the requirements established by the Regulation; see Art. 3 (15), Art. 28, and Annex I (see below).

[50] See: Regulation (EU) n. 910/2014, Art. 3 (11) and Art. 26.

[51] Regulation (EU) n. 910/2014, Art. 3 (12). As regards the qualified certificates for electronic signatures and the requirements for qualified electronic signature creation devices, see Art. 3 (15), Arts. 28–34 and Annex I-II.

[52] Which is provided for example in the Italian legislative decree no. 235/2010, Art. 1, lett. s).

the actual signature is applied to the document imprint obtained through the Hash function[53], as it allows the imputation of the document to that certain subject.[54]

In the digital signature, an asymmetric cryptographic technique is used consisting of a private key referable only to a natural person and a public key that allows any recipient of the message to open, read, and attribute that document to the sender.[55]

Finally, the most advanced types of electronic signatures require the use of variable codes, the so-called one-time password, OTP, communicated by the certifying subject to the user via app or sms.

The practical ease has been favoring the diffusion of the use of the electronic document at a legal level, particularly to sign contracts, send summons or defensive briefs, keep accounting records, etc.[56]

Regarding the legal effects of electronic signatures, the Regulation provides that:

(a) an electronic signature cannot be denied the legal effects and admissibility as evidence in legal proceedings for the sole reason of its electronic form or because it does not meet the requirements for qualified electronic signatures;
(b) the qualified electronic signature has legal effects equivalent to those of a handwritten signature;
(c) the qualified electronic signature based on a qualified certificate issued in one Member State is recognized as a qualified electronic signature in all other Member States.[57]

---

[53] The Hash function is a mathematical function which, applied to any text or computer document, results in an imprint consisting of several alphanumeric characters ranging from 5 to 20 which can only be referred to that given text. In other words, the Hash function transforms the writing into a brief computer summary; so, for example, the expression "I want to buy a Cartier watch" becomes "r2xm6hh". If a word, i.e., a comma or a point, were added or modified to the IT document, the imprint of the Hash function would be totally different: this, to guarantee the certainty of the integrity of the IT document. The characteristics of the Hash function are therefore: (1) public access, whereby anyone can perform the calculation if in possession of the original document; (2) possibility to trace the imprint from the document; (3) near zero probability that two different documents produce the same footprint.

[54] Cryptographic keys are of two types: (a) symmetric: a single key is used to close and open the document; this cryptographic technique is not fully reliable as it is easily decipherable by third parties unrelated to communication; (b) asymmetric: a key is used to close the document and a key to open it, and in no case can the same key be used to close and open the document.

[55] The digital signature can be generated in two ways, the first consisting of affixing the same to the document and the second by associating a key with the document. In the first case, both the plain text, in the example "I want to buy a Cartier watch", and the fingerprint deriving from the Hash function and from the application of the asymmetric key on it, appear on the screen. In the second case, however, the asymmetric key is applied directly to the document, without the Hash function being applied to it first. The preference for the first method outlined is justified for the already mentioned security reasons; one may see: Gambino et al. (2019), pp. 36 ff.

[56] In this regard, see e.g.: Uncitral (2009), pp. 1 ff.; Smedinghoff (2008), pp. 4 ff.

[57] See: Regulation (EU) no. 910/2014, Art. 25, par. 1–3.

Among the innovations introduced by the Regulation, the electronic seal stands out. It is similar to the electronic signature but created by a legal person to guarantee the origin and integrity of the data associated with it.[58]

Also, for the electronic seal, there is the definition of the three types: simple, advanced, and qualified electronic seal, which is based on a qualified certificate for electronic seal.[59]

Similarly to what is provided for electronic signatures, the electronic seal cannot be denied the legal effects and admissibility as evidence in judicial proceedings if it does not meet the requirements of the qualified electronic seal, and a qualified electronic seal enjoys the legal presumption of integrity and origin of the data to which it is associated.[60]

In addition, as with electronic signatures, a qualified electronic seal based on a qualified certificate issued in one Member State is recognized as a qualified electronic seal in all other Member States.[61]

In the click-wrap and browse-wrap contracts,[62] the conclusion is reached through a click on a screen containing the contractual terms in full, or simply by continuing to browse a website that contains a formula of implicit acceptance.[63]

Sometimes, contracts are executed even if the user does not have the possibility to access the terms of use before the purchase, provided that the opportunity is given to return the asset after examining the terms of the license.[64]

Click-wrap contracts were considered to be the online version of the standard contracts.[65] They are sometimes referred to as "pay now, terms after", since a party must consent to the agreement by clicking on a button before knowing, or without

[58]The electronic seal, defined as "data in electronic form, enclosed or connected by logical association with other data in electronic form to guarantee the origin and integrity of the latter," consists of a sort of virtual stamp useful to ensure the integrity and correctness of the data source of the electronic document on which it is affixed.

[59]See: Regulation (EU) n. 910/2014, Art. 3 (25)–(27), 35–40 and Annex III.

[60]Regulation (EU) n. 910/2014, Art. 35.

[61]See: Regulation (EU) no. 910/2014, Articles 35–36.

[62]In analogy with the shrink-wrap license. Most US courts were inclined to apply shrink-wrap licenses: see among others Hill v. Gateway 2000, Inc., 105 F.3d 1147 (7th Cir. 1997), and ProCD, Inc. v. Zeidenberg, 86 F.3d 1447 (7th Cir. 1996), but Klocek v. Gateway, Inc., 104 F.Supp.2d 1332 (D. Kan. 2000), refused to follow those precedents and declared that there was not enough demonstration of consent on an arbitration clause that was part of the agreement. See: Kim (2007), p. 837; Winn and Haubold (2002); Lemley (1995).

[63]In this regard, see: Winn and Bix (2006), p. 178; Mik (2009), p. 27.

[64]See, on this point: Kim (2007), p. 823.

[65]To this effect, see: Lemley (2006); Winn and Haubold (2002), p. 177; Kierkegaard (2007), p. 22, expressed doubts about the compatibility of the click-wrap agreements with the EU standards of the E-commerce Directive which require that the consumer can also memorize and maintain the contractual conditions.

reading, which terms will govern the contractual relationship and possibly how much it will have to pay.[66]

The browse-wrap agreements are simply formed because the user of a website continues navigation after being usually warned that the use of the website or just surfing itself means acceptance of the terms, without being required to demonstrate express consent.[67]

The European E-commerce Directive, at Art. 11, as mentioned, states that the recipient of the service must receive a series of information *ex ante*, and confirmation from the service provider that the order has been received.[68] For the rest, the validity of the click-wrap or browse-wrap agreements is subject to national laws.

In the United States, UCITA contains a very broad provision on the formation of the contract, according to which it can be formed in any way sufficient to demonstrate an agreement, including the offer and acceptance, the conduct of both parties, or the electronic agent operations that recognize the existence of a contract.[69]

From a comparative point of view, it should be noted once again that the courts of common law, and not the legislators, have made important contributions to the recognition of click-wrap and browse-wrap contracts.

The general tendency is to enforce them based on the formation of the contract and, when necessary, to use traditional doctrines such as unconsciousness to avoid unfair results.[70]

---

[66] To confirm their validity: I. LAN Sys., Inc. v. Netscout Serv. Level Corp., 183 F. Support 2d 328 (D. Mass. 2002); Feldman v. Google, Inc., 513 F. Supp. 2d 229 (ED Pa. 2007). See: Moringiello and Reynolds (2013), p. 463.

[67] In this case, the assent was characterized by Kim (2007), p. 817, as acquiescence rather than agreement. See also: Kunz (2003). As confirmation of validity, see: Pollstar v. Gigmania, Ltd., 170 F. Supp. 2d 974 (ED Cal. 2000); Register.com, Inc., v. Verio, Inc., 356 F.3d 393 (2d Cir. 2004); *contra*: Specht v. Netscape Communications Corp., 150 F. Supp. 2d 585 (SDNY 2011). The browse-wrap agreements may also be rolling contracts, and in Swift v. Zinga Game Network, Inc., 805 F. Supp. 2d 904 (ND Cal. 2011), the court found that the modified version of the agreement was applicable to the user. The case of contracts unilaterally modified and accepted through navigation appears recurrent in online consumer contracts. See recently: Becher and Benoliel (2020).

[68] On the other hand, the Directive clearly refers to the situation in which the user should pay something. In fact, many situations are repeated where the service is free, and the user only accepts the terms according to a click-wrap scheme.

[69] On the other hand, this formula appeared excessively unbalanced with a view to replacing the consent with the formality mentioned above, and caused the poor level of acceptance of the UCITA by the States.

[70] See, among others: Hines v. Overstock.com, Inc., 668 F. Supp. 2d 362, 366 (EDNY 2009); Bragg v. Linden Research, Inc., 487 F. Supp. 2d 593 (ED Pa. 2007); In re RealNetworks, Inc., Privacy Litigation, 2000 WL 631341 (ED Tex. 2000), and Brower v. Gateway 2000, Inc., 676 NYS 2d 569 (NY App. Div. 1998). For reviews and comments: Moringiello and Reynolds (2010). According to Gillette (2005), p. 983, the real problem is that judges will not be able to distinguish a term that is exploitative from a term inspired by an efficient risk allocation; since standard practices require legal compensation in electronic contracts and such remedies cannot derive from jurisprudence, the suggestion is that the appropriate forum for intervention is the administrative, not judicial; while Hillman and Rachlinski (2002) noted that online bargaining in standard format does

Legal scholars seem to confirm this orientation, even if there is a strong dissent on the specific question of compliance with the agreements in the absence of effective consent.[71]

In general, new forms of technology contracts are judged applicable by the majority of the courts, confirming the ability of contract law to address issues caused by technology.[72] In view of the trade-off between consent and speed, they exchange effective consent with the speed and facilitation of commercial transactions online.[73]

However, the click-wrap and browse-wrap contracts show that there are cases in which a contract is formed by altering the normal sequence of steps of the negotiation, when the consent of both parties is based on previous effective knowledge of the good or service and of the contractual conditions.[74]

Electronic agents are particular programs developed to perform different tasks also independently, including those for researching and correcting commercial offers, comparing them, collecting data and information, concluding contracts, etc.[75]

The use of electronic agents in bargaining gives rise to a break between the programming of the negotiating will and its externalization, even in the absence of the subjective alterity that characterizes the representation.[76]

---

not require different treatment in the digital age, while unconsciousness and the doctrines of consent are still a valid framework for analyzing the related contracts.

[71] See: Macaulay (2004); Braucher (2000); Bern (2004). Against those criticisms, mainly focused on the destruction of contract law based on consent and potential harm to consumers: Marotta Wurgler (2009), who has shown that in the software sector, at least on the US market, the terms of the end-user license agreements such as rolling contracts are not systematically in favor of the seller with respect to the terms included in the contracts available to users before the purchase. The "pay now, terms after" agreements, therefore, are not necessarily bad for users, be they professionals or consumers.

[72] Radin (2004), p. 3, notes that "these '-wrap' procedures are not 'agreements' in accord with the traditional rhetoric of 'consent' and 'meeting of the minds', but neither are most contracts in the contemporary offline world."

[73] In this perspective, see: Kim (2007), p. 800.

[74] See: Granieri (2017), p. 24; Savirimuthu (2005), p. 121.

[75] On the subject, see among others: Sartor (2009); Weitzenboeck (2001); Poggi (2000); Hayzelden and Bigham (1999); Lerouge (1999); Smed (1998).

[76] UCITA defines the electronic agent as "a computer program or electronic or automated means, used independently to initiate an action, or to respond to electronic message or performances, on the person's behalf without review or action by an individual at the time of the action or response to the message or performance," and "a person that uses an electronic agent that it has selected for making an authentication, performance or agreement, including manifestation of assent, is bound by the operations of the electronic agent, even if no individual was aware or reviewed the agent's operations or the results of the operations."

The regulatory definition contained in UCITA highlights the automatic nature of the electronic agent as a computer program characterized by the initiation of actions independently and the execution of the assigned tasks without the supervision of the interested party, and the imputability of the result to the user, who remains bound by it even if he is not aware of the transactions concluded or the related effects.

Considering that the electronic agent acts, while respecting the programming of its user in relation to a type of contract, with a margin of autonomy—increasingly broader with the development of machine learning and artificial intelligence[77]—it is necessary to question the mechanism of imputation and, therefore, the binding nature of the electronic agent for the user.[78]

The reconstructive proposals on the subject, which in any case submit the agreements thus stipulated to the governance of the contract regulation,[79] on one hand, converge on the current impossibility of attributing to the electronic agent a subjectivity in the proper sense, given the absence of a legal capacity and a patrimonial sphere.

On the other hand, there is a substantial dichotomy between those who trace the phenomenon back to the representation or figure of the *nuncius*,[80] and others who deny any dualism, solving the question of imputation based on the principle of self-responsibility, considering the electronic agent as an instrument of manifestation of the will of the human contracting party that makes use of it.[81]

A further reconstruction suggests a so-called intentional analysis, based on the postulate that the electronic agent, although not a legal subject, constitutes the term of a delegation relationship, the so-called cognitive delegation, with which the user entrusts the program with the task of entering into exchange relationships on his behalf.

To this end, then, the program performs "the necessary cognitive processes", so that the latter would be relevant for the law, while the user's cognitive states have no relevance.[82]

---

[77] See, among others: Linarelli (2019).

[78] On this point, see the United Nations Convention on the Use of Electronic Communications in International Contracts UNCITRAL of 23 November 2005, which in Art. 12 provides that: "A contract formed by the interaction of an automated system and a natural person, or by the interaction of automated message systems, shall not be denied validity on the sole ground that no natural person reviewed or intervened in each of the individual actions carried out by the automated message system or the resulting contract."

[79] In this perspective, see e.g.: Finocchiaro (2003).

[80] See e.g., in this regard: Sartor (2009).

[81] See, for example: Finocchiaro (2003). However, the qualification of the use of an electronic agent in terms of substitution in legal activity subverts the principles of the general theory of subjectivity, since there would be the hypothesis of a natural person who uses an unpersonified person to act in the exercise of an activity of legal relevance. Vice-versa, legislators require at least the ability to understand and want both in the representative and in the *nuncius* Thus, relevance is given to the subjective states of the representative and the latter is assumed as having financial autonomy, characteristics that are not found in electronic agents.

[82] See again: Sartor (2009). So, for example, the willful misconduct and error, regardless of a programming defect, would be those of the electronic agent and not the user. These defects of consent should not be understood in a subjective key, but in relation to the circumstances and the trust generated by the counterparty regarding the reasonable existence of the intention underlying the declaration.

However, such a reconstruction would require a complex identification of mechanisms suitable to accurately distinguish the will of the user from that of the electronic agent, as well as an identification of the rules on representation applicable to the latter which appears to be difficult practicability.[83]

Therefore, it seems more correct to find the basis of the criterion for attributing the action of the electronic agent in the principle of self-responsibility, regardless of the rules on substitution in legal activity which appear in this case entrusted to uncertain mechanisms.[84]

From a comparative point of view, the EU Directives haven't directly addressed the issue of electronic agents.[85] In the US, the UETA and the E-Sign provide for the formation of contracts through them, similarly to international sources such as the UNCITRAL Convention on the use of electronic communications in international contracts.[86]

Bargaining through electronic agents is currently taking place mainly in the business-to-business context. Its most widespread current version is that of machine-to-machine interactions on the so-called Internet of Things.[87]

Transactions are carried out by and within the information systems of two or more companies, with instantaneous exchanges and internal to the interconnected

---

[83] Considering that those rules which presuppose subjectivity, capacity, and patrimonial autonomy of the represented person are by definition inapplicable to her.

[84] In this sense, see: Teubner (2018).

[85] See: Poggi (2000), p. 265; Weitzenboeck (2001), p. 228; Kryczka (2005), p. 167. On the other hand, recently the European Parliament, in the Resolution of 16 February 2017 containing recommendations to the Commission concerning civil law rules on robotics (2015/2103 (INL)), and the European Bank for Reconstruction and Development, in the report Smart Contracts: Legal Framework and Proposed Guidelines for Lawmakers of October 2018, available on: https://www.ebrd.com, have raised the question of whether to update the regulatory framework to the existence of electronic agents with the capacity to independently enter into contracts and/or act as representatives of a contracting party. More generally on the EU approach to AI, see instead, lastly, the Proposal for a Regulation of the European Parliament and of the Council Laying Down Harmonised Rules on Artificial Intelligence (Artificial Intelligence Act) and Amending Certain Union Legislative Acts, Brussels 21.4.2021, COM(2021) 206 final. Its goal is to ensure that any AI improvements are based on rules that safeguard the functioning of markets and the public sector, and people's safety and fundamental rights. This is pursued through a legal framework which provides rules on four different levels of risk: unacceptable risk, high risk, limited risk, and minimal risk. Unacceptable risks are banned. High-risk AI systems are subject to strict obligations before they can be placed on the market. These measures include proper risk assessment and ongoing monitoring of dataset quality, as well as adequate human oversight. Limited-risk systems are subject to specific transparency obligations, requiring service providers, for example, to make users aware that they are interacting with a machine so that they can make an informed decision to continue or step back. Finally, minimal-risk systems are allowed to be used freely but may still be subject to voluntary codes of conduct, as well as to regulatory sandboxes to facilitate responsible innovation.

[86] On this point, see: Martin (2008), pp. 491–492; Kierkegaard (2007), p. 41; Sommer (2000), pp. 1145–1177.

[87] See: Höller et al. (2014), pp. 233 ff.; Sundmaeker et al. (2010); Lerouge (1999); Nimmer (1996), p. 213.

systems,[88] while the human parts only had a role in defining the general contractual framework a priori.[89]

Thus, in general so far legislators and regulators have avoided specific interventions on the subject, leaving it to private autonomy and the "new *lex mercatoria*".[90] Electronic agents, in fact, have not completely removed the role of consent and the human factor associated with the structuring of the contractual structure and the programming of the machines to execute the instructions.

The transaction itself may not be consensual, but its origins are, so the traditional rules of contract law shall apply to them.[91]

3.3 Complexity of Economic Relations and Contractual Incompleteness

In practice, it is frequently the case in which the concluded contracts prove to be incomplete, that is to say, they do not provide for the description and regulation of all the possible circumstances that may arise for the parties.

This happens more frequently in those complex and articulated negotiation operations through which the contracting parties intend to create a regulatory structure of interests not entirely typified by the legislator.[92]

Contractual figures which provide long-term obligations for the parties, then, may not consider circumstances which did not initially arise in the drafting and stipulation phase.

---

[88] However, there may be typical problems of traditional bargaining, such as the battle of forms when the two systems are programmed to issue and accept orders according to their standard terms; see again: Nimmer (1996), p. 232.

[89] According to Kobayashi (2005), the design of the business model by the parties is also instrumental in shaping the new scenario of electronic bargaining, while providing incentives to prevent opportunism. Savirimuthu (2005), p. 131, refers to this model of contract as "mediated consent". See also: Weitzenboeck (2001), p. 215, for a discussion on electronic agents according to the agency's regulation and a possible application of an objective theory of consent to the electronic agent. *Contra*: Radin (2000), p. 1130.

[90] UNCITRAL proposed a draft model law on the legal aspects of electronic data interchange and related media in 1995. In the United States, the American Bar Association worked on a model agreement many years ago: The Electronic Messaging Task Force, The Commercial Use of Electronic Data Interchange. A Report and Model Trading Partner Agreement (Business Lawyer, 1990, 45:1645–1749). See: Sabett (1996), pp. 530–531. Regarding the "new *lex mercatoria*", see *amplius* above in Chap. 2, Sect. 2.3.

[91] In this sense, see: Moringiello and Reynolds (2010), p. 485.

[92] Think, for example, of those contractual figures originated from the practices of the Anglo-Saxon countries that govern operations, commercial techniques and goods or services resulting from recently developed solutions.

In this perspective, US scholars have theorized the figure of the so-called relational contract, with a view to highlighting the importance of relational remedies compared to traditional contractual ones.[93]

In Europe, the so-called organizational contract paradigm has been proposed for the framing of long-term contractual cooperation, contract networks, etc.[94]

The incompleteness of the contract, therefore, produces as a consequence the emergence of conflicts between the contracting parties, who, during the execution of the contractual relationship, do not agree on the regulation of one or more supervening circumstances that affect their structure of interests.[95]

The traditional contract theory based on the consent of the contracting parties was based on the assumption of the completeness of the legal system. With reference to private autonomy, such a theory reconnected the regulation of the contractual relationship to the rules on the contract in general and typical contracts, as expressions of the will of the contracting parties.

However, the complexity of business, induced by economic development and technological innovation, and by the related incessant and progressive articulation of trade in goods and services, has shifted the attention of the interpreters to the concepts and functions of the cause in civil law, more recently formulated as economic function,[96] and the consideration in common law.

In this context, therefore, it is not sufficient to verify whether the scheme used by the parties is compatible with a contractual type, but it is necessary to identify, respectively, the meaning of the underlying economic operation in civil law and the functional counter-performance of the exchange in common law, with regard to all the purposes that determined the parties, even tacitly, at the conclusion of the contract.[97]

In current economic practice, however, the economic operation to which the parties aim, or the consideration at the basis of their relationship, are increasingly too complex to be exhausted into a single contractual regulation. So, new needs have emerged in business practice for considerably articulated contracts.

---

[93] See: Macneil (1969); Id. (1985); Id. (2000); Goetz and Scott (1981). Regarding the continuing relevance of contract law remedies, see: Eisenberg (1999); Baker and Choi (2015). On the relationship between long-term and relational contracts, see also: Hviid (2000).

[94] See: Grundmann et al. (2013). Regarding the phenomenon of cooperation between companies from a competitive point of view, so-called coopetition, one may refer to: Ghidini and Stazi (2015).

[95] See, among others: Rossi (2014); Hart (2008); Tirole (1999).

[96] The formulation of the cause as an "economic-individual function" of the contract, that is, of the economic interest that the contracting parties intend to achieve through the same, has been elaborated by civil law scholars. In this perspective, the cause is the element that connects the objective economic operation to the subjects who are the authors. The economic operation represents the *trait d'union* between the subjective and objective theory of the cause, and acts as a reference point both to analyze contractual cases with a particularly complex structure, and to fill the gaps and resolve the disputes that emerge during the relationship. See e.g., Gabrielli (2013), pp. 159 ff.

[97] See among others: Calleros (2013); Storme (1998); Lorenzen (1919).

Therefore, it is common for the economic operation and consideration to be pursued through or a plurality of functionally connected bargains, or incomplete contract(s) which shall be integrated and implemented over time.[98]

3.4 Interpretation and Integration of the Contract

Today's dynamics of economic relations and cross-border exchanges in the global market, then, give rise to advanced contractual models and articulated contractual operations, far from the typical figures envisaged by the legislator.[99]

The contract drafting technique tends to increasingly define the conventional regulation completely through contractual modules exported, or imposed by the strongest companies, beyond national borders, so as not to leave gaps—and therefore risks for contracting parties—on the key points of the economic operation.

The standardized offer of goods and services is often joined by an equally standardized adoption of contractual models, which sometimes report slavishly the norms of legislation.[100]

The tendency to establish in the text of the covenant regulation as many possible provisions that the relationship over time can generate derives from the willingness of the contracting parties to avoid incurring unexpected events.

In fact, they would risk interrupting the execution of the contractual obligation,[101] and give rise to the occurrence of a possible controversy that may require to be resolved using remedies unrelated to the contract.[102]

In this regard, an ever-increasing number of formal obligations—particularly information obligations—placed by the parties, especially by the proposing and/or professional subject, give rise to a "neo-formalism" of the contractual regulation.[103]

In the interpretation of the contract aimed at identifying the common intention of the parties of the negotiation, it is necessary to adopt a functional approach that looks

[98] The negotiation link takes place whenever the parties, in the exercise of their autonomy, give rise to separate contracts, contextually or otherwise. These contracts are characterized according to their cause and their negotiation type, to which they are subject. However, they are intended to be functionally connected to each other and mutually dependent, so that the events of one affect the others. In doctrine, see among others: Pannebakker (2013); Samoy and Loos (2012); Mitu Gulati et al. (2000).

[99] See, among others: Pannebakker (2013); Whitmore (1996).

[100] See e.g., European Commission, Standard contractual clauses for data transfers between EU and non-EU countries, 2001–2010, available at: https://ec.europa.eu/info/law/law-topic/data-protection/international-dimension-data-protection/standard-contractual-clauses-scc_en; Patterson (2010–2011).

[101] In this regard, see: Weisberg (1987).

[102] See e.g.: Triantis (2009); Macneil (1962).

[103] In this perspective, see: Murray Jr (2002); Charny (1999).

not only at the declarations in the contract text, but above all to the economic function or consideration pursued by the contracting parties.[104]

The hermeneutic procedure starts, therefore, from the literal analysis of the declaration, to grasp its objective meaning. Where necessary, then, it examines other extra-textual hermeneutic elements, the legal meaning of the declaration, and the common intention of the parties, to identify the economic function or consideration they pursue through the bargain.

In some cases, as mentioned in the previous section, the complex exchanges that characterize today's commercial relationships develop through transactions carried out with several functionally connected contracts.

Although this generally implies the unity of the evaluation of the negotiation operation and its possible defects, in some cases the invalidity of a stipulation will not overwhelm the entire operation.[105]

From the point of view of the relationship between interpretation and language, the various economic sectors are characterized by their own languages, based on peculiar terms and technicalities that are inserted in the contractual regulations by the contracting parties according to the negotiation operation put in place in the specific case.[106]

With reference to the language of telematic exchanges, the predominant use of the English language is immediately evident, which—together with the American contractual model often adopted by US large international companies—penetrates the legal language bringing with it its terms and neologisms.[107]

Another profile of particular relevance is that of the integration of the contract, which today is clearly distinct from its interpretation.[108]

The determinations of the parties expressing the contractual regulation may not reflect all the elements desired by them. Therefore, the content of the contract can be integrated with additional elements, not necessarily deriving exclusively from the intent of the parties but which in any case contribute to the common objective pursued by them.[109]

The integration represents the logical procedure aimed at identifying the settlement of an aspect of the contractual relationship not foreseen by the parties, due to an oversight, due to ignorance of certain circumstances, or because it is not foreseeable at the time of the conclusion of the contract. Consequently, the parties may be faced

---

[104] See, in this sense: Shavell (2006); Posner (2004).

[105] See among others: Samoy and Loos (2012). Indeed, some agreements, such as the option, the pre-emption right, the penal clause, the non-competition agreement etc., which according to some can be qualified in themselves as complete although ancillary contracts, if declared void they do not compromise the stability and effectiveness of the economic operation; see: Sammarco (2006), p. 149.

[106] In this regard, see e.g.: Weisberg (1987); Williman (1986).

[107] See: Zeno-Zencovich (2008), pp. 103 ff.; Walter (1988).

[108] See e.g.: Elofson (1996); Gillette (1990); Ayres and Gertner (1989).

[109] See: Yildrim (2019); Lewis and Roehrich (2009).

with obligations initially not foreseen or declined in a different way, with evident reflections on the dogmas of the binding and unchangeable nature of the agreements.[110]

In addition to the will of the parties, sources of integration of the contract may be the law, if the will of the parties has not been expressed in the opposite way, or the uses or equity, in the event of failure to express the will of the parties and absence of dispositive laws.

In Europe, for example, relevant legislative parameters may come from EU law and from the so-called European private law, with particular regard to the Principles of European Contract Law, which can be applied when required by law or by the parties.[111]

Particularly in Art. 6:102 of the PECL, it is stated that, together with the expressed clauses, the contract may contain "implicit clauses" which derive from the intention of the parties, from the nature and object of the contract, from good faith and correctness.

Internationally, Article 4.8 of the UNIDROIT Principles on international commercial contracts provides that if the parties have not agreed on an important term for the determination of their rights and duties, a clause appropriate to the circumstances may be inserted.

Such a clause shall be identified, keeping in mind the intention of the parties, the nature and purpose of the contract, the good faith and existing practices, and uses for that specific business.[112]

Furthermore, Articles 5.1 and 5.2 state that the contractual obligations may be expressed or implied and, in the event of gaps in the negotiating regulation, clauses appropriate to the circumstances may be added.

Such clauses shall also be identified with reference to the intention of the parties, the nature and purpose of the contract,[113] good faith, commercial practices and uses relating to that specific business.

The provisions therefore reiterate, among other things, the important role traditionally played in the matter by uses, whether they are contractual, that is contractual clauses, or normative, i.e. unwritten rules respected as legally binding rules.

---

[110] In this regard, see among others: Williams (2020); Yildrim (2019); Farnsworth (1968).

[111] The PECL contain multiple provisions relevant for the integration of the contract: see especially Arts. 1:101, 1:103, 1:105, 1:106. Of particular interest is the provision contemplated by Art. 4:109, relating to the excessive contractual imbalance, according to which, as an alternative to the option of annulment, at the request of the party entitled to ask for it, the judge can, if the remedy is adequate, modify the contract to harmonize it with what could have been agreed by the parties in respect of good faith and fairness. In a partially similar way, Art. 3.10 of the UNIDROIT Principles on international commercial contracts, basing any intervention on "Reasonable commercial standards of fair dealing" (without recalling good faith). See: Keirse (2011); Micklitz (2004); Lando (1992).

[112] Regarding the above provisions of the UNIDROIT Principles and their application in commercial practice, see: Bonell (2009).

[113] Therefore, where the contract is attributable to a specific type of negotiation, to the regulation of that type, which is generally adopted by the contracting parties for the purposes of the economic operation pursued.

Given their relevance, uses are in fact collected and classified by multiple market players, such as chambers of commerce, etc.[114]

Equity, then, represents a supplementary reference criterion for the purpose of equitable reconciliation of the interests of the parties. This may happen within the framework of a negotiating scheme for which it is not possible to identify the rule applicable to an event that gives rise to an economic imbalance of the synallagma, neither based on the agreement of the parties, nor of the law or customs.[115]

3.5 Good Faith and Contractual Contingency

The central parameter for the conclusion, interpretation, and execution of the contract is that of good faith. Good faith in a subjective sense precisely indicates a subjective state of those who ignore to infringe the rights of others.[116] Good faith in an objective sense refers to the rules of correctness which must be followed in fulfilling the obligation, in negotiations, in the interpretation, in the execution of the contract, etc.[117]

Interpretation in good faith means to understand the contract as two correct and respectful contracting parties would understand it.

Good faith excludes, in essence, that it is possible to try to leverage the literal meaning of single words or clauses, or the failure to insert certain clauses, to demand a literal and integral fulfillment of the contract, in contrast precisely with the good faith.[118]

At the same time, the principle of good faith allows to go beyond the will of the individual parties and to bind them to the objective meaning of their contractual declarations. In this perspective, good faith protects the assignment of the recipient of the declaration.[119]

The principle is widespread in various legal systems both of civil and common law, such as the German,[120] French,[121] and US ones.[122] It has been discussed whether it is possible to distinguish between the systems which attribute a central

[114] See e.g.: Gilson et al. (2014); Sacco and De Nova (2016), pp. 1390–1391.

[115] In this regard, see: Yildrim (2019); Valcke (2008); Posner (2004).

[116] For example, anyone who ignores the right to infringe the owner's rights is a good faith owner.

[117] Regarding the distinction, see: Hesselink (2011); Zimmermann and Whittaker (2000); Teubner (1998); Beatson and Friedmann (1997).

[118] On this point, see: Markovits (2014); Sacco and De Nova (2016), pp. 1367 ff.

[119] See e.g.: Kessler and Fine (1964); Gilmore (1954).

[120] See: § 242 BGB.

[121] Art. 1134 Civil Code.

[122] § 1-203 UCC. Regarding the duty to negotiate in good faith in US law and on the importance of the concept in the various common law systems, see: Houh (2003); Burton (1980); Summers (1968).

role to good faith and those which exclude its existence as a general principle, by limiting themselves to recognizing its relevance only in relation to certain specific cases or remedies.

According to the preferable reconstruction, it does not seem possible to identify such a clear distinction, particularly between the civil law and common law systems.[123]

Good faith plays a central role in some civil law systems, particularly in the German[124] and Italian systems.[125]

In Germany, § 242 BGB has always been a cornerstone of the system and has been fundamental for the adaptation of the BGB allowing the introduction of multiple contractual rules not foreseen by the legislator, such as protective duties, vexatious clauses, abuse of the law, contract review, etc.[126]

In Italy, while until recently legal scholars affirmed the scarce relevance of the general clauses, and particularly of the principle of good faith, the growing relevance of both the general clauses and the principle of good faith itself emerged.[127]

In the French legal system, notwithstanding its relevance, the existence of a general principle of good faith is controversial.[128]

In common law, although principles such as good faith are generally seen as pitfalls to the certainty of legal relationships between individuals, different remedies respond to the same needs, inspired by the same reference values.[129]

The criterion of good faith in an objective sense therefore represents the parameter for identifying and applying the tools aimed at realizing the reasonableness and efficiency of a legal system.[130]

---

[123] In this sense, see: Zimmermann and Whittaker (2000), pp. 7 ff.; Lando (2007), pp. 844 ff.

[124] In it, *bona fides* of Romanistic origin is connected with the Germanic notion of *Treu und Glauben*. The German Civil Code consecrates good faith in an objective sense, contemplating it as: (a) duty of the debtor to perform the services in accordance with objective good faith (§ 242 BGB); (b) contract interpretation criterion (§ 157 BGB); (c) criterion for assessing the unfair behavior of the party that prevented the fulfillment of the condition to its detriment and a prerequisite for considering the condition however fulfilled, or for assessing the behavior of the party that determined the fulfillment of the condition to its advantage and however, consider the condition as missed (§ 162 BGB); (d) criterion for justifying the debtor's refusal to perform a service disproportionately onerous in relation to the creditor's interest (§ 275, par. 2, BGB); (e) criterion for assessing the abusive nature of the clauses contained in the general contract conditions prepared by a professional operator and as a prerequisite for considering them ineffective (§ 307 ss. BGB); (f) criterion at the basis of the possibility of obtaining the adaptation of the contract to the change in the circumstances underlying it (§ 313 BGB), etc.

[125] In this regard, see: Zimmermann and Whittaker (2000), pp. 7 ff.; Lando (2007), p. 845; along with the seminal work of Jhering (1861).

[126] See, in particular: Bork and Wandt (2020).

[127] In this sense, see e.g.: Cabella Pisu and Nanni (1998).

[128] See: Ancel (2011); Zimmermann and Whittaker (2000), p. 33.

[129] See: Zimmermann and Whittaker (2000), pp. 15 and 36 ff.; Lando (2007), pp. 848 ff.

[130] Reasonableness is thus a point of substantial convergence between the common law and the civil law jurists. The first, starting from the perspective of remedies, assesses the case based on reasonableness. The second, starting from the perspective of rights, assesses whether the act constitutes a legitimate exercise of a right and otherwise can declare it contrary to good faith, abusive or generically unreasonable.

Good faith is the reference term for checking consistency between the purposes for which legal remedies are granted and those for which concretely those remedies are experienced.[131]

In this perspective, in Europe both the PECL and the Draft Common Frame of Reference[132] give wide emphasis to the objective good faith, establishing that the rules which compose them must be interpreted and developed independently and in accordance with their objectives, and that particular attention must be given the need to promote good faith and fairness, the certainty of contractual relations and uniformity of application.

Thus, more specifically, good faith is considered as: (1) a requirement to be respected in the conduct of the negotiations, in the determination of the content and in the conclusion of the contract;[133] (2) a criterion of interpretation of the contract;[134] (3) its integration criterion;[135] (4) a duty to be respected in the conduct of negotiations and in the conclusion of the contract.[136]

Similarly, the Common European Sales Law provides that the parties are required to act in good faith and fairness. The violation of this duty may: (a) preclude the party from exercising a right, remedy or exception of which it could otherwise make use of; or (b) make it liable for any damage deriving from the violation to the other party.[137] Furthermore, good faith is indicated as a criterion for interpreting and integrating the contract.[138]

On the remedies resulting from the violation of the duty of good faith, at European level the traditional distinction between the rules of conduct of the parties and the validity of the contract[139] tends to be overcome.[140]

---

[131] In this regard, see e.g.: MacMahon (2015).

[132] Principles, Definitions and Model Rules of European Private Law. Draft Common Frame of Reference (DCFR), prepared by the Study Group on a European Civil Code and the Research Group on EC Private Law (Acquis Group), Sellier, Munich, 2009. See: Emmert (2012); Somma (2009); Heidenmüller et al. (2008).

[133] See: Art. 1:102 PECL; Art. II.—1:102 DCFR.

[134] Art. 5:102, lett. g, PECL; Art. II.—8:102, par. 1, lett. g, DCFR.

[135] Art. 6:102, lett. c, PECL, which provides for the integration through implied terms; Art. II.—9: 101, par. 2, lett. c, DCFR.

[136] As well as specifically as a reference parameter in terms of remedies, through a series of provisions that indicate it as a criterion or presupposition to look at when applying remedies for violations or other contractual pathologies. See: Ricci (2013), pp. 636–641.

[137] Art. 2 CESL, which excludes the derogation of these provisions.

[138] See respectively Art. 59, lett. h), and 68.1, lett. c) CESL.

[139] So, the violation of the former could lead to the termination of the contract but would not be suitable to cause its invalidity. In this sense, see e.g.: Ancel (2011), pp. 95–96; *contra*: Perlingieri (2013), pp. 31 ff.

[140] Think of the aforementioned provision pursuant to Art. 2 CESL, as well as the provisions of the remedies for violations of good faith which include the obligation to pay compensation (Art. 2: 301 PECL and Art. II.—3: 301 DCFR), but also the cancellation of the contract concluded in error (Art. 4: 203 of the PECL, Art. II.—7: 201 of the DCFR and Art. 48 CESL) or for malice (Art. 4: 107 PECL, Art. II.—7: 205 DCFR and Art. 49 CESL) and the cancellation (Articles 4: 109 and 4: 110 PECL), or the ineffectiveness (Articles II.—9: 409 DCFR and Art. 79 CESL) of the unfair terms.

The above-mentioned provisions which deny the effects of the cases of violation of the duty of good faith, in fact, are now considered expressions of the rule affirmed on the matter.[141]

Finally, another profile of relevance of good faith is in the cases of contractual supervenience,[142] which modifies the balance between the services originally set by the contracting parties.

In this regard, many legal systems provide remedies such as rescission of the contract, termination due to excessive onerousness, or the possibility of requesting a revision of the amount of the consideration.[143]

In these hypotheses, one option is that of the renegotiation of the contract, with respect to which a wide theoretical elaboration and a consolidated practice have developed at international level.

The covenant adjustment of the contract can be pursued through various mechanisms, in particular automatic adjustment[144] clauses, renegotiation or unilateral modification clauses of the contract content, or devolution clauses of the variation to a third party.[145]

In common law, this type of contract adjustment mechanism is known as the hardship clause. It is characterized by the provision of the option to suspend the execution of the contract, with the consequent imposition of the conventional obligation to renegotiate in the presence of certain contingencies.[146]

Otherwise, such a clause may provide an automatism identified in detail to increase or decrease the economic advantages deriving from the contract. This automatism is activated when a change occurs in the context in which the contractual relationship is inserted, determined by an unforeseeable cause, not attributable to any party and of appreciable importance.[147]

The impulse to adapt the contractual conditions derives from the structure and function of long-term contracts, be they of duration or periodic execution, especially if in the context of relations between companies.[148]

---

[141] See, for example: Ricci (2013), pp. 644 ff. In the US system, see as well: MacMahon (2015), pp. 2066 ff.

[142] Regarding which, see e.g.: Barela (2012); Karampatzos (2005).

[143] In the Italian system, respectively, Art. 1447, 1467, and for example 1664 of the Italian Civil Code In doctrine, see: Gallo (2011); Gambino (2004). On judicial review in the German legal system, see: Köbler (1991); Larenz (1957).

[144] Consider, for example, the clauses for indexing pecuniary benefits.

[145] See, among others: Sirena and Patti (2020); Hillman (1987). The renegotiation clause, in particular, entrusts the overcoming of the imbalance between the performances or the difficulties of execution caused by contingencies upon reaching a revision agreement between the parties.

[146] In this regard, see: Schwenzer and Muñoz (2019); Fisher (2018).

[147] See: Perillo (1997); Maskow (1992); Oppetit (1974).

[148] On the subject, see: Pardolesi and Granieri (2005); Sen (1996); Horn (1981). If good faith can trigger the obligation for the parties to renegotiate, therefore, this only happens because renegotiation constitutes a legally relevant requirement, which is related to the necessary protraction of the contractual relationship over time.

In European private law, Art. 89 of the proposed regulation on a Common European Sales Law requires the parties to the sales contract—in the presence of unforeseen contingencies and not included in the contractual area or subject to a specific risk assumption, and such as to make the execution excessively burdensome—the obligation to enter into a negotiation aimed at modifying the content of the contract or dissolving it. If the negotiation fails, each party can turn to the judge to request the modification or the termination of the contract.[149]

A similar provision is found in Art. 6.2.3 of the UNIDROIT Principles and in Art. 6:111 of the PECL, according to which, if the parties do not find an agreement, the judge has the power to terminate the contract, or to modify it. This, to distribute "in a fair and equitable way the losses and the advantages deriving from the change of circumstances", to prevent the economic consequences of contingency from falling on only one of the parties.[150]

In German law § 313 BGB, in the presence of *Wegfall der Geschäftsgrundlage* (elimination of the business basis), provides for the *Anpassungsanspruch* (adjustment claim), where possible and payable, and otherwise the withdrawal from the contract, on the other hand, not providing for the *Neuverhandlungspflicht* (obligation to renegotiate).[151]

On the other hand, German jurisprudence, now in the light of European private law, continues to recognize the obligation to cooperate with a view to adapting the content of the contract to the circumstances that have arisen.[152]

The Dutch Civil Code reform of 1992, instead, introduced in Art. 6:258 BW the faculty of the parties to ask the judge to modify the contract, or alternatively the partial resolution, in the presence of unforeseen circumstances such as not to justify, based on reasonableness and fairness, the conservation of the original structure.[153]

In the Italian legal system, the thesis of the legal obligation to renegotiate is still opposed, and it is believed that the content of the obligation should be limited to soliciting the self-determination of the parties and not even making it an act due in the outcomes.[154]

Moreover, the renegotiation is also linked to the power relationships between the parties, as occurs in the case of the prohibition of abuse of economic dependence, which the jurisprudence considers may also justify the use of the sentence to fulfillment, possibly as a precautionary measure, if the violation of Art. 9 of law no. 192/1998 results in the arbitrary interruption of commercial relations.[155]

---

[149]Regarding the obligation to renegotiate in European private law, see: Collins (2011); Storme (2003).

[150]In this regard, see: Cabrillac et al. (2011).

[151]See: Piraino (2015), p. 595; Martinek (1998).

[152]In this regard, see: Lùttringhaus (2013).

[153]See: Busch (2002).

[154]See: Macario (2008), pp. 1061–1062.

[155]In this sense, see: Piraino (2015), pp. 596–597.

3.6 Contract Standardization and Disclosure Obligations

If traditionally the contract was mainly the result of a negotiation process between parties with symmetrical bargaining power,[156] this changed with the standardization of the contractual conditions that allowed the bargaining in the mass market at national and international level.

With the development of the information society and digital economy, this easier and faster way of contracting has changed the negotiation process, minimizing human involvement, and thus reducing transaction costs.[157]

Consequently, in recent decades, with the aim of restoring the balance of bargaining power compromised by standardization, a plethora of regulations have been adopted concerning the use of general terms and conditions or on the protection of consumers or other categories of weak contracting parties.[158]

Despite the considerable regulatory production that has resulted from the various legal systems, the principle of contractual freedom has evidently assumed a different and more limited role today, at least in the cases of contracts with weak contracting parties and electronic commerce, often based on so-called take it or leave it proposals.[159]

In this scenario, the ubiquity of the regulation of disclosure obligations, or disclosure regulation, is recognized almost unanimously by legal scholars.[160]

The question[161] of what the minimum information burden owed by the offeror is requires a comparative survey, aimed at identifying univocal ideas applicable to telematic transactions.

The known simplification, which sees in the Anglo-Saxon system the prevalence of legal principles of a liberal matrix, and in the Italian and French systems the centrality of *bona fides*, with consequent different attention towards the weak contracting party, does not consider the prevalent impact in the practice of rules

[156] In this regard, see among others: Parisi et al. (2017); Farnsworth (2006), pp. 911 ff.; von Mehren (2008).

[157] On the subject, see: Collins (2018); Cornelius (2018); Neumayer (2008); Patterson (2010–2011); Hillman and Rachlinski (2002); Pratt Jr. (1988).

[158] In this regard, see e.g.: Farnsworth (2006), pp. 912 ff.; Neumayer (2008); von Mehren (2008); one may also see: Stazi (2012a, b).

[159] In this sense, see: Woebbeking (2019), p. 107; Farnsworth (2006), pp. 912 ff.; Neumayer (2008).

[160] See, among others: Busch and De Franceschi (2018); Ben-Shahar and Schneider (2014); Id. (2011); Bar-Gill and Ben-Shahar (2013); Baldwin et al. (2012), pp. 119 ff.; Majone (1997).

[161] Of Ciceronian memory: the classic example was that of the trader who imported wheat from Alexandria to Rhodes in a period of famine, and who during the voyage at sea saw other boats, carrying the same goods. Arrived first in Rhodes, he could be silent about the arrival of other loads, thus making a profit on the sale price? According to Cicero, this would have been contrary to good faith (De Officiis, III, p. 319). Conversely, in the footsteps of Diogenes, St. Thomas (Summa theol., II, ii, lxvii, p. 3) considered it legitimate, thus grafting the rule of the *caveat emptor*.

that do not arise from state legal contexts, but rather aim at certainty, simplification and speed of exchange.[162]

In the French legal system, in the face of the growing perception of the injustice of an ineffective contractual model, there has been a progressive interpretative dilation in the legislative dictates in favor of the substantial rebalancing of the interests of the parties.

Starting from the rules relating to error and willful misconduct,[163] the jurisprudence of legitimacy introduced the general principle of the burden of information on the strong contracting party, which later crystallized in the legislation on the *contrat d'adhésion*.[164]

The presumption of good faith foreseen in Art. 2268 of the Civil Code, therefore, is substantiated in the lack of deception measured on the recipient, which is moreover *sui generis* in electronic exchanges.

In the Italian legal system, in addition to the information obligations in the Civil Code,[165] to those of EU origin referred to previously and to many others of similar origin provided for in sectoral regulations, the Consumer Code,[166] especially in Articles 22 and 48 ff., dictates a wide range of provisions on pre-contractual information that professionals are required to provide to consumers.

The Directive 2011/83/EU, in fact, extended these obligations beyond contracts negotiated away from business premises and remotely.[167]

---

[162] In this sense see, among others: Gambino (1999), pp. 311–312.

[163] Dictated before the 2016 reform to Articles 1110 and 1116 of the Civil Code, now Articles 1132–1139.

[164] See: Legrand (1986). In jurisprudence, on information obligations: Cass. civ., 3 February 1981, in *D.*, 1984, p. 457, with a note by Ghestin; on the inexcusable error: Cass. civ., 24 October 1972, in Bull. civ., III, n. 543, p. 396; on good faith among professionals: Cass. civ., November 24, 1976, in Bull. civ., I, 370, p. 291. The significant development, in IT matters, of the so-called *obligation précontractuelle d'information* has made it possible to distinguish the hypotheses related to the complexity of the asset covered by the contract, in which a subject is required to have a simple *avis*, from those in which there is an *obligation de reinsegnement*, that is, an obligation to objectively present the characteristics of the programs, the capacity of the machines and all the technical data concerning their products or services, up to situations in which there is a real *devir de conseil*, an objective suggestion that the seller must provide to the customer once he has learned his specific needs. See: Savatier (1972).

[165] That is, well before the doctrine of Law & Economics in the seventies of the last century theorized information asymmetry as the cause of market failure that legitimizes regulatory intervention; see among others: Schwarz and Wilde (1979).

[166] Legislative Decree 6 September 2005 n. 206, which contains the Consumer Code, OJ 8.10.2005, amended several times.

[167] For a broad examination of the provisions of the Directive and their application, see: European Commission (2017); Srivastava (2017); Helberger et al. (2013); Steennot (2013); Weathwerhill (2012).

Also in this case, the good faith, foreseen in the Art. 1337 of the Civil Code and partially implemented in Art. 1338, acts as a parameter for evaluating the deceptivity with respect to the recipient.[168]

At European level, regulation of information obligations developed in two phases.[169] The first phase was prior to the European policy of harmonization of national contract laws, especially contracts between consumers and professionals. It can be labeled as an "individualized contract" phase, in which the issue of information was dominated by good faith, from which communication or notice obligations to integrate often opaque contractual regulations were obtained.

The second phase developed with the European harmonization process. It can be defined as the "mass contract" phase, marked by the succession of regulatory interventions, often focused on the provision of disclosure obligations of specific elements of fact or law assumed as necessary information background of contracting parties.

The sectoral Directives on timeshare and consumer credit and the consumer rights directive 2011/83/EU, standardized not only content but also information obligations, through the provision of delivery of forms with predetermined content.[170]

Nowadays, the most relevant question seems to have become not so much the quantity of information, often rather counterproductive as excessive with the relative problem of the so-called "no reading", but their intelligibility to the recipient.[171]

Therefore, in the second phase of the information obligations there was a full awareness of the essentiality of the exhibition form and the punctuality of the information contents.

As mass bargaining has been the mainstay of consumer protection regulation, technological evolution, on the one hand, and the ever-increasing differentiation of products and services, on the other, constantly pose new challenges, boosting its development.[172]

The increase in information asymmetry, considered as a market failure, has led to believe that imperative interventions are needed on the information obligations front in terms of reallocation. This, both with reference to the individual contractual

---

[168] Conversely, by not imposing the obligation to disclose to the counterpart any information relating to the contract to be concluded, which would exclude the possibility of the information advantage and neglect the burden of self-information on each contracting party; on this point, see: Piraino (2015), pp. 331 ff.

[169] The centrality of the information profile in the European legal framework emerges in Art. 169, paragraph 1, TFEU, in which the promotion of information is indicated among the tasks of the Union for the purpose of consumer protection.

[170] See: Hall et al. (2012); Grundmann (2013).

[171] Regarding which, see: Ayres and Schwartz (2014); Bakos et al. (2014); Ben-Shahar (2009).

[172] See, among others: Smorto (2018).

relationship and in terms of market regulation with a view to the efficiency of the negotiating system.[173]

In the telematic field, the use in the negotiation of a language not traditionally known as the digital one, however, makes the definition of the relationship between the language and its expressive form of particular importance.

The problem of understanding the content of the electronic exchange is, in fact, preparatory to the scope of the principle of good faith and its application on an interpretative level.

In this sense, the dynamism of the telematic linguistic system,[174] which carries with it supernumerary information, even risks slowing down the time for a correct and transparent contact with the service or content provider.[175]

As part of the individual contractual relationship, the imposition of information obligations on the professional is aimed at rebalancing, at least partially, a relationship deemed unequal, due to the concentration in one of the parties of the so-called information advantage.

This is considered existing whenever one party has a large amount of relevant information on the object and elements of the contract which are generally unknown to the counterparty, as well as the power to determine the negotiating content by guiding the results of the relationship.[176]

In the current globalized and digital economic environment, with the multiplication and amplification of bargaining power and information advantage, information obligations are becoming increasingly important.

Thus, for example, European private law, first, provides an integrated protection system that connects information obligation to content requirements. constraints and constraints of form, as a protective framework of the weak contracting party.

Moreover, European private information law does not only stem from the pre-contractual dimension: the information obligations are displaced at every stage of the contract, including its execution.[177]

Finally, in terms of remedies, there are contrasting phenomena. On the one hand, except for the information on the right of withdrawal, with the controversial figure of the extension of the exercise term, there is no specification of the remedies for the breach, without prejudice to the ordinary route of damages.

On the other hand, there is a tendency towards a progressive, overcoming the criterion of identifying remedies for failure to fulfill obligations based on the

[173]Regarding the dual function of disclosure obligations in European private law as aimed at rebalancing the individual contract but also as tools for market regulation, see: Delfos-Roy (2011); Wihlelmsson (2005); Giliker (2005).

[174]In this regard, see Mital and Elliman (1994).

[175]See, among others: Helberger et al. (2013), pp. 40–41.

[176]See e.g.: Zeno-Zencovich (2021), pp. 268 ff.; Smorto (2018), pp. 437–438.

[177]This extension is of considerable importance also with respect to the usefulness of the criterion of good faith.

distinction between validity rules and correctness rules, going as far as invalidating protection.[178]

3.7 Technology as a Tool and/or Object of the Relationship

Through digital technologies, not only the conclusion, but also the execution of the contract can be carried out entirely online, for example when the agreement allows the user to access resources or download digital content.[179]

The development of cloud computing has substantially changed the offer of digital content, especially software, making the supply consequent to the offer of services and license agreements rather than sales.[180]

When the subject of a contract becomes digital or digitized, technology is no longer only a means of reaching an agreement, but it is also its content, a phenomenon which clearly highlights the issue of the protection of intellectual property online.

Moreover, this implies that the technology can be used to apply the proprietary regime on the resources shared by the owner, with the possibility of modeling the rights and prerogatives of the same according to a scheme defined no longer legally by legislators, but technologically by private actors of the market.

The advent of digital rights management systems, or DRMs, has brought technology to take on a new additional role, which poses even more complex issues. This role is not only facilitating, but also regulatory, with the consequent risk of erosion of the analogous role of contract law.[181]

---

[178] See: Tutt (2013); Storme (2006).

[179] Storage capacity, software, databases, audio-visual content, etc.

[180] European Court of Justice, UsedSoft v. Oracle International, July 3, 2012, C-128/11, in which the Court stated that the effect of exhaustion is produced even when the user has paid to download a copy of a software product and her rights have unlimited duration. The same problem has been raised by some US courts, regardless of whether a contract that the seller calls a "license" should rather be a sale, which would require the application of Art. 2 of the UCC; see: Softman Products Co. v. Adobe Sys., Inc., 171 F. Supp. 2d 1075 (CD Cal 2001). In doctrine, see: Winn and Bix (2006), p. 180. As mentioned *above* in Sect. 3.1, Radin (2000), p. 1135, notes that the real world is populated by contracts-as-products, rather than by contracts-as-consensus, and this argument should make us more prepared to consider not entirely unusual situations in which consent is only presumed.

[181] In the European Union, see Directive 2001/29/EC of the European Parliament and of the Council of 22 May 2001 on the harmonization of certain aspects of copyright and related rights in the information society, OJ 22.6.2001, L 167/10, Arts. 6 and 7. From this unexpected role comes a challenge for spaces of freedom traditionally recognized to users, such as the doctrine of fair use in the United States and exceptions and limitations in Europe. Radin (2000), p. 12, notes that DRMs "bypass the state's structuring of the legal infrastructure of exchange. The DRMS is like an infallible 'injunction' controlled completely by one party." Sommer (2000), p. 1222, stresses that digital rights management is much more precise than traditional intellectual property and facilitates price discrimination in commercial transactions, which is more difficult with physical resources.

Thus, technology joins national and supranational law in the creation of rules for the protection of rights in online exchanges. The standardization and/or regulation processes through technology, in fact, can be faster and more effective than legislative interventions.[182]

In this scenario, the European Union has followed a more proactive regulatory path than the United States, aimed at governing the development of innovation with limited confidence in the virtues of market forces.

Consistent with this view, the legislation has been less intense with regard to business-to-business transactions, in which the parties tend to be more aware.[183]

In the United States, the regulatory approach has tended to be milder so far, both for a perception of digital technologies with a positive outlook for innovation and growth, and for greater adherence to the *laissez-faire* criterion.

Therefore, the most significant contributions in this matter come from the courts and from the adaptation of the traditional doctrines of contract law.

The legislators intervened only where necessary, with specific approaches, while in the case of attempts of wider interventions the reaction was negative, as in the case of UCITA.[184]

In conclusion, in the context of regulatory competition, the US approach and the role of the courts has resulted in an element of competitive advantage.[185]

The European Union, for its part, has recently been further increasing its commitment to creating a uniform framework for online contracts, with growing

The jurisprudence of the European Union testifies how digital management systems can be used unilaterally to remove freedom from users far beyond the proprietary and legal regime. See for example in this regard: European Court of Justice Nintendo v. PC Box, 23 January 2014, C-355/12, which states that in the event that the technological measures prevent or limit not only the acts that require the authorization of the owner of the right under this directive, but also acts that do not require such authorization, the court must verify whether the application of the measures complies with the principle of proportionality, and in particular if, in the current state of technology, the first effect could be achieved without producing this latter effect or producing it to a lesser extent. Regarding the subject, see: Ficsor (2010); Lucchi (2006); Burk and Cohen (2001); one may also see: Stazi (2012a, b). On the relationship between technology, contract, and ownership, see again: Radin (2004), p. 10, who highlights how the advent of digital rights management systems has the potential to reconfigure the regulatory profile of the contract just as the advent of ubiquitous sovereignty regimes has the potential to reconfigure the regulatory framework of ownership.

[182] In this sense, see: Sommer (2000), p. 1221; Radin (2000), p. 1152. Regarding the functions and limits of techno-regulation as an aid tool for the law, see: Leenes (2012), with the reference doctrine referred to therein and above in Sect. 2.1, including especially: Lessig (1999); Reidenberg (1998); one may also see: Stazi (2020), pp. 148 f.

[183] See, among others: Granieri (2017), p. 27; Ramberg (2001), p. 450.

[184] In this sense, see: Moringiello and Reynolds (2013), pp. 499 f., who note that: "Not only has contract law rejected hard-and-fast rules, but when legislators have attempted to codify some of those rules, the courts have softened them. Contract law has survived because it is firm enough to give guidance to those who use it to order their daily lives, and flexible enough to permit change when needed"; see also: Radin (2000), p. 1147.

[185] See: Winn and Bix (2006), p. 179; Winn and Haubold (2002), p. 568; Kim (2007), p. 801.

attention to the hypothesis in which technology is not only an instrument but also an object of the relationship.[186]

On the other hand, as soon as the adoption of the new rules mentioned above was registered, technological evolution already poses a new challenge: the so-called smart contracts, which will be analyzed in the next chapters.

References

Ancel P (2011) Les sanctions du manquement à la bonne foi contractuelle en droit français à la lumière du droit québecois. Revue Juridique Thémis 45:87–113

Atiyah PS (1989) An introduction to the law of contract, 4th edn. Oxford University Press, Oxford

Ayres I, Gertner RH (1989) Filling gaps in incomplete contracts: an economic theory of default rules. Yale Law J 99:87–130

Ayres I, Schwartz A (2014) The no-reading problem in consumer contract law. Stanf Law Rev 66: 545–610

Baker S, Choi A (2015) Contract's role in relational contract. Virginia Law Rev 101:559–607

Bakos Y et al (2014) Does anyone read the fine print? Testing a law and economics approach to standard form contracts. J Leg Stud 43:1–35

Baldwin R, Cave M, Lodge M (2012) Understanding regulation, 2nd edn. Oxford University Press, Oxford

Barela V (2012) Comparative analysis of the evolution of the termination of contract. Comparazione e diritto civile:1–19

Bar-Gill O, Ben-Shahar O (2013) Regulatory techniques in consumer protection: a critique of European consumer contract law. Common Mark Law Rev 50:109–125

Beale H et al (2019) Cases, materials and text on contract law, 3rd edn. Hart, Oxford

Beatson J, Friedmann D (eds) (1997) Good faith and fault in contract law. Clarendon, Oxford

Becher SI, Benoliel U (2020) Sneak in contracts: an empirical and legal analysis of unilateral modification clauses in consumer contracts. Georgia Law Rev 55:657–729

Bell J, Boyron S, Whittaker S (1998) Principles of French law. Oxford University Press, Oxford

Ben-Shahar O (2009) The myth of the "Opportunity to Read" in contract law. Eur Rev Contract Law 5:1 ff.

Ben-Shahar O, Schneider CE (2011) The failure of mandated disclosure. Univ Pa Law Rev 159: 647–749

Ben-Shahar O, Schneider CE (2014) More than you wanted to know. The failure of mandated disclosure. Princeton University Press, Princeton

Bern RC (2004) "Terms Later" contracting: bad economics, bad morals, and a bad idea for a uniform law, judge Easterbrook notwithstanding. J Law Policy 12:641–796

Bonell MJ (2009) An international restatement of contract law: the Unidroit principles of international commercial contracts, 3rd edn. Transnational Publishers, Ardsley

Bork K, Wandt M (2020) "Utmost" good faith in German contract law. Zeitschrift für die gesamte Versicherungswissenschaft. https://link.springer.com/article/10.1007/s12297-020-00478-6

Braucher J (2000) Delayed disclosure in consumer E-Commerce as an unfair and deceptive practice. Wayne Law Rev 46:1806–1868

[186] See, in particular, the EU directives 2019/770 and 2019/771, regarding which see above at Sect. 2.4. For a *caveat* regarding the risks of an excessive focus on the subject of the report, see: Sein (2017), pp. 109 f.

Burk DL, Cohen JE (2001) Fair use infrastructure for copyright management systems. Harv J Law Technol 51:41–83
Burnstein MR (1996) Conflicts of the net: choice of law in transnational cyberspace. Vanderbilt J Transnatl Law 29:75–116
Burton SJ (1980) Breach of contract and the common law duty to perform in good faith. Harv Law Rev 94:369–404
Busch D (2002) Sub art. 6:111. In: Id et al (eds) The principles of European contract law and Dutch law. A commentary. Kluwer, The Hague, pp 285 ff.
Busch C, De Franceschi A (2018) A granular legal norms: big data and the personalization of private law. In: Mak V, Tjong Tjin Tai E, Berlee A (eds) Research handbook of data science and law. Edward Elgar, Cheltenham, pp 408–424
Cabella Pisu L, Nanni L (eds) (1998) General clauses and principles in the jurisprudential argument of the nineties. Cedam, Padua
Cabrillac R et al (2011) The duty to renegotiate an international sales contract under CISG in case of hardship and the use of the Unidroit principles. Eur Rev Priv Law 19:101–154
Calleros CR (2013) Cause, consideration, promissory estoppel, and promises under deed: what our students should know about enforcement of promises in historical and international context. Chic-Kent J Int Comp Law 13:83–120
Charny D (1999) The new formalism in contract. Univ Chic Law Rev 66:842–857
Collins H (2011) Good faith in European contract law. Oxf J Leg Stud 14:229–254
Collins H (ed) (2018) Standard contract terms in Europe. A basis and a challenge for European contract law. Wolters Kluwer, Alphen aan den Rijn
Cornelius KB (2018) Standard form contracts and a smart contract future. Internet Policy Rev 7:1 ff.
Delfos-Roy Y (2011) The PEICL and the duty of disclosure. Eur Rev Priv Law 19:71–86
Dumortier J (2016) Regulation (EU) No 910/2014 on electronic identification and trust services for electronic transactions in the internal market (eIDAS Regulation). https://papers.ssrn.com/sol3/papers.cfm?abstract_id=2855484
Eisenberg MA (1999) Why there is no law of relational contracts. Northwest Univ Law Rev 94: 805–812
Elofson J (1996) The dilemma of changed circumstances in contract law: an economic analysis of the foreseeability and superior risk bearer tests. Columbia J Law Soc Probl 30:1 ff.
Emmert F (2012) The Draft Common Frame of Reference (DCFR) – the most interesting development in contract law since the code civil and the BGB. Indiana University Robert H. McKinney School of Law Research Paper No. 2012-08. https://papers.ssrn.com/sol3/papers.cfm?abstract_id=2,025,265
European Commission (2017) Study on the application of the Consumer Rights Directive 2011/83/EU. Publications Office of the European Union, Luxembourg
European Union (2002) The principles of European Contract Law 2002 (Parts I, II, and III). https://www.jus.uio.no/lm/en/pdf/eu.contract.principles.parts.1.to.3.2002.portrait.a4.pdf
Farnsworth EA (1968) Disputes over omission in contracts. Columbia Law Rev 68:860–891
Farnsworth EA (2006) Comparative contract law. In: Reimann M, Zimmermann R (eds) The Oxford handbook of comparative law. Oxford University Press, Oxford, pp 900 ff
Fasciano P (1997) Internet electronic mail: a last bastion for the mailbox rule. Hofstra Law Rev 25: 971–1004
Ficsor M (2010) Protection of 'DRM' under the WIPO 'Internet Treaties': interpretation, implementation and application. In: Stamatoudi I (ed) Copyright enforcement and the internet. Wolters Kluwer, Alphen aan den Rijn, pp 257–302
Finocchiaro G (2003) The conclusion of the electronic contract through "software agents": a false legal problem? Brief considerations. Comput Law Secur Rev 19:20–24
Finocchiaro G, Bomprezzi C (2020) A legal analysis of the use of blockchain technology for the formation of smart legal contracts. MediaLaws 111–135
Fisher JC (2018) Contract variation in the common law: a critical response to Rock Advertising v MWB Business Exchange. Common Law World Rev 47:196–207

Flume W (1979) Allgemeiner Teil des bürgerlichen Rechts. In: Das Rechtsgeschäft, vol II, 3rd edn. Springer, Berlin, p 657

Gabrielli E (2013) "Economic operation" and contract theory. Giuffrè, Milan

Gallo P (2011) Revisione e rinegoziazione del contratto, in Digesto delle discipline privatistiche – Sezione civile – Sesto aggiornamento. Utet, Turin, pp 804–821

Gambino AM (1999) Il contratto telematico. In: Bigiavi W (ed) Giurisprudenza sistematica di diritto civile e commerciale, vol 2. Utet, Turin, pp 1460 ff.

Gambino F (2004) Problemi di rinegoziare. Giuffrè, Milan

Gambino AM, Stazi A (2021) Contract automation from telematic agreements to smart contracts. Italian Law J 7:97–115

Gambino AM, Stazi A, Mula D (2019) Diritto dell'informatica e della comunicazione, 3rd edn. Giappichelli, Turin

Ghestin J (1988) Traité de droit civil: Les obligations: Le contrat: Formation. Librairie Générale de Droit et de Jurisprudence, Paris

Ghidini G, Stazi A (2015) Coopetition: the role of IPRs. In: Beldiman D (ed) Innovation, competition and collaboration. Edward Elgar, Cheltenham, pp 15–22

Ghirardelli A (2015) Rules of engagement in the conflict between businesses and consumers in online contracts. Oregon Law Rev 93:719–770

Giliker P (2005) Unifying European contract law: identifying a European pre-contractual obligation to inform. Camb Yearb Eur Leg Stud 7:135–159

Gillette C (1990) Commercial relationships and the selection of default rules for remote risks. J Leg Stud 19:535–582

Gillette CP (2005) Pre-approved contracts for internet commerce. Houston Law Rev 42:975–1013

Gilmore G (1954) The commercial doctrine of good faith purchase. Yale Law J 63:1057–1122

Gilson RJ, Sabel C, Scott RE (2014) Text and context: contract interpretation as contract design. Columbia Law and Economics Working Paper No. 385. https://papers.ssrn.com/sol3/papers.cfm?abstract_id=2394311

Goetz CJ, Scott RE (1981) Principles of relational contracts. Virginia Law Rev 67:1089–1150

Goldman E (2019) Online contracts. In: Id (ed) Internet law: cases and materials. Santa Clara University, Santa Clara, pp 45 ff.

Granieri M (2017) Technological contracts. In: Monateri PG (ed) Comparative contract law. Edward Elgar, Cheltenham, pp 408–450. https://papers.ssrn.com/sol3/papers.cfm?abstract_id=2666191 (pp 1 ff.)

Grundmann S (2013) The EU Consumer Rights Directive: optimizing, creating alternatives, or a dead end? Uniform Law Rev 18:98–127

Grundmann S, Cafaggi F, Vettori G (2013) The organizational contract. From exchange to long-term network cooperation in European contract law. Routledge, London

Hall E et al (2012) The Consumer Rights Directive. An assessment of its contribution to the development of European consumer contract law. Eur Rev Contract Law 8:139–166

Hardy IT (1993) The proper legal regime for "Cyberspace". Univ Pittsburgh Law Rev 55:993–1056

Hart O (2008) Incomplete contracts. In: Durlauf SN, Blume LE (eds) The new Palgrave dictionary of economics, 2nd edn. Palgrave Macmillan, London

Hayzelden A, Bigham J (eds) (1999) Software agents for future communication systems. Springer, Berlin

Heidenmüller H et al (2008) The common frame of reference for European private law – policy choices and codification problems. Oxf J Leg Stud 28:659–708

Helberger N et al (2013) Digital content contract for consumers. J Consumer Policy 36:37–57

Hesselink MW (2011) The concept of good faith. In: Hartkamp AS et al (eds) Towards a European civil code, 4th edn. Wolters Kluwer, New York, pp 619 ff.

Hillman RA (1987) Court adjustment of long-term contracts: an analysis under modern contract law. Duke Law Journal:1–33

Hillman RA, Rachlinski JJ (2002) Standard form contracting in electronic age. N Y Univ Law Rev 77:429–495

Höller J et al (2014) From machine-to-machine to the internet of things. Introduction to a new age of intelligence. Elsevier, Amsterdam

Holmes S (2010) Stevens v. Publicis: the rise of "No E-Mail Modification" clauses? Wash J Law Technol Arts 6:67–82

Horn N (1981) Neuverhandlungspflicht. AcP 181:255–288

Houh EMS (2003) Critical interventions: toward an expansive equality approach to the implied doctrine of good faith in contract law. Cornell Law Rev 88:1025–1096

Hviid M (2000) Long-term contracts and relational contracts. In: Bouckaert B, De Geest G (eds) The encyclopaedia of law and economics, vol III. Edward Elgar, Cheltenham, pp 46–72

Irti N (1998) Scambi senza accordo. Rivista trimestrale di diritto e procedura civile 52:347–364

Jhering R (1861) Culpa in contrahendo oder Schadenersatz bei nichtigen oder nicht Perfection gelangten Vertragen. Jherings Jahrbùcher fùr die Dogmatik des bùrgerlichen Rechts, IV, Fischer, Jena, pp 1 ff.

Karampatzos A (2005) Supervening hardship as subdivision of the general frustration rule: a comparative analysis with reference to Anglo-American, German, French and Greek Law. Eur Rev Priv Law 13:105–147

Keirse ALM (2011) European impact on contract law: a perspective on the interlinked contributions of legal scholars, legislators and courts to the Europeanization of contract law. Utrecht Law Rev 7:34–51

Kessler F, Fine E (1964) Culpa in Contrahendo, bargaining in good faith, and freedom of contract: a comparative study. Harv Law Rev 77:401–449

Kierkegaard SM (2007) E-Contract formation: US and EU perspectives. Shider J Law Commerce Technol 3:12 ff.

Kim NS (2007) Clicking and cringing. Oregon Law Rev 86:797–863

Kim NS (2012) The duty to draft reasonably and online contracts. In: DiMatteo L et al (eds) Intercommercial contract law: a transatlantic perspective. Cambridge University Press, Cambridge

Kobayashi I (2005) Private contracting and business models of electronic commerce. Univ Miami Bus Law Rev 13:161–216

Köbler R (1991) Die "clausula rebus sic stantibus" als allgemeiner Rechtsgrundsatz. Mohr Siebeck, Tübingen

Kötz H (2012) Vertragsrecht, 2nd edn. Mohr Siebeck, Heidelberg

Kryczka K (2005) Electronic contracts and the harmonization of contract laws in Europe – an action required, a mission impossible? Eur Rev Priv Law 13:149–170

Kunz K (2003) Browse-Wrap Agreements: validity of implied assent in electronic form agreements. Bus Lawyer 59:279–312

Lando O (1992) Principles of European contract law: an alternative to or a precursor of European legislation? Am J Comp Law 40:573–585

Lando O (2007) Is good faith an over-arching general clause in the principles of European contract law? Eur Rev Priv Law 15:841–853

Larenz K (1957) Geschäftsgrundlage und Vertragserfüllung. Beck, Munich

Leenes RE (2012) Framing Techno-Regulation: an exploration of state and non-state regulation by technology. Tilburg Law School Research Paper No. 10/2012. https://papers.ssrn.com/sol3/papers.cfm? abstract_id=2182439

Legrand P (1986) Pre-contractual disclosure and information: English and French law compared. Oxf J Leg Stud 6:322–352

Lemley MA (1995) Intellectual property and shrinkwrap licenses. South Calif Law Rev 68:1239–1294

Lemley MA (2006) Terms of use. Minn Law Rev 91:459–483

Lerouge JF (1999) The use of electronic agents questioned under contractual law: suggested solutions on a European and American level. Marshall J Comput Inf Technol Privacy Law 18:403–433

LeRoy Miller R, Jentz GA (2010) Business law today. Cengage Learning, Boston

Lessig L (1999) Code and other laws of cyberspace. Basic Books, New York
Lew DA (1998) Contract formation under the UNIDROIT principles of international commercial contracts, UCC, restatement, and CISG. Uniform Commercial Code Law J 30:249–332
Lewis MA, Roehrich J (2009) Contracts, relationships, integration: towards a model of the procurement of complex performance. Int J Procurement Manag 2:125–142
Linarelli J (2019) Advanced artificial intelligence and contract. Uniform Law Rev 24:254–259
Lorenzen ER (1919) Causa and consideration in the law of contracts. Yale Law J 28:621–646
Lucchi N (2006) Digital media & intellectual property. Springer, Berlin
Lùttringhaus JD (2013) Verhandlungspflichten bei Störung der Geschäftsgrundlage. Ein Beitrag zur Dogmatik und Durchsetzung von Anpassungsanspruch und Verhandlungspflichten nach § 313 Abs. 1 BGB. AcP 213:266–298
Macario F (2008) Revisione e rinegoziazione del contratto. Enciclopedia del diritto, Annali, II. Giuffrè, Milan, pp 1026 ff.
Macaulay S (2004) Freedom of contracts: solutions in search for a problem? Wisconsin Law Rev:777–820
MacMahon P (2015) Good faith and fair dealing as an underenforced legal norm. Minn Law Rev 99:2051–2110
Macneil IR (1962) Power of contract and agreed remedies. Cornell Law Rev 47:495–528
Macneil IR (1964) Time of acceptance: too many problems for a single rule. Univ Pa Law Rev 112: 947–979
Macneil IR (1969) Whither contracts? J Leg Educ 21:403–418
Macneil IR (1985) Relational contract: what we do and do not know. Wisconsin Law Rev:483–526
Macneil IR (2000) Relational contract theory: challenges and queries. Northwest Univ Law Rev 94: 877–908
Majone G (1997) The new agencies: regulation by information. J Eur Publ Policy 4:262–275
Maniruzzaman AFM (2001) Formation of international sales of contracts: a comparative perspective. Int Bus Law J 29:483–489
Markovits D (2014) Good faith as contract's core value. In: Klass G, Letsas G, Saprai P (eds) Philosophical foundations of contract law. Oxford University Press, Oxford, pp 272–293
Marotta Wurgler F (2009) Are "Pay Now, Terms Later" contracts worse for buyers? Evidence from software license agreements. J Leg Stud 38:309–343
Martin CH (2008) The electronic contracts convention, the CISG, and new sources of E-Commerce law. Tulane J Int Comp Law 16:467–503
Martinek M (1998) Die Lehre von den Neuverhandlungspflichten. Bestandsaufnahme, Kritik … und Ablehnung. AcP 198:329–400
Maskow D (1992) Hardship and force majeure. Am J Comp Law 40:657–669
Micklitz HW (2004) The principles of European contract law and the protection of the weaker party. J Consumer Policy 27:339–356
Mik E (2009) The effectiveness of acceptances communicated by electronic means, or – does the postal acceptance rule apply to email? J Contract Law 26:1–29
Mital V, Elliman D (1994) Semantic models and knowledge representation. Document assembly and evidence analysis: two approaches to hypertext. Comput Sci Law, 150 ff.
Mitu Gulati G, Klein WA, Zolt EM (2000) Connected contracts. UCLA Law Rev 47:887–948
Moringiello JM (2005) Signals, assent and internet contracting. Rutgers Law Rev 57:1307–1350
Moringiello JM, Ottaviani J (2016) Online contracts: we may modify these terms at any time, right? Business Law Today, May 2016, pp 1–4
Moringiello JM, Reynolds WL (2010) Electronic contracting cases 2009–2010. Bus Lawyer 66:175 ff.
Moringiello JM, Reynolds WL (2013) From Lord Coke to internet privacy: the past, present and future of the law of electronic contracting. Maryland Law Rev 72:452–500
Mouly C (1990) La formation du contrat. In: Derains Y, Ghestin J (eds) La Convention de Vienne sur la vente internationale et les incoterms, Librairie Générale de Droit et de Jurisprudence, Paris, pp 55–82

Murray JE Jr (1988) An essay on the formation of contracts and related matters under the United Nation Convention on contracts for the international sale of goods. J Law Commerce 8:11–51
Murray JE Jr (2002) Contract theories and the rise of neoformalism. Fordham Law Rev 71:869–913
Neumayer KH (2008) Contracting subject to standard terms and conditions. In: International encyclopedia of comparative law: contracts in general, VII/2. Mohr Siebeck, Tübingen, pp 8 ff.
Nimmer RT (1996) Electronic contracting: legal issues. Marshall J Comput Inf Law 14:211–246
Oppetit B (1974) L'adaptation des contrats internationaux aux changements de circonstances: la clause de hardship. Journal du droit international, 794–814
Owsia P (1994) Formation of contract. A comparative study under English, French, Islamic and Iranian Law. Kluwer, London
Pannebakker E (2013) Offer and acceptance and the dynamics of negotiations: arguments for contract theory from negotiation studies. Erasmus Law Rev:131–141
Pardolesi R, Granieri M (2005) The dimension of time on language and legal thought. Some preliminary notes on long term contracting in the comparative legal discourse. In: Pozzo B (ed) Ordinary language and legal language. Giuffrè, Milan, pp 219 ff.
Parisi F, Cenini M, Luppi B (2017) Enforcing bilateral promises: a comparative law and economics perspective. In: Monateri PG (ed) Comparative contract law. Edward Elgar, Cheltenham, pp 145 ff.
Patterson M (2010–2011) Standardization of standard-form contracts: competition and contract implications. William Mary Law Rev 52:327–414
Peel E (2015) Treitel: the law of contract, 14th edn. Thomson, London
Perillo J (1997) Force majeure and hardship under the UNIDROIT principles of international commercial contracts. Tulane J Int Comp Law 5:5–28
Perlingieri G (2013) The non-existence of the distinction between rules of conduct and validity in Italian-European law. ESI, Naples
Piraino F (2015) La buona fede in senso oggettivo. Giappichelli, Turin
Planiol M, Ripert G (1953) Traité pratique de droit civil français, 2nd edn. Librairie Générale de Droit et de Jurisprudence, Paris
Poggi CT (2000) Electronic commerce legislation: an analysis of European and American approaches to contract formation. Virginia J Int Law 41:224 ff.
Posner RA (2004) The law and economics of contract interpretation, John M. Olin Program in Law and Economics Working Paper No. 229. https://core.ac.uk/download/pdf/192872169.pdf
Pratt WF Jr (1988) American contract law at the turn of the century. S C Law Rev 39:415–464
Radin MJ (2000) Humans, computers, and binding commitments. Indiana Law J 75:1125–1162
Radin MJ (2004) Regulation by contract, regulation by machine. J Inst Theor Econ 160:1–15
Ramberg CH (2001) The E-Commerce Directive and formation of contract in a comparative perspective. Eur Law Rev 26:429–450
Rawls A (2009) Contract formation in an internet age. Columbia Sci Technol Law Rev 10:200–231
Reed C (2000) Internet law: texts and materials. Butterworths, London
Reidenberg JR (1998) Lex Informatica: the formulation of information policy rules through technology. Tex Law Rev 76:553–594
Ricci F (2013) Buona fede e rimedi. Contratto e impresa Europa 18:632–647
Rossi MA (2014) Incomplete contracts. In: Marciano A, Ramello GB (eds) Encyclopedia of law and economics. Springer, London
Sabett RV (1996) International harmonization in electronic commerce and electronic data interchange: a proposed first step toward signing on the digital dotted line. Am Univ Law Rev 46: 511–536
Sacco R, De Nova G (2016) Il contratto, 4th edn. Utet, Turin
Sammarco P (2006) I nuovi contratti dell'informatica. Sistema e prassi. Cedam, Padua
Samoy I, Loos MBM (eds) (2012) Linked contracts. Intersentia, Cambridge

Sartor G (2009) Cognitive automata and the law: electronic contracting and the intentionality of software agents. Artif Intell Law 17:253–290

Savatier R (1972) Les contracts de conseil professionel en droit privè. Dalloz, pp 140 ff.

Savirimuthu J (2005) Online contract formation: taking technological infrastructure seriously. Univ Ottawa Law Technol J 2:105–143

Schlesinger RB, Bonassies PG (1968) Formation of contracts: a study of the common core of legal systems. Dobbs Ferry, New York

Schwarz A, Wilde L (1979) Intervening in markets on the basis of imperfect information: a legal and economic analysis. Univ Pa Law Rev 127:630–682

Schwenzer I, Muñoz E (2019) Duty to renegotiate and contract adaptation in case of hardship. Uniform Law Rev 24:149–174

Sein K (2017) What rules should apply to smart consumer goods? Goods with embedded digital content in the borderland between the digital content directive and "Normal" contract law. JIPITEC 8:96–110

Sen A (1996) Termination clauses in long-term contracts. J Econ Manag Strategy 5:473–496

Shavell S (2006) On the writing and the interpretation of contracts. J Law Econ Organ 22:289–314

Sirena P, Patti FP (2020) Hardship and renegotiation of contracts in the prospective recodification of Italian Civil Law. Bocconi Legal Studies Research Paper No. 3706159. https://papers.ssrn.com/sol3/papers.cfm?abstract_id=3706159

Smed S (1998) Intelligent software agents and agency law. Santa Clara Comput High Technol Law J 14:503–507

Smedinghoff TJ (2008) The legal challenges of implementing electronic transactions. Uniform Commercial Code Law J 41:3–34

Smith SA (2006) Atiyah's Introduction to the Law of contract, 6th edn. Clarendon, Oxford

Smits JM (2017) Contract law: a comparative introduction. Edward Elgar, Cheltenham

Smorto G (2018) Protecting the weaker parties in the platform economy. In: Davidson N, Finck M, Infranca J (eds) The Cambridge handbook of the law of the sharing economy. Cambridge University Press, Cambridge, pp 431–446

Somma A (ed) (2009) The politics of the draft common frame of reference. Kluwer, The Hague

Sommer JH (2000) Against cyberlaw. Berkeley Technol Law J 15:1145–1232

Srivastava A (2017) The new EU Consumer Rights Directive: an empirical study on compliance issues by e-tailers. J Bus Law:282–309

Stazi A (2004) La pubblicità commerciale online. Giuffrè, Milan

Stazi A (2012a) Digital copyright and consumer/user protection: moving toward a new framework? Queen Mary J Intellect Prop 2:158–174

Stazi A (2012b) Intellectual property and consumer protection: towards a new framework? Diritto Mercato Tecnologia. https://www.dimt.it/index.php/it/culturaindustriaproprieta/10527-70intellectual-property-and-tutela-de-consumers-to-a-new-framework

Stazi A (2020) Genetically modified organisms and sustainable development: regulatory approaches, access to resources and traceability. BioLaw J, 127–149

Steennot R (2013) The right of withdrawal under the Consumer Rights Directive as a tool to protect consumers concluding a distance contract. Comput Law Secur Rev 29:105–119

Storme ME (1998) The binding character of contracts – causa and consideration. In: Hartkamp AS et al (eds) Towards a European Civil Code, 2nd edn. Kluwer/Ars aequi, Nijmegen/The Hague, pp 239–254

Storme ME (2003) Good faith and the contents of contracts in European private law. Electron J Comp Law 7:1–13. http://www.ejcl.org/71/art71-1.html

Storme ME (2006) Freedom of contract: mandatory and non-mandatory rules in European contract law. Juridica Int, 34–44

Summers RS (1968) "Good Faith" in general contract law and the sales provisions of the Uniform Commercial Code. Virginia Law Rev 54:195–267

Sundmaeker H et al (2010) Vision and challenges for realizing the internet of things, publications office of the European Union, Brussels
Teubner G (1998) Legal irritants: good faith in British law or how unifying law ends up in new divergences. Mod Law Rev 61:11–32
Teubner G (2018) Digital legal entities? On the private status of autonomous software agents. Ancilla Iuris:106–149
Tirole J (1999) Incomplete contracts: where do we stand? Econometrica 67:741–781
Triantis GG (2009) The evolution of contract remedies (and why do contracts professors teach remedies first?). Harvard Public Law Working Paper No. 09-69. https://papers.ssrn.com/sol3/papers.cfm?abstract_id=1512636
Tutt A (2013) On the invalidation of terms in contracts of adhesion. Yale J Regul 30:440–474
Uncitral (2009) Promoting confidence in electronic commerce: legal issues on international use of electronic authentication and signature methods, United Nations, Vienna. https://www.uncitral.org/pdf/english/texts/electcom/08-55698_Ebook.pdf
Valcke C (2008) Contractual interpretation at common law and civil law: an exercise in comparative legal rhetoric. In: VNeyers J (ed) Exploring contract law. Hart, Oxford, pp 77–114
von Mehren A (2008) A general view on contract. In: International encyclopedia of comparative law: contract in general, vol VII/1. Mohr Siebeck, Tübingen
Walter C (1988) Computer power and legal language: the use of computational linguistic, artificial intelligence, and expert systems in the law. Charles Walter, New York
Watnick V (2004) The electronic formation of contracts and the common law "Mailbox Rule". Baylor Law Rev 56:175–204
Weathwerhill S (2012) The Consumer Rights Directive: how and why a quest for "coherence" has largely failed. Common Mark Law Rev 49:1279–1317
Weill A, Terré F (1986) Droit civil, Les obligations, 4th edn. Dalloz, Paris
Weisberg RH (1987) When lawyers write. Little Brown, Boston
Weitzenboeck E (2001) Electronic agents and the formation of contracts. Int J Law Inf Technol 9: 204–234
Weitzenboek EM (2001) Electronic agents and the formation of contracts. Int J Law Technol 9: 204–234
Whitmore G (1996) Globalisation of contract law: rules for commercial contracts in the 21st century. N Z Law J 52:52–53
Wihlelmsson T (2005) European rules on pre-contractual information duties? ERA Forum 6:16–25
Wijayasriwardena D (2016) Consent in online contracts – mindless or mindful? Queen Mary School of Law Legal Studies Research Paper No. 234/2016. https://papers.ssrn.com/sol3/papers.cfm?abstract_id=2783793
Williams S (2020) Contracts as systems. Del J Corp Law 45:219–278
Williman D (1986) Legal terminology: an historical guide to the technical language of law. University of Toronto Press, Lewiston
Williston S (1957) Contracts. Thomson, New York
Winn JK, Bix BH (2006) Symposium: cyberpersons, propertization, and contract in the information culture: diverging perspectives on electronic contracting in the U.S. and EU. Cleveland State Law Rev 54:175–189
Winn JK, Haubold J (2002) Electronic promises: contract law reform and E-Commerce in a comparative perspective. Eur Law Rev 27:567–588
Woebbeking MK (2019) The impact of smart contracts on traditional concepts of contract law. JIPITEC 10:106–113
Yildrim AC (2019) Interpretation of contracts in comparative and uniform law. Wolters Kluwer, Alphen Aan den Rijn

Zeno-Zencovich V (2008) Freedom of expression: a critical and comparative analysis. Routledge, London

Zeno-Zencovich V (2021) "Smart contracts", "granular norms" and non discrimination. In: Busch C, De Franceschi A (eds) Algorithmic regulation and personalized law. CH Beck/Hart/ Nomos, Munich/Oxford/Baden-Baden, pp 264–278

Zimmermann R, Whittaker S (eds) (2000) Good faith in European contract law. Cambridge University Press, Cambridge

Zweigert K, Kötz H (1998) An introduction to comparative law, 3rd edn. Clarendon Press, Oxford

Chapter 4
Smart Contracts: Legal Issues and First Regulatory Approaches

4.1 Distributed Ledger Technologies and Blockchain: Features and Operation

In recent years, the development of distributed ledger technologies[1] and in particular of Blockchain technology[2] is making it possible the drafting and growing

[1] A distributed ledger technology is a consensus mechanism for geographically distributed, shared, and synchronized digital data without a central administrative authority or centralized data store. The distributed registry database is shared on multiple computers called "nodes" of a peer-to-peer network, where each of them replicates and saves an identical copy of the registry. Each individual node in the network processes every transaction, reaching its own conclusions and voting on them, with a view to ensuring that the majority agrees. Once this consensus is reached, the distributed registry is updated, and all nodes keep their identical copy of it. See: Distributed ledger, in Wikipedia, available at: https://en.wikipedia.org/wiki/Distributed_ledger; UK Government Chief Scientific Adviser (2016).

[2] The Blockchain is a distributed, shared, encrypted and tamper resistant database, which acts as a tendentially irreversible and incorruptible public archive of information. It allows for the first time unrelated persons to reach a consensus on the occurrence of a particular transaction or event without the need for a supervisory authority. By allowing the transfer of information, data or digitized properties to others in a secure, protected and unchangeable way, this technology allows to give rise, in particular, to: (1) digital currencies, so-called cryptocurrencies, also not supported by any government agency, called Bitcoin, Ethereum, Litecoin, etc.; (2) self-imposed digital contracts, so-called smart contracts, the execution of which does not require any human intervention; (3) decentralized markets that aim to operate independently of regulation; (4) decentralized communication platforms aimed at being very difficult to intercept; (5) digitized resources that can be controlled as digital properties, so-called smart properties. In the first regulatory approaches to the subject, regarding which see further below at Sect. 4.5, according to the regulation adopted in Arizona, Blockchain is a distributed ledger technology that uses a distributed, decentralized, shared and replicated ledger, which can be public or private, authorized or without permission, based on cryptographic tokens or without them (cryptographic tokens are virtual currency representations that reside on a Blockchain and represent an asset or utility). The log data is encrypted, tamper resistant, reliable, and verifiable. The state of Vermont, then, defined the Blockchain as a mathematically secure, chronological, and decentralized consensus register or database, managed through

A. Stazi, *Smart Contracts and Comparative Law*,
https://doi.org/10.1007/978-3-030-83240-7_4

diffusion of so-called "smart contracts".[3]

The concept indicates digital contracts coded through computer algorithms, in which the execution and application of contractual conditions occur automatically without the need for human intervention.[4]

A Blockchain technology platform is generally a database which is shared, decentralized, distributed, encrypted, transparent and tamper-resistant, for transactions recorded by a computer network.[5]

Every Blockchain is encrypted and organized into smaller data sets called "blocks".[6] Each block contains information on a certain number of transactions, a reference to the previous block in the chain, and a response to a complex mathematical problem that is used to validate the data associated with that block, according to the "rules of consent" established in the algorithm.[7]

A copy of the Blockchain is stored on every computer on the network and these computers, called "nodes", synchronize periodically to make sure that all have the same shared database, that is, a distributed registry that can be shared and confirmed by anyone with the appropriate permissions.[8]

To ensure that only legitimate transactions are recorded on a Blockchain platform, the network confirms that the new transactions are valid and do not invalidate previous transactions. A new block of data will be added to the end of the

Internet interaction, peer-to-peer or other network. In doctrine, see: De Filippi and Wright (2015), pp. 2 ff.; Bustillos (2013); Benkler (2006), pp. 62 ff.

[3]The concept is due to the theoretical elaboration of the American computer science and law researcher Nick Szabo in some writings of the nineties of the last century (1997, 1996, 1994).

[4]In this regard, see: Szabo (1997), cit. See likewise, regarding the way in which the representation of contractual obligations as computer data allows new contractual properties, including "calculable" contractual conditions: Surden (2012). The smart contract, then allows to join together the time of the agreement with the performance of the contract; see: DiMatteo et al. (2019), pp. 1 ff.; Diedrich (2016), pp. 3 ff.

[5]See: Blockchain, in the Bitcoin Foundation Wiki, available at: https://en.bitcoin.it/wiki/Block_chain.

[6]In this regard, see: Blocks, in the Bitcoin Foundation Wiki, available at: https://en.bitcoin.it/wiki/Blocks.

[7]All operations in the Blockchain are validated through a fingerprint created by means of a particular cryptographic function, the "hash function", which is used to compress the information/transaction data in a specific fixed length format. In the Blockchain, this function is used to create a link between each block, inserting the hash of the previous block into the next block of the chain. Therefore, if some data is changed in a certain block, each subsequent block will change, allowing the detection of changes to any part of the data in each block of the chain. See: Bonneau et al. (2015), p. 4.

[8]See: Gambino et al. (2019), pp. 185–186; Szostek (2019), pp. 34 ff.; De Caria (2019), p. 733; Nakamoto (2009), p. 3. This provides the platform with considerable resilience. Given that the same copy of the Blockchain is stored by multiple computers connected to the network, even if a certain number of computers do not work or are damaged at a given moment, the shared database can be recreated in its entirety; see: De Filippi and Wright (2015), p. 7.

Blockchain only after the network computers reach consensus on the validity of the transaction.[9]

Consensus within the network is achieved through various voting mechanisms, the most common of which is called "proof of work", which depends on the amount of processing power provided respectively by the computers connected to the network.[10]

There are other types of consensus mechanisms currently under development and dissemination, such as the so-called "proof of stake" or "proof of interest". This consensus mechanism is less intensive from a computational point of view, and therefore of energy expenditure, compared to the proof of work.

The "proof of stake" mechanisms do not require any specific processing power. Rather, voting rights depend on the amount of resources, for example cryptocurrencies, respectively held by computers connected to the network.[11]

After a block has been added to the Blockchain, it generally can no longer be eliminated, and the transactions contained therein are accessible and verifiable by everyone on the network.

This results in a permanent log that all computers on the network can use to coordinate an activity or verify an event. Anyone can check the database, but nobody is able to edit it.[12]

Such a technology, therefore, in principle, provides a decentralized, fast, flexible, and highly secure means of recording any type of transaction and the history of previous transactions in a distributed ledger, often based on open-source software that is publicly available.[13]

Generally, the database is open to all participants, except in cases of non-public Blockchain. In fact, there are different Blockchain models that provide for different authorization levels. Most of them are public, so-called permissionless.[14]

---

[9] In this regard, see: Franco (2014), p. 15.

[10] The consent mechanism so-called proof of work requires that some computers on the network, referred to as "miners", solve computationally intensive mathematical puzzles, while others verify that the solution to that riddle does not match a previous transaction. To incentivize miners to invest computational power, the first miner to solve the mathematical problem is rewarded through the issue of cryptocurrency or transaction fees. In this regard, see: Bonneau et al. (2015), pp. 2–4; Proof of Work, in the Bitcoin Foundation Wiki, available at: https://en.bitcoin.it/wiki/Proof_of_Work.

[11] See: Proof of Stake, in Bitcoin Foundation Wiki, available at: https://en.bitcoin.it/wiki/Proof_of_Stake.

[12] See: De Filippi and Wright (2015), p. 8. This, except in exceptional cases, to which reference will be made below and in Sect. 4.2.

[13] In this sense, see: De Caria (2019), p. 733.

[14] Such as the Bitcoin and Ethereum platforms. Unlike the Bitcoin system, designed to send money safely, the main feature of the Ethereum protocol is that of allowing the development and management of smart contracts, through a separate environment from the network to operate protected from external interference called Ethereum Virtual Machine, and with the ability to create a representation of any asset or information in the form of a token. In the public Blockchain, in addition to the absence of permits to participate, the source code is made public to allow developers

To use the Blockchain in sectors with specific characteristics and regulations such as the financial one, so-called permissioned infrastructures have been developed.

These can be, on the one hand, of the "shared permission" type, or *consortium*, in which the consent process is controlled by a pre-selected set of nodes, but everyone can sign the transactions and access the shared register without having to access the registers of other members.

On the other hand, they can be "private" platforms, where similarly there are pre-selected nodes that act as validators, often managed by an organization, but the transactions can only be viewed by those who are allowed access to the platform.[15]

Here, two main features of Blockchain technology need to be recalled. First, the data recorded on a Blockchain platform are distributed within a network and are cryptographically protected. Consequently, it is very difficult to hack the system without using considerable resources.

Second, therefore, once recorded, the data on a Blockchain are resistant to tampering, that is, they can be considered as tendentially immutable and perpetual.[16]

On the other hand, it should be noted that there are different types of Blockchains and none of them are truly unassailable or infallible. Conversely, each of them has its own specificities and weaknesses.[17]

In this regard, it is important to focus on the consensus mechanism within a Blockchain, whose *raison d'etre* is the keeping of a uniform register of all transactions. Consent can be achieved through several methods.

One of these, as mentioned, is the "proof of work", which allows most users to modify the Blockchain in a democratic and unilateral way. Consequently, this method shows weaknesses in cases where a participant, or a group, manages to gain possession of a significant part of the overall computational power of the specific Blockchain platform in question.[18]

As for the immutability of a Blockchain platform, then, this does not mean that it is invulnerable. In fact, in theory it is possible to violate or even destroy the platform, even if it is difficult, or more plausibly it can be overcome by a higher platform. In addition, a Blockchain platform could also be abandoned due to the effect of time, if nobody used it anymore.[19]

As for the relationship between the development of Blockchain technology and law, according to some scholars Blockchain would produce something similar to what happened with the advent of the Internet and the related decentralized

---

around the world, after reaching consensus, to modify and improve it. See: R3, Norton Rose Fullbright (2016), p. 11.

[15] In this regard, also for examples of these platforms, see e.g.: Buterin (2015).

[16] See among others: Erbguth (2017), pp. 2 ff.

[17] See: Jaccard (2017), p. 6.

[18] In such cases, the remedy that would remain for most of the participants in that Blockchain platform would be a collective decision of "bifurcation", or fork. This, for example, will make it possible to delete a certain transaction from the platform, as happened because of the attack to "The DAO" platform (regarding which, see below Sect. 4.2). See: Juels and Marino (2016), pp. 151 ff.

[19] On this point, see: Jaccard (2017), p. 7.

communication layers, such as TCP/IP and HTTP, which highlighted the relevance, or according to some even prevalence, of the so-called Lex Informatica.

In this perspective, the progressive diffusion of the Blockchain would give rise to a further regulatory system, the so-called Lex Cryptographia, which would be characterized by a set of rules managed through self-executed and decentralized smart contracts and potentially autonomous organizations.[20]

Although such an approach is not shareable as it completely presents a phenomenon that is actually only partially incident on the overall regulation of emerging legal issues on the matter, one of the main consequences of the Blockchain could actually be a rapid expansion of what Lawrence Lessig called "architecture", that is the computer code, hardware, software and the related operating rules that limit our behavior, which in the case of the Blockchain are essentially substantiated in the basic rules of the platform used.[21]

From these rules derives, at least, a redefinition of the ways in which laws and regulations are drafted, implemented, and applied, with significant consequences also in terms of judicial control.[22]

4.2 Smart Contracts: Peculiarities, Legal Issues and First Applications

Distributed ledger and Blockchain technologies allow, by virtue of their immutability, to create "smart contracts", characterized by the self-execution of contractual clauses without the need for human intervention and generally excluded the possibility of interrupting such execution or modifying the content,[23] except for the *caveats* mentioned above or the hypotheses of multi-signature or self-destruction.[24]

---

[20] In this sense, see: De Filippi and Wright (2015), pp. 48 ff.; Szostek (2019), pp. 25 ff.

[21] For example, in the case of the Ethereum platform, it can refer to: https://www.ethereum.org/use.

[22] In this perspective, see: Lessig (2006), p. 24.

[23] Among legal scholars, the concept of smart contract gives rise to a multitude of definitions without a consensus has yet been reached on a shared definition. See e.g.: Zeno-Zencovich (2021), pp. 264–270; Finocchiaro and Bomprezzi (2020), pp. 115–117; Weber (2019), pp. 301–303; Szostek (2019), pp. 110 ff.; De Caria (2019), p. 734; Herian (2018), pp. 16–17; Cong and He (2018), p. 11; Raskin (2017), pp. 304 ff.; Catchlove (2017), p. 6; Künnapas (2016), pp. 111 ff.

[24] Multi-signature verification technology, or "multisig", allows a smart contract to stop executing until several parties have signed the transaction with their private keys. These can include not only the parts of the smart contract, but also an external third party, a so-called referee; see: Werbach and Cornell (2017), p. 345; Buterin (2014a). In addition, the code of most smart contracts contains a so-called kill switch. Solidity, the language used to write smart contracts on the Ethereum Blockchain, allows an operation called self-destruction, which removes the smart contract code from the Blockchain; see: Eenmaa-Dimitrieva and Schmidt-Kessen (2019), pp. 84–85; Introduction to Smart Contracts, available at: http://solidity.readthedocs.io/en/develop/introduction-to-smart-contracts.html#self-destruct.

This entails clear advantages, especially in cases of absence of a relationship of trust such as those in which the parties are remote, for example in international agreements. The legal effects of contracts are thus automated, in general irrevocably and basically without the need for judicial intervention.[25]

In some cases, "smart contracts" represent the implementation of a previous contractual agreement in the legal sense, the clauses of which are formalized in the so-called computer source code.[26]

Therefore, the contracting parties have the advantage of structuring their relationships and performances in a more efficient and self-executive way, regardless of the ambiguity of natural language.[27]

In other cases, smart contracts introduce new codified relationships which are both defined and automatically applied by the computer code, but are not linked to any underlying contractual right or obligation.[28]

To the extent that a Blockchain allows the implementation of self-executed transactions, the parties can freely transact with each other, without the technical need to enter into a traditional contractual agreement.

On the other hand, regardless of the technical necessity, the legal need to draw up a smart contract in writing can be configured to make its clauses legally binding and applicable at a judicial level.[29]

---

[25] See, among others: Jaccard (2017), p. 7. The development of smart contracts is expanding rapidly. In recent years, several open-source projects, such as Ethereum, Counterparty, Mastercoin etc., have been developed to create programming languages that allow the creation of smart contracts increasingly sophisticated. Using these programming languages, more and more smart contract models are being developed which can be used, also at a transnational level, for example to: (a) allow employees to be paid also on an hourly or daily basis with the taxes deducted in real time; (b) administer musical royalties instantly with distributions provided to authors and performers in real time; (c) recharge electric vehicles by processing the deposit of a deposit, enabling the recharging station and returning the remaining funds at the end of the recharge, etc.; in this regard see, among others: De Filippi and Wright (2015), p. 12; Steinmetz (2017); Ream et al. (2016); Wallach (2014).

[26] The source code, in computer science, is the text of an algorithm of a program written in a programming language by a programmer in the programming phase. It therefore defines the execution flow of the program itself. See: Source code, in Wikipedia, available at: https://it.wikipedia.org/wiki/Codice_sorgente.

[27] Thus, for example, a smart contract was created to simulate the mechanism for a public funding campaign, the so-called crowdfunding, with fifty-six lines of computer code (see: http://www.mintchalk.com/c/68f3e). The creation of smart contract models, then, could in practice result in a reduction in the role of jurists when the contract is formed, especially with respect to those more easily modeled.

[28] In this regard, see among others: Chamber of Digital Commerce – Smart Contracts Alliance (2018), pp. 10 ff.

[29] See: De Filippi and Wright (2015), p. 11, who noted that, while initially smart contracts were developed mainly to automatically execute derivatives, options, futures, and swaps, they were subsequently used to facilitate the sale of goods on the network between unrelated persons without the need for a centralized organization. In this sense, they cite the example of OpenBazaar, an open-source service aimed at creating a decentralized global market in which people can buy and sell products directly, without intermediation costs or centralized control (see: https://openbazaar.org).

However, a smart contract is not immutable in all possible scenarios. As mentioned above, first, the Blockchain could be "forked" by most users.

Second, the code of smart contracts can contain various functions that allow a certain range of flexibility.[30]

Still, the recording of smart contracts on a Blockchain platform usually comes at a cost.[31] Consequently, the IT code of these contracts cannot be too long and explicit.

This in fact avoids the inclusion of detailed and complex clauses in smart contracts, as vice versa is commonly the case especially in the context of common law but increasingly also at an international level.[32]

In this book, in consideration of the characteristics mentioned so far, the smart contracts examined are those commonly associated with the Blockchain technology platform, which provides the ecosystem within which the idea proposed by Nick Szabo in the nineties of the last century can be realized.[33]

Still, however, except for the classification that will be proposed later, the concept is misleading because it gives rise to confusions and simplifications.

This, on the one hand, as the objective of its proponent was to identify an analogy in terms of structure between law and information technology, and not to come to assimilate them as often proposed in the subsequent debate on the topic.[34]

On the other, as one of the purposes of smart contracts appears to be to emancipate users from traditional intermediaries, or "trusted third parties", which include legal practitioners such as judges, lawyers, etc.[35]

---

[30] For example, functions such as "call"—which accepts an arbitrary number of arguments of any kind, "enums"—a way to create a user-defined type, "self-destruct", and variable functions that allow the smart contract to process external inputs; see: Juels and Marino (2016), pp. 151 ff. (for technical operation, see: https://solidity.readthedocs.io/en/v0.4.21/types.html).

[31] For example, called "gas" on the Ethereum platform (see: https://ethereum.stackexchange.com/questions/3/what-is-meant-by-the-term-gas).

[32] On this point, see again: Jaccard (2017), p. 7.

[33] See: Szabo (1996); Id. (1994), who stated that the objectives of such contracts would have consisted in fulfilling contractual obligations such as payment terms, privileges, confidentiality and even execution, and in minimizing both harmful and accidental exceptions and the need for trusted intermediaries. Related economic objectives, he added, would include reducing fraud losses, enforcement and arbitration costs, and other transaction costs. See also: R3, Norton Rose Fullbright (2016), p. 8.

[34] Referring to the theorization of the so-called Lex Informatica emerged in American doctrine since the nineties of the last century as a natural extension of the Lex Mercatoria to cyberspace (already mentioned above in Sect. 2.1). In this regard, see: De Filippi and Wright (2015), pp. 45 ff.; Marrella and Yoo (2007); Lessig (1999); Reidenberg (1998); Johnson and Post (1996). On the Blockchain and smart contracts and the relative theorization of a so-called Lex Cryptographia, see especially: De Filippi and Wright (2018), pp. 193 ff. In a similar vein, for a proposal on mutual rapprochement between law and computer code, see: Werbach (2018a), pp. 536 ff.

[35] In this regard, see: Jaccard (2017), p. 3.

In a technical sense, it is possible to define smart contracts as computer protocols that self-execute by applying the lines of the computer code for which they have been programmed.[36]

Eventually, if an economic function recognized by the legal system in which they are intended to carry out their effects is pursued through them, they allow the automation of the relevant prose—as a truly contractual case in a legal sense—according to a logic of "if/then".[37]

In practice, they operate by means of software, the computer code of which contains instructions and data for the execution of agreements between the parties and is stored on a distributed register.[38]

From a technical point of view, therefore, a smart contract is simply a sequence of computer code. However, processing generally requires four elements to function properly:

1. The computer source code, which contains all the details of the desired transaction, in which the term "transaction" describes the transfer of information relating to money, data, etc. for the purposes of the economic operation pursued.
2. The wallet, that is, the digital space in which the cryptographic keys are kept. On the one hand, a private key that allows users to access certain goods and/or activities, so-called crypto-property, and allows user to check her account.[39] On the other, a public key, whose function is to authenticate the owner of the messages and encrypt them.[40] Finally, the private key and the public key are paired to allow for secure communication.
3. A storage file, a digital space in which a transaction is stored before it is registered, which most often takes place on a Blockchain.
4. The register in which the transaction is stored, usually also on a Blockchain.

A smart contract program is run from a so-called network. miners, who, once the consensus on the outcome of the execution has been reached, consequently update the status of the contract on the Blockchain. In this way, users can send or receive money, data, etc. through a contract.[41]

Based on the capabilities of the Blockchain, therefore, smart contracts operate autonomously, transparently, tamper-proof and tendentially immutable.[42]

These features allow the contracting parties several significant advantages, compared to traditional contracts: they can rely on contractual promises that are stored in

[36] See: De Filippi and Wright (2018), pp. 33 ff.; Buterin (2013).

[37] In this regard, see: Hazard and Haapio (2017).

[38] In this sense, see: Jaccard (2017), p. 4.

[39] Externally Owned Account.

[40] The address of the externally owned account derives from the last twenty bytes of the public key.

[41] See: Jaccard (2017), pp. 5–6; Essebier and Wyss (2017); Juels et al. (2016).

[42] See, among others: De Filippi and Wright (2018), p. 72; Linardatos (2019), p. 2; Heckelmann (2018), p. 505; Schrey and Thalhofer (2017), p. 1432.

the smart contract, i.e., the transaction protocol automatically executed without recourse to judicial intervention, and must not trust the counterparty.

This allows them to take calculated risks, even in areas where the parties are not directly opposed to each other, but which are often characterized by anonymity and application risks, as usually happens in e-commerce and international contracts.[43]

Consumers or users, in particular, could benefit significantly from these advantages, since they usually face difficulties and/or costs for which they neglect to assert their rights in court.[44]

In addition, smart contracts entail the possibility of reducing transaction costs, by performing some functions currently performed by online intermediaries such as Amazon, eBay, PayPal, etc.[45]

The standardized smart contracts allow the parties to incorporate the commercial practice in their agreement, bypassing the need for explicit but redundant negotiation.[46]

Automated enforcement or compensation has the potential to reduce the amount of litigation, increasing certainty and reducing performance monitoring costs.[47] In general, therefore, smart contracts give rise to a further reduction in human intervention and formalization of the contract.[48]

Compared to traditional contracts, again, smart contracts increase the speed with which contractual relationships can be performed.

Since they do not depend on the paper and the related procedural steps and can be performed in real time, they also allow for cost savings and faster execution compared to paper contracts.[49]

Finally, smart contracts offer an alternative to one of the most characteristic aspects of contractual drafting: the intrinsic ambiguity of natural language.[50]

Words often have multiple meanings and interpretations, and in many cases ambiguous language can make it easier for the parties to enter into a contractual agreement, creating flexibility in terms of contractual performance.[51]

However, ambiguity and editorial shortcomings can also be used by parties wishing to free themselves from contractual conditions that they no longer want to

[43] See: Ryan (2017), pp. 14 ff.

[44] In this perspective, see: Borgogno (2019), pp. 8 ff.; Fries (2018), p. 88.

[45] See: Borgogno (2019), pp. 13 ff.; Sokolov (2018), p. 11; Mik (2017), p. 277; Goldman Sachs (2016).

[46] On this point, see: Sklaroff (2017), pp. 282 ff.

[47] In this regard, see: Werbach and Cornell (2017), pp. 318 and 352 ff.; McJohn and McJohn (2017).

[48] On this point, see e.g.: Savelyev (2017), pp. 120 ff.

[49] See: De Filippi and Wright (2015), p. 25.

[50] See, among others: Raskin (2017), p. 324; Farnsworth (1967). *Contra*, regarding the ambiguity of the language and operational mechanisms of smart contracts, see: Grimmelmann (2019).

[51] In this regard, see: Gergen (1992), p. 1006; Hadfield (1984).

honor.[52] The smart contract provides a binding solution to this phenomenon, by incorporating the legal provisions in the computer code.[53]

However, although smart contracts can facilitate the execution of complex agreements with greater clarity and speed, they also present several new issues and challenges for trade law and practice.

A first question that can arise is that of the identification of the other contracting party, if the Blockchain allows anonymous, or rather pseudonymous transactions,[54] such as in the case where transactions are recorded with reference to an IP or wallet address of cryptocurrencies.[55]

The codification of the clauses in the IT language could lead to a limitation of the possible contents of the smart contracts, linked to the possibility of automation of the contractual prose according to the if/then logic.[56]

This is linked to the risk that the code, drawn up by IT specialists, incorrectly reports the provisions of the contractual agreement between the parties, or may operate differently from what was planned, with the related question of imputation of responsibilities.

Furthermore, there is the issue of the risk of non-understanding of smart contracts by the parties and legal practitioners.[57]

In fact, the connection between the text in computer code and one written in natural language is increasingly widespread in practice.

The smart contract, then, can have the same content of the contract in natural language, so-called split contracting, or they can be the specification or execution of the other, so-called hybrid agreement.[58]

From an execution standpoint, smart contracts implement a zero-tolerance policy by default, in which the parties have no choice but to execute the contract.

Contrary to traditional contracts, in which the parties can decide whether or not to fulfill their obligations, the smart contract cannot be violated. Once the contracting

[52] In this sense, see: Burnham et al. (2009).

[53] Thus: De Filippi and Wright (2015), p. 25. Regarding the impact of the computer code on contractual ambiguity see also e.g.: Ogilvie (1992), p. 531.

[54] Pseudonymity refers to the possibility that although a person is not identifiable by her real name, such identification can still take place through the acquisition of further information on the same, such as a pseudonym, an IP address, a bank account number, etc.; on the subject, see: Article 29 Data Protection Working Party, Opinion 05/2014 on Anonymisation Techniques, WP 216, 10 April 2014, available at: https://ec.europa.eu/justice/article-29/documentation/opinion-recommendation/index_en.htm, pp. 20 ff.

[55] On this point, see: European Bank for Reconstruction and Development, Clifford Chance (2018), pp. 22–23; Franco (2014), pp. 209 ff.

[56] See: Cardozo Blockchain Project (2018), pp. 8 ff; Werbach and Cornell (2017), pp. 365 ff.; Giancaspro (2017), p. 832; Mik (2017), p. 292.

[57] Regarding these profiles, see: DiMatteo and Poncibò (2019), p. 815; Giancaspro (2017), pp. 830 ff.; Mik (2017), pp. 281 ff.

[58] On this point, see: European Bank for Reconstruction and Development, Clifford Chance (2018), pp. 17 ff.; De Filippi and Wright (2018), pp. 76 ff.; Allen (2018), pp. 307 ff.

parties have agreed to be bound by a certain clause, the computer code binds them to it without possibility of breach.[59]

In a system regulated by self-imposed smart contracts and other technical agreements, there is less need for judicial intervention, because the way the rules were defined—the computer code—is the same tool through which they are applied.[60]

This raises the question of what is legally or technically binding. While contract law provides a series of safeguards to protect the parties, and in particular consumers, by allowing them to invalidate the contract or make it inapplicable, smart contracts operate within their own closed technological framework.

Although the implementation of basic contractual guarantees and consumer protection rules in smart contracts is theoretically possible, in practice it can be complex given the formalized and deterministic nature of the computer code.[61]

Still, although most of the data comes from the Blockchain or from other databases connected to it, some smart contracts, for the purpose of their execution, may have to acquire data from outside the Blockchain.

This creates the need to make use of reliable external sources, the so-called "oracles", which represent interfaces between contracts and the outside world.[62]

Therefore, reliable oracles that support and can satisfy a wide range of data requests are of paramount importance for many smart contracts.[63]

On the other hand, this phenomenon requires the guarantee that the oracle is reliable and effectively third, and that there are no interferences or threats to security during the acquisition of data from the same.[64]

Another problematic issue concerns the need to intervene on a smart contract in the event that an injunction issued by the judicial authority must be carried out.

In general, apart from the exceptions mentioned above, given the impossibility of interrupting the execution of a smart contract, the realization of this result may take place in the hypothesis of a private Blockchain which provides for blocking mechanisms of execution under the responsibility of certain predefined nodes.

The areas of application of smart contracts are numerous. They can be used, at least in theory, in all cases where economic activities are related to the Internet and some events can be verified digitally.[65]

---

[59] Except that of course the parties could terminate the contract if they decided not to remain tied to it.

[60] From the merger of law and computer code, therefore, it follows that the only way to violate the law is to effectively break the code.

[61] See: Cutts (2019); De Filippi and Wright (2015), p. 26.

[62] An example of smart contracts activated by external inputs is that of the insurance policies proposed by AXA and Etherisc, insurance companies that offer policies that compensate travellers who suffer delays or airline cancellations. Flight information is acquired automatically and in real time by an oracle company indicated in the contract and compensation is paid automatically.

[63] In this sense, see: Sokolov (2018), p. 10; Zhan (2016).

[64] On this point, see: Mik (2017), pp. 292–293.

[65] In this regard, see: Linardatos (2019), pp. 9 ff.; Breidenbach and Glatz (2018), pp. 111 ff.; Governatori et al. (2018).

By virtue of the growing interconnection of devices, sensors, etc. through the Internet of Things, this phenomenon affects ever wider areas.[66]

In addition to the financial and insurance sectors in which digital bargaining already plays a central role, the use of smart contracts is developing in sectors such as art, entertainment, agri-food, energy, sharing economy, etc.[67]

Of course, contracts that relate to access to digital content, and are therefore easily translatable into software, represent privileged use cases for smart contracts.[68]

The ability of Blockchain and smart contracts to manage data from a variety of unreliable sources per se, moreover, appears likely to make them fundamental tools for the development of the Internet of Things.

It will consist of billions of networked devices, not all reliable and some even harmful. These devices need a central reference point that can help facilitate coordination between machines that is private, secure, and independent of trust.[69]

To this end, devices and other material properties can be registered on a Blockchain and, using smart contracts, transformed into "smart properties", such as for example Non-Fungible Tokens or NFTs,[70] thus allowing the control of material properties on the network, also through other machines.

A Blockchain can archive the relationship between Internet-enabled machines at any time and the smart contracts can allocate the corresponding rights and obligations of the connected devices.

In addition, different relationships and credentials can be encoded in the Blockchain regarding certain cryptographically activated resources, such as key locks or smartphones, to ensure that only certain people have access to the property's features at any time.[71]

Furthermore, the coordinating power of the Blockchain also allows the execution and interconnection of a variety of smart contracts that interact with each other in a decentralized and distributed way.

---

[66] See: Wendehorst (2016).

[67] In this regard, see: Chamber of Digital Commerce (2016); Unsworth (2019); Prinz and Schulte (2017), pp. 27 ff.; Gatz (2017).

[68] This would allow the generalized implementation of a so-called metered Internet, in which the actions are linked to micro-payments through related smart contracts. Since cryptocurrencies and smart contracts significantly reduce transaction costs, in particular, they allow artists, musicians, authors, etc. to automatically collect royalties related to copyrights on their works each time they are viewed or used. In this regard, see: De Filippi and Wright (2015), pp. 29 ff.; Wallach (2014); Fischer (2009). An application of specific importance, in this sense, is that of the distribution of music, as for example in the cases of Ujo Music, which allows artists to publish music online and collect the entire proceeds of sales, and Artlery, which guarantees the artist a percentage for each transfer of ownership of the work occurred via smart contract.

[69] See: Rejeb et al. (2019); Reyna et al. (2018).

[70] Regarding which, see among others: Fairfield (2021).

[71] In this regard, see: De Filippi and Wright (2015), pp. 14–15.

It is therefore possible to associate multiple smart contracts to form decentralized organizations, which operate according to specific rules and procedures defined by contracts and algorithms.[72]

Using a decentralized organization based on Blockchain, people and machines, or a combination of them, can coordinate through a series of smart contracts, without the need to incorporate them into traditional corporate entities.

Governance can be reached as well by recording transactions directly on Blockchain, reducing operating costs while providing more transparent and verifiable decisions paths.[73]

The spread of decentralized autonomous organizations, or DAOs, which enter into contractual relationships with individuals or other machines, can give rise to a complex ecosystem of autonomous agents that interact with each other according to a set of predetermined, codified, and self-application rules.[74]

On the other hand, the first applications have shown the risks to which similar organizations may be exposed and the relative persistent need for an adequate protection system, as emerged for example in the case of the cyber-attack on "The DAO" platform.[75]

---

[72] Thus, realizing the theory according to which the firm consists of a collection of contracts and relationships, on which see among others, also regarding the relationship between business organization and transaction costs: Williamson (2002); Jensen and Meckling (1976); Coase (1937).

[73] In particular, corporate governance models can be replicated by distributing decision-making power to multiple parties using multiple signature technology, which prevents the execution of an action until multiple parties agree on a transaction; on this point, see: De Filippi and Mauro (2014); Buterin (2014c).

[74] In this regard, see: De Filippi and Wright (2015), pp. 15 ff.; Buterin (2014b).

[75] In 2016, a group of developers associated with the Ethereum Blockchain had created a crowdfunding distributed platform called "The DAO". in which corporate governance and operations would be conducted automatically through smart contracts. Users promised an Ethereum cryptocurrency sum in exchange for tokens that gave them the authority to vote on projects to be financed. Funding organizations would sign up through another interface and collect Ethereum if they received enough votes. In just a few weeks, the platform users had committed an amount of Ethereum cryptocurrency worth more than 150 million dollars. Users were registered to participate in the DAO on a website which stated explicitly in its terms of service that the smart contract on the Ethereum Blockchain was the legal supervisory authority, and any document or explanation readable by humans, including those on the website, they were offered for educational purposes only and did not interfere with the terms expressed by the DAO code established on the Blockchain. A few weeks after the launch of the project, an attacker took advantage of an error in the DAO code to steal Ethereum worth more than 60 million dollars. Although it was clearly an attempted theft, the deal was done through a series of smart contracts that were formally valid within the rules of The DAO. Even if the stolen funds were temporarily quarantined in an account and not immediately disbursed, from the point of view of the smart contracts system, the transactions were perfectly legitimate. Therefore, even if a judge had ordered the restitution of the funds, no one could execute that order: there was no legal or technical way to recover the funds without compromising the whole system. In the end, the leaders of the Ethereum platform had to convince most of the nodes of the platform to put in place a so-called hard fork, which divided the entire Ethereum Blockchain into two incompatible paths. Only through this intervention, which effectively ended the DAO project and partly undermined trust in the Ethereum platform, was it possible to return the stolen funds. See:

4.3 Legal Nature of Smart (Legal) Contracts

Although the term "smart contract", as mentioned, originates in the nineties of the last century, the definition of the concept remains controversial.[76] In particular, one of the most discussed profiles turns out to be the fundamental question of their legal relevance.

Although the computer code of a smart contract can be considered a kind of *sui generis* regulation, as its operating rules produce effects similar to the legal ones,[77] the law and the code form different systems, which evolve autonomously in terms of normativity and logic, regulating the first social relationships and the other an information system.[78]

Not everything that is executable is legally relevant. A smart contract can, for example, be used to: (a) carry out a non-contractual process, for example a voting procedure online; or (b) provide for the performance of a service such as the payment of a cryptocurrency based on an agreement that has already taken place outside the network.

Otherwise, it (c) may represent the actual contract itself, sometimes unilateral and predefined by one of the parties; or (d) where it makes use of artificial intelligence algorithms, give rise to the definition, modification, or integration of the contractual content itself.[79]

In hypotheses (c) and (d), therefore, the smart contract represents a legally relevant contractual agreement, and not a mere act of execution as in hypothesis (b).[80]

It is true that, as highlighted by several scholars, the automatic execution of the contract does not necessarily require the Blockchain but can be based on more traditional technologies.

For example, vending machines typically deliver the desired merchandise after receiving payment. The bank customer withdraws the money from the ATM using a card recognized by the ATM circuit. Automatic blocking of credit cards online is activated whenever suspicious activity occurs.[81]

Werbach and Cornell (2017), pp. 138 ff.; Rohr (2019), pp. 87 ff.; Kolber (2018), p. 200 ff.; DiMatteo and Poncibò (2019), pp. 821–822; Grimmelmann (2019), pp. 18 ff.

[76] Think, for example, of the different definitions adopted in the first US regulations on the subject, referred to: Cardozo Blockchain Project (2018), pp. 23 ff.

[77] On this point, see: Black (2002), pp. 25 ff.

[78] In this regard, see e.g.: Graber (2012).

[79] Which, as will be specified below, does not represent an essential feature of the smart contract, but can be integrated on a subsidiary basis.

[80] On the problematic profiles of the relationship between smart contracts and contractual agreements, see among others: Kasprzyk (2018); Kõlvart et al. (2016), pp. 133 ff.; European Bank for Reconstruction and Development, Clifford Chance (2018), pp. 6 ff.; R3, Norton Rose Fullbright (2016), pp. 5 ff.

[81] On these examples and for consequent criticisms of the autonomy of the smart contract concept, see: Zeno-Zencovich (2021); Möslein (2019).

On the other hand, the examples cited represent executions of clauses and/or limited or mechanical aspects, behind performance or at least action of a human counterpart,[82] or performance under pre-existing contracts[83] and/or for security reasons aimed at protecting the performance of the contract.[84]

With smart contracts, automation appears for the first time able to affect *not only clauses or modules*,[85] but also *the entire contract from conclusion to execution.*

Conversely, not everything that is legally relevant is executable. There are a series of contractual clauses that cannot be programmed and executed through the computer code, as ambiguous or interpretable, such as fairness and good faith, utmost diligence, etc.[86]

Furthermore, a computer code will not consider the possible nullity of a legal contract unless instructed to do so. Its system is based, in fact, on its own rules and will execute the agreement only according to the configuration of its algorithms, regardless of the legal rules.

Consequently, the phenomenon of smart contracts registered on a distributed ledger such as Blockchain is problematic, as discrepancies can occur between the two legal and information technology systems which can lead to the application of illegal smart contracts.[87]

In this context, while some scholars propose distinctions between smart contracts, smart contract codes and legal smart contracts,[88] others believe that smart contracts are independent of law.[89]

As computer scientists and economists have shown on several occasions, it is possible to talk about smart contracts without even considering the question of their legal nature.

This is because they, despite the wording "contract", are not necessarily seen as a legal issue, at least as far as the Blockchain is concerned, so much so that from many sides both legal and smart nature have been discussed.[90]

From the information technology point of view, the term smart is an operational definition that indicates the use of algorithms and computer programs. The term contract, for its part, indicates that they are used for the purpose of fulfilling certain

[82] Think of the traditional example of vending machines.

[83] This is the case with the ATM, which operates behind human action.

[84] As in the hypothesis of the block of the credit card.

[85] In the context of smart contracts, by the way and in favor of the prospect of modularization of the contract, see: Werbach (2018a), pp. 543 ff.

[86] In this regard, see: Giancaspro (2017), p. 832; Mik (2017), p. 292.

[87] In this sense, see: Jaccard (2017), p. 8.

[88] See: Blemus (2017), pp. 1 13 ff.; International Swaps and Derivatives Association, Linklaters (2017), pp. 4 ff.

[89] In this sense, see: Savelyev (2017), pp. 17 ff.; Breidenbach and Glatz (2018), pp. 115 ff.

[90] See e.g.: Zeno-Zencovich (2021); Pardolesi and Davola (2019); Kolber (2018); MONAX, Smart Contracts, available at: https://monax.io/learn/smart_contracts.

obligations, exercising certain rights, or taking control of certain goods within a distributed register.

To clarify the distinction between the information technology phenomenon and the smart contract relevant in a legal sense, some scholars propose to replace the term smart contract with the concept of smart legal contract, which would precisely indicate the way in which legally relevant contracts can be expressed and executed through the software.[91]

The computer code at the basis of the smart contract, therefore, is essentially an infrastructure for the conclusion and execution of a contract, in the same way as the vending machine, website, or app that offers the user the possibility of accepting contractual terms.[92]

The use of the term smart reflects the fact that the code of the smart contract ensures that certain elements are automatic and self-executed according to predefined conditions.

The smart (legal) contract, in fact, can examine whether particular states have occurred and, in this case, trigger a predetermined action.[93]

Thus, a smart contract in the legal sense, or smart legal contract, is a contractual agreement drawn up and implemented through an IT code. This agreement implies the creation of legal obligations for the parties. Once the agreement is codified and activated, the algorithms guarantee the execution of the promises, except for the use of judicial protection.[94]

Therefore, if smart contracts in a technical sense per se do not necessarily have legal relevance,[95] however, smart contracts do not operate in a legal vacuum.[96] As regards legally relevant acts, the law is generally applicable.

Ultimately, in these cases the term could be understood in the way that Nick Szabo originally coined it, limiting itself to affirming the greater functionality of smart contracts compared to non-codified contracts without distancing from the law.

---

[91] In this regard, see: Clack et al. (2016), p. 2.

[92] In this perspective, one may also see e.g.: Gambino and Stazi (2021); Stazi (2019).

[93] See: International Swaps and Derivatives Association, Linklaters (2017), p. 5. Although the smart contract can be automated at the IT level, some parties may require human input and control; see: Clack et al. (2016), p. 2.

[94] In this sense, see again: Clack et al. (2016), p. 2, who propose the definition—also accepted by European Bank for Reconstruction and Development, Clifford Chance (2018), p. 6—according to which: "A smart contract is an automatable and enforceable agreement. Automatable by computer, although some parts may require human input and control. Enforceable either by legal enforcement of rights and obligations or via tamper-proof execution of computer code"; see also: De Caria (2019), pp. 746–747; Sokolov (2018), p. 14.

[95] The description of smart contracts as "deposit objects on the account" on the website of the Ethereum Blockchain platform shows precisely that smart contracts do not always have to be contracts in a legal sense.

[96] See: DiMatteo and Poncibò (2019), pp. 814 ff.; Jaccard (2017), p. 9, who highlight the continuing hierarchical superiority of the legal system with respect to the rules of the computer code, with particular reference to judicial control and restorative remedies; see also: Werbach (2018a), pp. 528 ff.; De Filippi and Wright (2018), p. 78; Bacon et al. (2017).

In this perspective, smart contracts are "a set of promises, specified in digital form, including the protocols within which the parties carry out these promises." The term smart does not imply, even if it does not exclude, instead, the use of artificial intelligence.[97]

Similarly, other scholars stressed that smart contracts (a) are not simply digital contracts—many of which rely on trusted authorities to reach consensus and execution—(b) nor do they imply artificial intelligence, regardless of what their name may[98] suggest, and that smart contracts (c) do not "think" like a lawyer or an artificial intelligence might be able to do. The smart contracts, however, automatically perform the lines of computer code for which they were programmed.[99]

Considering what has been specified so far, a smart contract can be defined as an automated mechanism that performs its defined functions when certain preliminary conditions are met.[100]

In a legal sense, it consists in the digital coding of a contract or parts of it.[101] Its legal assessment, therefore, depends on the law applicable to the contract below.[102]

Although most of the smart contracts are also prepared in the form of a related written agreement or electronic in natural language,[103] the conclusion of a contract and its digital representation in a smart contract may also coincide.[104]

In this book, the analysis focuses on the case of the smart contract in the legal sense, with the related questions it poses about the institution and the applicable contractual regulation.

---

[97] In this regard, see: Szabo (1996).

[98] Rather, it has been argued that on the contrary they are robotic, that their "intelligence" can be questioned precisely because they do not contain artificial intelligence in themselves, and therefore that the term smart contracts is somewhat deceptive; see: Cong and He (2018), p. 11; Lauslahti et al. (2017), pp. 3 ff.

[99] Thus: Jaccard (2017), pp. 3–4.

[100] See, among others: De Caria (2019), p. 737; Lauslahti et al. (2017), p. 17.

[101] See: De Filippi and Wright (2018), p. 79; Linardatos (2018), p. 87.

[102] In this sense, see: Woebbeking (2019), p. 109; Splinder and Woebbeking (2019); Kaulartz and Heckmann (2016), p. 622.

[103] It should be noted, in fact, that the smart contract can take various forms. In particular, it may consist of: (a) a contract entirely in computer code; (b) a code contract with a separate natural language version; (c) a natural language contract with coded services; (d) a natural language contract with a coded payment mechanism. In this regard, see: Sokolov (2018), p. 14; Cardozo Blockchain Project (2018), pp. 4 f.; International Swaps and Derivatives Association, Linklaters (2017), p. 13.

[104] See: Raskin (2017), p. 322; Allen (2018), p. 309; Linardatos (2018), p. 89.

4.4 Distinction from Other Cases

Smart contracts have some characteristics in common with other cases, from which they must be distinguished.

The best-known hypothesis of assimilation, as recalled by the same creator of the concept of smart contracts,[105] is that with vending machines.[106] However, although in both cases the services are automated, it is possible to stop the vending machine, while in general it is not possible to block the execution of the smart contract.[107]

Furthermore, the vending machine application can only be used for simple and unilateral transactions,[108] while the smart contracts are more sophisticated and can also substantiate a multilateral agreement if two or more parties agree something, incorporate an agreement in the code and they insert it in the Blockchain.[109]

Another hypothesis often associated with smart contracts in the common law doctrine is that of the so-called self-help, that is, a legally permissible conduct that people commit to avoid the compulsion of the law and without the assistance of a governmental or judicial authority to prevent or remedy a civil liability.[110]

In particular, some scholars assimilate smart contracts to one of the technological forms of self-help called start switch.[111] Although both technologies do not involve a third party to enforce an agreement, the start switch does not deal with the substance of the contract and is a separate device that helps a party prevent or remedy a civil liability.[112]

The concept of smart contract is broader than those of self-help and start switch. First, the computer code of the smart contract is an indivisible part of the contract, which makes it smart. Second, the smart contract code and the Blockchain are aimed

---

[105] See: Szabo (1997), who compared them to virtual vending machines.

[106] The first known meeting between law and vending machines occurred in the seventeenth century, when the free-speech agitator Richard Carlile invented the book vending machine to counteract censorship. He believed that a contract would form between a human being and a machine, but his argument was not accepted, and he was convicted of selling blasphemous literature through the device; see: Segrave (2012), pp. 4–5.

[107] In this regard, see: Savelyev (2017), p. 17.

[108] A vending machine is essentially a contract with the bearer: anyone with coins can participate in an exchange with the seller. The lock and other security mechanisms protect the coins and contents from external agents, enough to allow the vending machines to operate in a wide range of areas. Once the coins or banknotes have been inserted into the machine, the value is transferred, and no third-party involvement is required in the process. On this point, see the English leading case Thornton v Shoe Lane Parking Ltd [1971] 2 QB 163.

[109] In this regard, see: Sokolov (2018), p. 17.

[110] See: De Caria (2019), pp. 745–746; Sokolov (2018), p. 16; Raskin (2017), pp. 333 ff.

[111] In this sense, see again: Raskin (2017), pp. 333 ff.

[112] The starter switch can track the scheduled payments of the buyer or tenant of a vehicle under a loan or rental agreement, and prevent the vehicle from starting if a scheduled payment is not received by its due date or within an applicable grace period. Similarly, a smart contract can be programmed with the help of an IoT device incorporated in the vehicle to prevent its use. In this regard, see: Möslein (2019), pp. 11 ff.; Hudson and Laudicina (2006).

at ensuring the fulfillment of promises and not at preventing or remedying a civil liability.[113]

Similarly, the smart contract is a larger case than that of the escrow agreement, or letter of credit. Both in the smart contract and in the guarantee deposit, in fact, the money or the property would be transferred to the parties only after a detailed verification of compliance with the specific conditions of the agreement.

The difference is that smart contracts, in addition to not providing the involvement of a third-party guarantor, have much wider application areas than guarantee deposits.[114]

Compared to the letter of credit,[115] while both have in common the characteristic of guaranteeing compliance, the letter of credit is only an additional agreement to the main one and is not necessary.

Furthermore, the letter of credit generally involves a third party, usually a bank, which guarantees the performance, while in the smart contract the fulfillment is guaranteed by technical means and not by third parties.[116]

For some smart contracts, the contract conclusion procedure can be the same as the click-wrap or browse-wrap agreements.[117] However, while these can be interrupted at any time, the smart contract code once activated generally cannot be interrupted.[118]

In addition, they mainly impose negative obligations,[119] while smart contracts are flexible in this regard.[120] Finally, similarly to the agreements via vending machine, the electronic agreements mentioned above are essentially unilateral contracts, while smart contracts can be multilateral.[121]

As regards, then, cases of electronic contracts that appear to be the most immediate antecedents of smart contracts, since the seventies of the last century, in exchanges between companies, the Electronic Data Interchange system has been used to automatically regulate supplies.[122]

The EDI agreements, however, are based on traditional contractual texts transposed on a different medium. The agreement remains a written text, which can be

---

[113] See: Sokolov (2018), p. 16; Werbach and Cornell (2017), pp. 354 ff.

[114] See again: Sokolov (2018), p. 15; Werbach and Cornell (2017), pp. 344 ff.

[115] That is, a document which ensures that a seller will receive a payment up to the amount indicated if certain conditions are met.

[116] However, the letter of credit can be incorporated into the smart contract. See: Sokolov (2018), p. 15; McJohn and McJohn (2017), pp. 205–206.

[117] Regarding which see above, in Sect. 3.2.

[118] See: Sokolov (2018), p. 18; Werbach and Cornell (2017), pp. 335 ff.

[119] For example, do not perform specific activities while using the service or do not object to certain activities performed by the service provider.

[120] On this point, see: Savelyev (2017), p. 12.

[121] See: Chopra and White (2011), p. 37.

[122] In this regard, see: Reed (2012), pp. 267 ff.; R3, Norton Rose Fullbright (2016), p. 15; Feick and Packer (2008); Radin (2000); Boss (1992); Pfeiffer (1992).

read and interpreted by any reader and whose execution is in any case left to an additional action, even if not automated.[123]

Subsequently, contracts have begun to be drawn up to be automatically executed by the machines and, therefore, in a language different from the natural one, but understandable for the computer.

These are the so-called data-oriented contracts, and therefore computable contracts, that is, contracts in which the parties express one or more terms and conditions of the agreement as data so that they are executable by a computer, possibly after evaluating the fulfillment or not of certain conditions provided by the agreement.[124]

The representation of the contractual content in computer code terms has opened the way for automation: it has become possible that the software itself intervenes dynamically in a negotiation relationship, based on the combination of a set of predefined instructions provided to the program.[125]

The real predecessor of smart contracts on Blockchain can be considered the so-called Ricardian contract, a method to register a document as a contract in a legal sense and connect it securely to other systems, for example accounting, to link the contract to a financial transaction, such as a payment, etc.

The Ricardian contract is essentially a contractual model aimed at codifying the elements that define the legal agreement also in a format that can be elaborated and executed by the software.

Unlike the smart contract, therefore, the function of the Ricardian contract is to allow the digitalization of the intentions of the parties and their connection to a financial transaction before the execution of the contract.[126]

Smart contracts represent, indeed, an evolution of telematic contracts and cybernetic contracts.[127] In the electronic contract, the use of the computer connected to the Internet constitutes the means to transmit the proposal of a contract and receive its acceptance, and in the cybernetic contract the parties express their will in the software instructions leaving the electronic agent the definition of the content and any contractual integration or modification.

In the smart contract the use of the distributed ledger such as Blockchain technology characterizes the contract for total disintermediation from the human

[123]See e.g. again: Boss (1992).

[124]In this regard, see: Surden (2012), pp. 629 ff. Regarding the different levels of contracts negotiated and/or subsequently integrated by algorithms, in addition to referring to the analysis proposed above in Sect. 3.2 on electronic agents, see: Scholz (2017); Casey and Niblett (2016). For a critical approach to the concept of smart contracts and a reconversion of the smart contract to the data-driven one, see: Zeno-Zencovich (2021); Hsiao (2017). In a critical sense with respect to the novelty of the effects of smart contracts with respect to previous practice and their contractual relevance, see also: Pardolesi and Davola (2019); Kolber (2018).

[125]See among others: Gambino and Stazi (2021); Surden (2012).

[126]In this regard, see: Chohan (2017); Grigg (2004), pp. 25 ff., who conceived it based on the Ricardo financial instrument exchange platform.

[127]With regard to which, see the analysis proposed above in Sect. 2.2.

factor, through a database which is shared, decentralized, distributed, encrypted, tamper resistant[128] and automatically run.

4.5 First Regulatory Approaches in Comparative Law

There is no international legal framework specifically dictated for smart contracts.[129] The fact that there is no specific regulation does not mean that existing regulations and general principles cannot be applicable to them, or that they are not regulated at all.[130]

In several legal systems,[131] some initial regulatory approaches have been or are being adopted.

In the United States, although the Statute of Frauds, UCC, UETA, and E-Sign Act, already seem to allow the use of smart contracts,[132] several states have started to issue laws aimed at clarifying the execution of smart contracts in the context of legal agreements, presumably to attract potential entrepreneurs who develop applications and services based on Blockchain technology.

Thus, Arizona, California, Illinois, Nevada, Tennessee, and Ohio, have introduced specific provisions stating that documents placed on a Blockchain are electronic documents within the meaning of the UETA.[133]

However, the general definitions of electronic records and electronic agent contained in the UETA and in the E-Sign Act appear to include the use of smart contracts to create binding legal agreements.

---

[128] Apart from the exceptions mentioned above in Sect. 4.2.

[129] See among others: Mukherjee (2018).

[130] In this sense, see: De Caria (2019). p. 739; regarding the Chinese system, see: Wang and Lei (2019), p. 940. For further considerations on the applicability of the existing regulation to the new forms of commercial interaction offered by technology, one may also see: Stazi (2004).

[131] In this regard, see: Joint Economic Committee Congress of the United States (2018), pp. 218 ff.

[132] As noted in: Cardozo Blockchain Project (2018), pp. 22 ff., pursuant to the Statute of Frauds and the UCC, the parties will be able to rely on a smart contract to create legally binding agreements, if the smart contract outlines the material terms of the agreement and the parties digitally sign it through a voluntary act, or even more if the parties include the reference to a "hybrid" contract that contains standard legal prose connected to the related smart contract algorithms. Even if a legal agreement based on a smart contract is deemed not to comply with the Statute of Frauds or the requirements of the UCC—for doubts in this regard, see: Sokolov (2018), pp. 26–27—the parties that attempt to contest the applicability of this contract should face a complex legal path by virtue of the ample provisions of the UETA and E-Sign.

[133] See: 2017 Ariz. HB 2417 44-7061; 2018 Cal. AB 2658; Nev. Rev. Stat. Ann. § 719.090; 2018 Ohio. SB 220 1306.01; 2018 Tenn. SB 1662 47-10-202. Regarding Blockchain and UETA, see: Bosco (2019).

Therefore, the amendments adopted by the states have been criticized as they would be likely to make the use of smart contracts complex, creating ambiguity within the legislation.[134]

As these state regulations, especially those of Arizona, California, and Tennessee, contain technical terms such as "distributed ledger technology", "cryptoeconomics", "decentralized ledger", etc. to describe the Blockchain and smart contracts—terms that currently do not have a clear and shared meaning—the courts should interpret these definitions referring to the intent of the legislator, giving rise to consequent questions on the meaning and application of the amendments.[135]

In addition, by changing the state legislation implementing the UETA to broadly define Blockchain-based documents as electronic signatures, as Arizona and Tennessee have done, states can face the risk of pre-emption under the E-Sign Act.[136]

Thus, where states deem it necessary to adopt legislation that affirms the applicability of smart contracts, they should adopt a limited approach similar to that adopted by Nevada and Ohio, limiting themselves to affirming that a Blockchain, defined in the broadest and forward-looking possible meaning, can qualify as an electronic document, and therefore that the electronic signatures and smart contracts recorded on it are legally valid and binding.

Conversely, states that have not adopted the UETA such as New York, Washington and Illinois should amend their state laws to recognize the use of smart contracts to carry out commercial transactions.[137]

In the European context, the EU institutions have started to wonder about the possible adoption of uniform legislation that can guarantee a homogeneous approach with respect to the various problems arising from the use of Blockchain and smart contracts.

---

[134] In this sense, see: Cardozo Blockchain Project (2018), p. 24; Chamber of Digital Commerce et al. (2018); Rohr (2019), pp. 74 ff.; Dell'Erba (2018).

[135] So, again: Cardozo Blockchain Project (2018), p. 25.

[136] As mentioned above in Sect. 2.5, by virtue of the peculiar mechanism of pre-emption that regulates the relationship between the E-Sign and the UETA provisions, the E-Sign Act gives way to the state laws on electronic signature only if they are consistent with the UETA, or if alternative procedures or requirements for the use and/or acceptance of electronic signatures do not require or give greater relevance or legal effectiveness to the application of a specific technology for the creation, storage, communication or authentication of electronic documents or electronic signatures. Thus, by changing the state regulations implementing the UETA to broadly define Blockchain and smart contracts, states risk—based on a textual interpretation of the E-Sign Act—attributing greater legal relevance than it had been previously granted to defined technology, to give rise to pre-emption in favor of federal law. On this point, see: Svikhart (2017), pp. 105 ff.

[137] Bills have been introduced in the states of New York and Illinois that define blockchain in relation to electronic documents and signatures (2018 Ill. HB5553; 2018 NY SB 8858). Further bills have been presented in several other states. A picture of the state of the art is available on: https://www.sagewise.io/smart-contracts-state-legislation. In doctrine, see: De Caria (2019), pp. 737 ff.; Svikhart (2017), pp. 103 ff.; Catchlove (2017), p. 2.

Therefore, some initiatives aimed at promoting the study of these phenomena and cross-border cooperation have been started, without so far reaching binding interventions.

Among others,[138] specifically relevant for smart contracts is a resolution of the European Parliament of October 2018, in which the Parliament invited the European Commission to promote the development of technical standards in collaboration with the relevant international organizations,[139] and to conduct an in-depth analysis of the potential and legal implications, including those relating to jurisdiction, and the legal framework existing in the various Member States in relation to the applicability of smart contracts.[140]

Then, the Parliament invited the Commission, should potential obstacles to the use of such contracts emerge in the digital single market, to take appropriate measures to assess whether these obstacles are proportionate, while noting that legal certainty can also be enhanced through legal coordination or mutual recognition between Member States on the matter, with the obvious intention of respecting their autonomy in contract law.[141]

Among the Member States of the European Union, the Republic of Malta has adopted the most organic legislation so far,[142] defining the smart contract as "a form of technology arrangement consisting of – (A) a computer protocol; or (B) an agreement concluded wholly or partly in an electronic form, which is automatic and enforceable by computer code, although some parts may require human input

---

[138] In particular, on the one hand, the launch in February 2018 by the European Commission, with the support of the European Parliament, of the Observatory and the EU Blockchain Forum, aimed at analyzing the issues and highlighting the most important technologies and to reinforce the commitment made at European level by those involved in the sector. On the other, the creation in April 2018 of a European Blockchain Partnership, on the initiative of twenty-two European countries to which five others have been added, in order to collaborate with the institutions and the EU Observatory-Forum to avoid a fragmented approach of the various players in the sector and to consolidate Europe's role in the development and diffusion of technology.

[139] Such as International Organization for Standardization (ISO), International Telecommunication Union (ITU), European Committee for Standardization (CEN), and European Committee for Electrotechnical Standardization (CENELEC).

[140] European Parliament Resolution of 3 October 2018 on distributed ledger and blockchain technologies: building trust through disintermediation (2017/2772 (RSP)).

[141] On the need to provide for the compatibility of smart contracts with contract law rules, see also: European Parliamentary Research Service (2017), p. 15. For a framework of contract law at European level and on the complex path of harmonization and attempted standardization on the matter, also with specific regard to the digital context, in addition to referring to the doctrine mentioned above in Sect. 2.4, see e.g.: Grundmann (2018); De Franceschi (2016).

[142] The Maltese legislative framework, definitively approved in July 2018, consists of three texts: the Virtual Financial Assets Act, the Malta Digital Innovation Authority Act and the Innovative Technology Arrangements and Services Act, respectively Act XXX, XXXI and XXXIII of 2018. In particular, Act XXX, Art. 2, provides a very broad definition of Distributed Ledger Technology as: "a database system in which information is recorded, consensually shared, and synchronized across a network of multiple nodes."

and control and which may also be enforceable by ordinary legal methods or by a mixture of both."[143]

The approach adopted appears to be acceptable both for the distinction between smart contracts in the information technology sense and those likely to give rise to a legal constraint, and for the affirmation of their possible execution either through the computer code or through the use of jurisdictional remedies.

Italy, unlike other countries which limited to dictate provisions on specific[144] aspects, introduced a legislation specifically relating to technologies based on distributed ledgers and smart contracts.[145]

First, similarly to what happened in the US state models, definitions have been provided for both technologies based on distributed ledgers,[146] and the smart contract, defined as "a computer program that operates on technologies based on distributed registers and whose execution automatically constrains two or more parts based on effects predefined by them."

This definition, on the one hand, mentions execution and automatic constraint by failing to specify whether they refer to smart contracts in an information technology sense or in a legal sense.[147]

On the other hand, in this second hypothesis, it raises important questions regarding both the issues of when the effects are predefined on the one hand only as a unilateral contract, and of the moment when the contractual obligation arises.[148]

According to the Italian law, smart contracts can meet the requirement of the written form after computer identification of the interested parties, through a process having the requirements to be set by the Agency for Digital Italy.[149]

---

[143] Act XXX of 2018, cit., Art. 2.

[144] For example, in France, see Ordonnance no. 2016-520 du 28 avril 2016 relative aux bons de caisse and the Ordnance no. 2017-1674 du 8 décembre 2017 relative à l'utilisation d'un dispositif d'enregistrement électronique partagé pour la représentation et la transmission de titres financiers, which allowed the use of the Blockchain for the registration and transfer of unlisted financial securities as an alternative to the traditional registration in accounting and corporate books. In this regard, see: R3, Norton Rose Fullbright (2016), pp. 40–41; Muka Tshibende (2019), p. 874.

[145] Law 11 February 2019, n. 12, Art. 8-*ter*, entitled "Technologies based on distributed registers and smart contracts."

[146] Defined as "IT technologies and protocols that use a shared, distributed, replicable, simultaneously accessible, architecturally decentralized registry on cryptographic bases, such as to allow the recording, validation, updating and archiving of data both in clear and further protected by cryptography verifiable by each participant, not alterable and not modifiable." As noted previously in Sect. 4.2, on the other hand, the characteristics of non-alterability and unchangeability are not absolute.

[147] Worthy of positive note in these definitions, on the other hand, are the markedly functional approach and the absence of technical-operational terms, of which the risk of ambiguity and/or obsolescence has been mentioned above with regard to the US state models.

[148] On these issues, see below, at Sect. 5.2.

[149] Through guidelines to be adopted within 90 days from the date of entry into force of the law, but which so far have not been adopted. The provision is in line with Art. 20, par. 1-*bis*, of the Digital Administration Code, contained in the Legislative Decree no. 82/2005, which establishes the

In the same sense, the storage of a computer document using technologies based on distributed ledgers produces the legal effects of the electronic time validation referred to in Article 41 of EU e-IDAS regulation.[150]

Therefore, a full recognition of the legal and judicial effects of the smart contract is envisaged between the interested parties according to a qualified electronic time validation,[151] which, pursuant to the e-IDAS Regulation, if issued in a Member State, is recognized as such in all Member States.[152]

4.6 Applicable Law and Jurisdiction

While a national agreement, concluded by national entities and to be executed only on the national territory, would be clearly subject to the corresponding national law and jurisdiction would be determined according to the procedural law of the country in question, in international trade smart contracts can create significant problems if applicable law and competent jurisdiction are not clearly established in the agreement.[153]

In the United States, matters relating to the choice of law are generally a competence of individual state law and jurisprudence.

In general, when the parties to an agreement have expressly selected the law of a particular state, or if the judge concludes from the provisions of an agreement that the parties wished to apply the law of a specific state, the rights and obligations provided for apply precisely in that state.[154]

---

conditions for which an electronic document is suitable to satisfy the requirement of the written form.

[150] EU Regulation no. 910/2014, regarding which one may see above, at Sect. 3.2.

[151] Which, pursuant to Art. 41, par. 2, of the e-IDAS Regulation enjoys the presumption of accuracy of the date and time it indicates and the integrity of the data with which this date and time are associated.

[152] E-IDAS regulation, Art. 41, par. 3. To this end, the technologies must possess the technical standards whose definition has been entrusted also in this case to the Agency for Digital Italy. This should have happened within 90 days of the entry into force of the law, but so far, they have not been adopted. This, in line with what was foreseen in the modification of the Digital Administration Code pursuant to Legislative Decree no. 217/2017, which had extended the validity of the electronic document also to the case in which it is signed with an electronic signature different from the digital one, qualified or advanced, provided that it respects the technical standards identified by the Agency for Digital Italy through specific guidelines.

[153] In this regard, see: De Caria (2019), p. 748. In general, the parties to an agreement can contractually select the law applicable to a smart contract. However, in some jurisdictions, for example the United States (see below) or Spain, the applicable law selected by the parties must have some connection with the parties or the business concerned. See Chamber of Digital Commerce – Smart Contracts Alliance (2018), p. 28.

[154] See: American Law Institute, Restatement (Second) of Conflicts of Law, 1971, § 187.

However, US courts do not apply the chosen state law if: (a) the state does not have a "substantial" relationship with one of the parties and there is no reasonable basis for the parties' choice; or (b) the application of the law of the chosen State would be contrary to a fundamental policy of a state that has a materially greater interest than the chosen state.[155]

In the absence of an explicit selection of the applicable law, the applicable law should be that of the state that has the most significant relationship with the transaction and the parties, based on the place of the contract, the place of negotiation, the place of fulfillment, the location of the object of the contract, and the domicile, residence, nationality, place of incorporation or place of business of the parties.[156]

In the European Union, where the parties to a smart contract are located in different Member States and have not chosen a specific law, the so-called Regulation Rome I can help determine applicable law based on certain principles.[157]

A contract for the provision of services or the sale of goods is governed by the law of the country in which the provider or seller has his habitual residence.[158] Property rights are generally linked to the law of the country where the property is located.[159]

In the case of financial instruments traded in a multilateral trading system, a contract that brings together or facilitates the matching of third party buying and selling interests in financial instruments in accordance with non-discretionary rules and governed by a single law is regulated by the same.[160]

For consumer contracts, the law of the country where the consumer has his permanent address will apply.[161]

In residual cases where the smart contract is not covered by any of the other criteria or where more than one is applicable, the law of the country in which the party performing the characteristic performance has her habitual residence will apply, or otherwise the law of the country with which the contract has the closest connection.[162]

[155] In determining the applicable state law, courts can consider the relationship between the parties and the way the contract was presented, the offer structure, acceptance, and consideration, to assess whether there was a "dominant party" who made a "take it or leave it" offer. See: American Law Institute, Restatement (Second), cit., § 187 and Comments; Chamber of Digital Commerce – Smart Contracts Alliance (2018), p. 29.

[156] See: American Law Institute, Restatement (Second), cit., § 188.

[157] EC Regulation no. 593/2008 on the law applicable to contractual obligations, arts. 4–6.

[158] Thus: EC Regulation n. 593/2008, cit., Art. 4, par. 1, lett. a)–b).

[159] EC Regulation n. 593/2008, cit., Art. 4, par. 1, lett. c).

[160] EC Regulation n. 593/2008, cit., Art. 4, par. 1, lett. h).

[161] See: EC regulation n. 593/2008, cit., Art. 6.

[162] EC Regulation n. 593/2008, cit., Art. 4, par. 2–4.

Beyond these provisions, given the multiple and often new characteristics of the smart contracts,[163] the parties can avoid the uncertainties relating to the applicable law by indicating it in advance in the contract.[164]

Similarly, in terms of jurisdiction,[165] especially until there is sufficient clarity on the implementation of a smart legal contract, the Blockchain platforms or the parties may provide in the smart contracts arbitration clauses, or performance recovery or automatic interruption mechanisms,[166] to further limit the need for recourse to the judicial authority or to facilitate the execution of arbitration or judicial decisions.[167]

4.7 Profiles of Law & Economics

The area of contract law is of particular interest to Law and Economics scholars, since it is the legal regime that applies to the agreements between the parties underlying the trade, which is in turn a socially desirable activity for economic well-being.[168]

The economic function of contract law, as is known, is considered the prevention of inefficient opportunistic behavior between the parties engaged in economic exchanges.[169]

In the Law and Economics literature on contracts, therefore, regarding the mechanisms that determine the optimal amount of cooperation in economic exchanges between individuals, two strands and so two different environments for bargaining are distinguished: one relating to contract law, and the other on the relational mechanisms that induce cooperation between individuals.[170]

A common characteristic between the legal and relational environments of the contracts is that trust, based on the remedies available in the event of default by the

[163] For example, with regard to the design of the related Blockchain platform, to its economic operation, to its technical complexity, to the number of participants, to the geographical location, etc.; see: Arner et al. (2018), pp. 1387 ff.

[164] In the natural language version, since it is not a self-executable clause from the computer code. In this sense, see: Rühl (2019).

[165] For all the reasons of necessary coordination with the legal system highlighted so far, although as said according to the original concept, smart contracts are not put in place with a view to depending on a judicial intervention; see: Savelyev (2017), pp. 20 ff.

[166] For example, to allow the recovery of funds or other assets by giving the smart contract access to certain accounts financed by the parties.

[167] In this sense, see: Herian (2020), p. 23; De Caria (2019), pp. 748–749; Chamber of Digital Commerce – Smart Contracts Alliance (2018), pp. 30 ff.

[168] See, among others: Posner (2011), pp. 29 ff.; Hermalin et al. (2007), pp. 7 ff.

[169] In this regard, see e.g.: Cooter and Ulen (2012), pp. 284 ff. About four centuries ago, Thomas Hobbes described the impossibility of binding agreements in the absence of the law, as a necessary system to ensure that the parties can trust each other; see: Hobbes (1651).

[170] In this sense, see: Eenmaa-Dimitrieva and Schmidt-Kessen (2019), pp. 77 ff.; Posner (2011), pp. 96 ff.

counterparty, is considered as a necessary determinant to push the parties to cooperate and start commercial relationships.[171]

In a legal contractual environment, the parties can draw up contracts including *ex ante* the necessary terms relating to the performance and other obligations that prefigure the remedies imposed by the courts in case of non-performance of the service.

In a relational context, it is the social norms of a community, such as commercial customs or religious rules, which determine the formation and execution of the contract.

In addition, a series of control instruments are available in both environments *ex post* to ensure compliance with the agreements.[172]

With the advent of distributed ledger technologies, Blockchain and smart contracts, a third environment has been identified in the most recent literature, the so-called bargaining without trust, particularly connected to public Blockchains, without a particular legal-social context of protection under which to enter into contracts, since contract law or other instruments for the regulation of contracts are not available or reliable.[173]

From this perspective, the Blockchain's trustless contract environment for smart contracts offers a different alternative for the execution of the contract: the execution through technology.[174]

Before the Blockchain, there were two main mechanisms that helped create the trust needed for economic exchanges: (a) peer-to-peer; (b) Leviathan.[175]

In environments of trust peer-to-peer, the parties entering into an economic transaction trust that the other party will not behave opportunistically, since social norms are in place that encourage both parties to fulfill their obligations.[176]

Leviathan's environments of trust generally refer to trust that is based on centralized coercive power, for example the law applied by administrative or judicial

[171]In this regard, see: Werbach (2018b), pp. 17 ff.; Dasgupta (1988), pp. 49 ff.; Arrow (1972) pp. 357 ff.

[172]See: Eenmaa-Dimitrieva and Schmidt-Kessen (2019), pp. 77 ff.; Dixit (2007), pp. 63 ff.; Baker et al. (2002); Feinman (2000); Eisenberg (1999), pp. 805 ff.; Macneil (1978); Id. (1969), pp. 403 ff. Regarding the so-called relational contracts, see also above in Sect. 3.3.

[173]Thus again: Eenmaa-Dimitrieva and Schmidt-Kessen (2019), pp. 78–79, who mention how in terms of reliability, for example in the case of anonymity, even if there is a contractual right, the identity of the parties or of a party of the contract is not known, so a potential actor may not be able to trace the counterparty against whom to assert their rights.

[174]See: Möslein (2019); Hunn (2019); Leenes (2012); one may also see: Stazi (2020), pp. 319 ff.

[175]In this regard, see: Werbach (2018b), pp. 25 ff.

[176]Peer-to-peer trusted environments are generally limited to cohesive communities that share a common feature such as profession, culture, etc.

bodies,[177] although they can also be generated by private intermediaries who have the power to enforce contracts among the people who refer to them.[178]

On the Blockchain, both permissionless and permissioned,[179] trust between the parties as in the peer-to-peer model, or trust in a central authority or intermediary as in the Leviathan model, is not necessary for economic exchange.[180]

Therefore, smart contracts can lead to exchanges and markets where previously, due to the lack of trust, this was not the case.[181]

In permissioned Blockchains, on the other hand, relationships of trust can also be similar to those in legal or relational contractual environments.[182]

By virtue of their uniform nature, independent of the peculiarities of different jurisdictions and socio-economic contexts, smart contracts can facilitate trade on a transnational level.

Conversely, in a global context, as known by the practice of telematic contracts,[183] contract law would have difficulty in ensuring the application of the agreements, due to the limited and/or complex application of jurisdiction in many cases.[184]

On the other hand, in the face of the efficiency gains deriving from the characteristics of the Blockchain described so far and in the previous paragraphs,[185] smart contracts can also give rise to risks of efficiency losses.

---

[177] In today's societies, Leviathan's trust, that is the law, has intervened to fill the gaps in trust that have been left by the reduction of trust peer-to-peer; on this point, see: Werbach (2018b), pp. 25 ff.; Putnam (2000), pp. 135 ff.

[178] In the digital environment these include, for example, payment processors such as credit card companies, PayPal, or Stripe, which ensure payment and take credit risk in exchange for a commission.

[179] As noted above in Sect. 4.1, the basic technologies that make up the Blockchain—that is: (a) the distributed computer network that maintains a chronological database of all transactions (the register), and (b) the use of cryptographic keys and a network maintenance protocol (the mechanism of consent)—can be designed in different ways depending on the type of Blockchain necessary for the specific purpose. The choice between managing a permissionless or permissioned blockchain has implications for: (1) the identifiability of the people who carry out transactions; (2) the selection of nodes and dimensions of the network, as well as the related costs; (3) the peculiarity of the consent mechanism; (4) the transparency of the block content transactions. See: Eenmaa-Dimitrieva and Schmidt-Kessen (2019), pp. 71 ff.

[180] See: Werbach (2018b), pp. 28 ff.; Reijers et al. (2016). However, on the continuing importance of trust, in programmers, in oracles, etc., see: Herian (2020), pp. 24–25; Zou et al. (2019); DiMatteo and Poncibò (2019), p. 820.

[181] In this regard, see: Werbach and Cornell (2017), p. 333.

[182] See: Eenmaa-Dimitrieva and Schmidt-Kessen (2019), p. 81.

[183] With regard to which see above, in Sect. 2.2.

[184] In this sense, see: Werbach (2018b), pp. 160 ff.; Eenmaa-Dimitrieva and Schmidt-Kessen (2019), p. 82; Bacon et al. (2017), pp. 29 ff.

[185] Regarding which, see: Giancaspro (2017), pp. 830 ff., who notes the possible costs due to computer coding, the risks of its malfunctioning and the understanding of smart contracts by legal operators; McKinney et al. (2018); Kiviat (2015), p. 574; Fairfield (2014).

In this sense, first, the execution of smart contracts takes place even if from a legal point of view the contract is not valid. Therefore, smart contracts do not have the function provided by the courts in the case of traditional contracts to adjust *ex post* the results due to defects *ex ante* in the consent of the parties.[186]

Similarly, from the point of view of legal capacity, whose economic function is to cure market failures deriving from deviations from individual rationality,[187] smart contracts cannot verify whether a party had the ability to enter into a contract, unless there is no identity verification system in place in the case of permissioned Blockchain.[188]

Furthermore, while the automatic nature guarantees the execution of the contract and eliminates the risks of default in many cases, it also makes it difficult to fulfill a contract when it would be efficient.

Sometimes, however, especially in common law countries, in cases where the costs of executing the contract are greater than its value contractual violations are considered efficient and accepted despite the illegality, provided that the defaulting party compensates the damage to the victim.[189]

Also, from the perspective of Law & Economics, therefore, in consideration of the risks of efficiency losses, even in the context of smart contracts traditional judicial control remains a fundamental instrument of corrective action.[190]

References

Allen JG (2018) Wrapped and stacked: 'Smart Contracts' and the interaction of natural and formal languages. Eur Rev Contract Law 14:307–343

Arner DW, Buckley RP, Zetsche DA (2018) The distributed liability of distributed ledgers: legal risks of blockchain. Illinois Law Rev, 1361–1407

Arrow K (1972) Gifts and exchanges. Philos Publ Aff 1:343–362

Bacon J et al (2017) Blockchain demystified. Queen Mary School of Law Legal Studies Research Paper No. 268/2017. https://ssrn.com/abstract=3091218

Baker G, Gibbons R, Murphy KJ (2002) Relational contracts and the theory of the firm. Q J Econ 117:39–84

Benkler Y (2006) The wealth of networks. How social production transforms markets and freedoms. Yale University Press, New Haven

Black J (2002) Critical reflections on regulation. Aust J Leg Philos 27:1–35

Blemus S (2017) Law and blockchain: a legal perspective on current regulatory trends worldwide. Revue Trimestrielle de Droit Financier, 1–15

---

[186] See: Savelyev (2017), p. 19; Werbach and Cornell (2017), pp. 160 ff.

[187] In this regard, see: Cooter and Ulen (2012), pp. 342 ff.

[188] See: Eenmaa-Dimitrieva and Schmidt-Kessen (2019), pp. 83–84, who point out that in any case it would be difficult to imagine how a smart contract can identify a temporary incapacity, for example in case of intoxication.

[189] In this regard, see among others: Posner (2011), pp. 149 ff.; Coleman and Kraus (1986).

[190] See again: Eenmaa-Dimitrieva and Schmidt-Kessen (2019), p. 87; Werbach (2018a), pp. 489 ff.; Id. (2018b), pp. 149 ff.

Bonneau J et al (2015) Research perspectives and challenges for Bitcoin and cryptocurrencies. IEEE Symposium on Security and Privacy, IEEE, Piscatay. https://ieeexplore.ieee.org/abstract/document/7163021

Borgogno O (2019) Usefulness and dangers of smart contracts in consumer and commercial transactions. In: DiMatteo LA, Cannarsa M, Poncibò C (eds) The Cambridge handbook of smart contracts, blockchain technology and digital platforms. Cambridge University Press, Cambridge. https://papers.ssrn.com/sol3/papers.cfm?abstract_id=3350128

Bosco AJ (2019) Blockchain and the Uniform Electronic Transactions Act. Bus Lawyer 74:243–252

Boss AH (1992) Electronic data interchange agreements: private contracting toward a global environment. Northwest J Int Law Bus 13:31–70

Breidenbach S, Glatz F (2018) Rechtshandbuch Legal Tech, 1. Auflage. CH Beck, Munich

Burnham SJ et al (2009) Transactional skills training: contract drafting-beyond the basics. Trans Tennessee J Bus Law 10:253–295

Bustillos M (2013) The Bitcoin boom. The New Yorker: Annals of Technology, April 2013

Buterin V (2013) Ethereum white paper: a next-generation smart contract and decentralized application platform. https://github.com/ethereum/wiki/wiki/White-Paper

Buterin V (2014a) Bitcoin multisig wallet: the future of Bitcoin. Bitcoin Magazine, March 2014. https://bitcoinmagazine.com/articles/multisig-future-bitcoin-1394686504

Buterin V (2014b) DAOs, DACs, DAs and more: an incomplete terminology guide. Ethereum Blog, May 2014. https://blog.ethereum.org/2014/05/06/daos-dacs-das-andmore-an-incomplete-terminology-guides

Buterin V (2014c) Multisig: the future of Bitcoin. Bitcoin Magazine, March 2014. https://bitcoinmagazine.com/11108/multisig-future-bitcoin

Buterin V (2015) On public and private blockchain. Ethereum Blog, August 2015. https://blog.ethereum.org/2015/08/07/on-public-and-private-blockchains

Cardozo Blockchain Project (2018) Research Report #2: "Smart Contracts" & legal enforceability, October 2018. https://cardozo.yu.edu/sites/default/files/Smart%20Contracts%20Report%20%232_0.pdf

Casey AJ, Niblett A (2016) Self-driving contracts. Univ Toronto Law J 66:429–442

Catchlove P (2017) Smart contracts: a new era of contract use. https://papers.ssrn.com/sol3/papers.cfm?abstract_id=3090226

Chamber of Digital Commerce (2016) Smart contracts: 12 use cases for business & beyond a technology, legal & regulatory introduction, December 2016. https://digitalchamber.org/policy-positions/smart-contracts

Chamber of Digital Commerce et al (2018) Joint statement in response to state "Smart Contracts" legislation, April 2018. https://digitalchamber.org/wp-content/uploads/2018/07/Smart-Contracts-letter-cover.png

Chamber of Digital Commerce – Smart Contracts Alliance (2018) Smart contracts: is the law ready? September 2018. https://digitalchamber.org/smart-contracts-whitepaper

Chohan UW (2017) What is a Ricardian contract? https://papers.ssrn.com/sol3/papers.cfm?abstract_id=3085682

Chopra S, White LF (2011) A legal theory for autonomous artificial agents. University of Michigan Press, Ann Arbor

Clack CD, Bakshi VA, Braine L (2016) Smart contract templates: foundations, design landscape and research directions. Cornell University Library. https://arxiv.org/abs/1608.00771

Coase RH (1937) The nature of the firm. Economica 4:386–405

Coleman J, Kraus J (1986) Rethinking the theory of legal rights. Yale Law J 95:1335–1371

Cong LW, He Z (2018) Blockchain disruption and smart contracts. NBER Working Papers 24399. https://papers.ssrn.com/sol3/papers.cfm?abstract_id=2985764

Cooter R, Ulen T (2012) Law and economics, 6th edn. Pearson, London

Cutts T (2019) Smart contracts and consumers. LSE Legal Studies Working Paper No. 1/2019. https://papers.ssrn.com/sol3/papers.cfm?abstract_id=3354272

Dasgupta P (1988) Trust as a commodity. In: Gambetta D (ed) Trust: making and breaking cooperative relations. Blackwell, Oxford, pp 49–72
De Caria R (2019) The legal meaning of smart contracts. Eur Rev Priv Law 26:731–752
De Filippi P, Mauro R (2014) Ethereum: the decentralized platform that might displace today's institutions. Internet Policy Review, August 2014. http://policyreview.info/articles/news/ethereum-decentralised-platform-might-displacetodays-institutions/318
De Filippi P, Wright A (2015) Decentralized blockchain technology and the rise of Lex Cryptographia. https://papers.ssrn.com/sol3/papers.cfm?abstract_id=2580664
De Filippi P, Wright A (2018) Blockchain and the law: the rule of code. Harvard University Press, Cambridge
De Franceschi A (ed) (2016) European contract law and the digital single market. Intersentia, Cambridge
Dell'Erba M (2018) Demystifying technology. Do smart contracts require a new legal framework? Regulatory fragmentation, self-regulation, public regulation. Univ Pa J Law Publ Aff. https://papers.ssrn.com/sol3/papers.cfm?abstract_id=3228445
Diedrich H (2016) Ethereum: blockchains, digital assets, smart contracts, decentralized autonomous organizations. Wildfire, Bristol
DiMatteo LA, Poncibò C (2019) Quandary of smart contracts and remedies: the role of contract law and self-help remedies. Eur Rev Priv Law 26:805–824
DiMatteo LA, Cannarsa M, Poncibò C (2019) Smart contracts and contract law. In: Id (eds) The Cambridge handbook of smart contracts, blockchain technology and digital platforms. Cambridge University Press, Cambridge, pp 1 ff.
Dixit A (2007) Lawlessness and economics: alternative modes of governance. Princeton University Press, Princeton
Eenmaa-Dimitrieva H, Schmidt-Kessen MJ (2019) Creating markets in no-trust environments: the law and economics of smart contracts. Comput Law Secur Rev 35:69–88
Eisenberg MA (1999) Why there is no law of relational contracts. Northwest Univ Law Rev 94: 805–812
Erbguth J (2017) Lösung Blockchain-basierter Konflikte. In: Schweighofer E et al (eds) Trends and communities of legal informatics. Proceedings of the 20th International Legal Informatics Symposium IRIS 2017. Österreichische Computer Gesellschaft, Wien
Essebier BJ, Wyss DA (2017) Von der Blockchain zu Smart Contracts. Jusletter, 24 April 2017
European Bank for Reconstruction and Development, Clifford Chance (2018) Smart contracts: legal framework and proposed guidelines for lawmakers, October 2018. https://www.ebrd.com
European Parliamentary Research Service (2017) How blockchain technology could change our lives, February 2017. https://www.europarl.europa.eu/RegData/etudes/IDAN/2017/581948/EPRS_IDA(2017)581948_EN.pdf
Fairfield J (2014) Smart contracts, Bitcoin bots, and consumer protection. Washington Lee Law Rev Online 71:35–50
Fairfield J (2021) Tokenized: the Law of non-fungible tokens and unique digital property. Indiana Law J (fothcoming)
Farnsworth EA (1967) "Meaning" in the law of contracts. Yale Law J 76:939–965
Feick T, Packer D (2008) EDI (Electronic Data Interchange) for libraries, publishers, and agents: the reality show – SUSHI, ONIX and? Serials Librarian 54:261–264
Feinman JM (2000) Relational contract theory in context. Northwest Univ Law Rev 94:737–748
Finocchiaro G, Bomprezzi C (2020) A legal analysis of the use of blockchain technology for the formation of smart legal contracts. MediaLaws, 111–135
Fischer F (2009) Saving journalism, a farthing at a time. The Guardian, 19 May 2009. http://www.guardian.co.uk/commentisfree/2009/may/18/news-online-payment-journalism
Franco P (2014) Understanding Bitcoin: cryptography, engineering and economics. Wiley, Hoboken
Fries M (2018) Smart contracts: Brauchen schlaue Verträge noch Anwälte? Anwaltsblatt, 86–90

Gambino AM, Stazi A (2021) Contract automation from telematic agreements to smart contracts. Italian Law J 7:97–115

Gambino AM, Stazi A, Mula D (2019) Information and communication law, 3rd edn. Giappichelli, Turin

Gatz F (2017) Blockchain – Bitcoin – smart contracts – Anwendungsmöglichkeiten. In: Blocher W, Heckmann D, Zech H (eds) DGRI Jahrbuch 2016. Otto Schmidt, Cologne, pp 83 ff.

Gergen MP (1992) The use of open terms in contract. Columbia Law Rev 92:997–1081

Giancaspro M (2017) Is a 'Smart Contract' really a smart idea? Comput Law Secur Rev 33:825–835

Goldman Sachs (2016) Blockchain: putting theory into practice. https://github.com/bellaj/Blockchain/blob/master/Goldman-Sachs-report-Blockchain-Putting-Theory-into-Practice.pdf

Governatori G et al (2018) On legal contracts, imperative and declarative smart contracts, and blockchain systems. Artif Intell Law 26:377–409

Graber CB (2012) Internet creativity, communicative freedom and a constitutional rights theory response to "Code is Law". In: Pager S, Candeub A (eds) Transnational culture in the internet age. Edward Elgar, Cheltenham, pp 135–164

Grigg I (2004) The Ricardian contract. In: IEEE (ed) Proceedings of the First IEEE International Workshop on Electronic Contracting, IEEE Computer Society, Washington. http://iang.org/papers/ricardian_contract.html

Grimmelmann J (2019) All smart contracts are ambiguous. Penn J Law Innov 2:1–22

Grundmann S (ed) (2018) European contract law in the digital age. Intersentia, Cambridge

Hadfield GK (1984) Judicial competence and the interpretation of incomplete contracts. J Leg Stud 23:159–184

Hazard J, Haapio H (2017) Wise contracts: smart contracts that work for people and machines. In: Schweighofer E et al (eds) Trends and communities of legal informatics. Proceedings of the 20th International Legal Informatics Symposium IRIS 2017. Österreichische Computer Gesellschaft, Wien, pp 425–432

Heckelmann M (2018) Zulässigkeit und Handhabung von Smart Contracts. Neue Juristische Wochenschrift 71:504–510

Herian R (2018) Legal recognition of blockchain registries and smart contracts. *EU* Blockchain Observatory and Forum. https://www.eublockchainforum.eu/knowledge

Herian R (2020) Smart contracts: a remedial analysis. Inf Commun Technol Law 30:17–34

Hermalin B, Katz A, Craswell R (2007) Contract law. In: Polinsky AM, Shavell S (eds) Handbook of law and economics, vol 1. Elsevier, Amsterdam, pp 3–138

Hobbes T (1651) Leviathan, 1651, repr. CreateSpace, Scotts Valley, 2016

Hsiao JIH (2017) Smart contract on the blockchain-paradigm shift for contract law. US-China Law Rev 14:685–694

Hudson TB, Laudicina DJ (2006) The emerging law of starter interrupt devices. Bus Lawyer 61: 843–854

Hunn PGL (2019) Smart contracts as techno-legal regulation. J ICT 7:269–286

International Swaps and Derivatives Association, Linklaters (2017) Whitepaper on smart contracts and distributed ledger – a legal perspective, August 2017. https://www.isda.org/2017/08/03/smart-contracts-and-distributed-ledger-a-legal-perspective

Jaccard GOB (2017) Smart contracts and the role of law. Jusletter IT, November 2017. https://papers.ssrn.com/sol3/papers.cfm?abstract_id=3099885

Jensen MC, Meckling WH (1976) Theory of the firm: managerial behavior, agency costs and ownership structure. J Financ Econ 3:305–360

Johnson DR, Post D (1996) Law and borders-the rise of law in cyberspace. Stanf Law Rev 48: 1367–1402

Joint Economic Committee Congress of the United States (2018) The 2018 Joint Economic Report – Report of the Joint Economic Committee Congress of the United States on the 2018 Economic Report of the President, Chapter 9: Building a Secure Future, One Blockchain at a Time, March 2018. https://www.congress.gov/115/crpt/hrpt596/CRPT-115hrpt596.pdf, pp 201 ff.

Juels A, Marino B (2016) Setting standards for altering and undoing smart contracts. In: Alferes JJ et al (eds) Rule technologies. Research, tools, and applications – proceedings of the 10th international symposium RuleML 2016. Springer, Cham, pp 151–166
Juels A, Kosba A, Shi E (2016) The ring of gyges: investigating the future of criminal smart contract. In: Weippl E (ed) Proceedings of the 2016 ACM SIGSAC conference on computer and communications security. ACM, New York, pp 283–295
Kasprzyk K (2018) The concept of smart contracts from the legal perspective. Rev Comp Law 34: 101–118
Kaulartz M, Heckmann J (2016) Smart contracts – Anwendungen der Blockchain-Technologie. Computer und Recht 32:618–624
Kiviat TI (2015) Beyond Bitcoin: issues in regulating blockchain transactions. Duke Law J 65:569–608
Kolber AJ (2018) Not-so-smart blockchain contracts and artificial responsibility. Stanf Technol Law Rev 21:198–236
Kõlvart M, Poola M, Rull A (2016) Smart contracts. In: Kerikmäe T, Rull A (eds) The future of law and eTechnologies. Springer, Berlin, pp 133–147
Künnapas K (2016) From Bitcoin to smart contracts: legal revolution or evolution from the perspective of de lege ferenda. In: Kerikmäe T, Rull A (eds) The future of law and eTechnologies. Springer, Berlin, pp 111–113
Lauslahti K, Mattila J, Seppälaä T (2017) Smart contracts – how will blockchain technology affect contractual practices? ETLA Reports No 68, 2017. https://pub.etla.fi/ETLA-Raportit-Reports-68.pdf
Leenes RE (2012) Framing techno-regulation: an exploration of state and non-state regulation by technology. Tilburg Law School Research Paper No. 10/2012. https://papers.ssrn.com/sol3/papers.cfm? abstract_id=2182439
Lessig L (1999) Code and other laws of cyberspace. Basic Books, New York
Lessig L (2006) Code and other laws of cyberspace. Version 2.0. Basic Books, New York
Linardatos D (2018) Smart contracts – einige klarstellende Bemerkungen. Kommunikation & Recht 21:85–92
Linardatos D (2019) Smart contracts: some clarifying remarks from a German legal point of view. https://papers.ssrn.com/sol3/papers.cfm?abstract_id=3193588
Macneil IR (1969) Whither contracts? J Leg Educ 21:403–418
Macneil IR (1978) Contracts: adjustment of long-term economic relations under classical, neoclassical, and relational contract law. Northwest Univ Law Rev 72:854–905
Marrella F, Yoo CS (2007) Is open source software the new Lex Mercatoria? Vanderbilt J Int Law 47:807–837
McJohn SM, McJohn I (2017) The commercial law of Bitcoin and blockchain transactions. Uniform Commercial Code Law J 47:187 ff.
McKinney SA, Landy R, Wilka R (2018) Smart contracts, blockchain, and the next frontier of transactional law. Washington J Law Technol Arts 13:313–347
Mik E (2017) Smart contracts: terminology, technical limitations and real world complexity. Law Innov Technol 9:269–300
Möslein F (2019) Legal boundaries of blockchain technologies: smart contracts as self-help? In: De Franceschi A et al (eds) Digital revolution – new challenges for law. CH Beck, Munich, pp 313–326
Muka Tshibende LD (2019) Contract law and smart contracts: property and security rights issues. Eur Rev Priv Law 26:871–883
Mukherjee A (2018) Smart contracts – another feather in UNCITRAL's Cap. Cornell Int Law J Online, February 2018. http://cornellilj.org/smart-contracts-another-feather-in-uncitrals-cap
Nakamoto S (2009) Bitcoin: a peer-to-peer electronic cash system. https://bitcoin.org/bitcoin.pdf
Ogilvie JWL (1992) Defining computer program parts under learned hand's abstractions test in software copyright infringement cases. Mich Law Rev 91:526–570

Pardolesi R, Davola A (2019) What is wrong in the debate about smart contracts. https://papers.ssrn.com/sol3/papers.cfm?abstract_id=3339421
Pfeiffer HKC (1992) The diffusion of electronic data interchange. Physica-Verlag, Heidelberg
Posner R (2011) Economic analysis of law, 8th edn. Aspen Publishers, New York
Prinz W, Schulte AT (eds) (2017) Blockchain und Smart Contracts: Technologien, Forschungsfragen und Anwendungen. Fraunhofer-Gesellschaft, Stuttgart
Putnam R (2000) Bowling alone: the collapse and revival of American Community. Simon & Schuster, New York
R3, Norton Rose Fullbright (2016) Can smart contracts be legally binding contracts?, November 2016. https://www.nortonrosefulbright.com/en-it/knowledge/publications/a90a5588/can-smart-contracts-be-legally-binding-contracts
Radin MJ (2000) Humans, computers, and binding commitment. Indiana Law J 75:1131–1162
Raskin M (2017) The law and legality of smart contracts. Georgetown Law Technol Rev 1:305–341
Ream J, Chu Y, Schatsky D (2016) Upgrading blockchains. Smart contract use cases in industry. Deloitte Insights, June 2016. https://www2.deloitte.com/insights/us/en/focus/signals-for-strategists/using-Blockchain-for-smart-contracts.html
Reed C (ed) (2012) Computer law, 7th edn. Oxford, Oxford University Press
Reidenberg JR (1998) Lex Informatica: the formulation of information policy rules through technology. Tex Law Rev 76:553–593
Reijers W, O'Brolchàin F, Haynes P (2016) Governance in blockchain technologies & social contract theories. Ledger 1:134–151
Rejeb A, Keogh JG, Treiblmaier H (2019) Leveraging the internet of things and blockchain technology in supply chain management. Future Internet 11:1–22
Reyna A et al (2018) On blockchain and its integration with IoT. Challenges and opportunities. Futur Gener Comput Syst 88:173–190
Rohr JG (2019) Smart contracts and traditional contract law, or: the law of the vending machine. Cleveland State Law Rev 67:71–88
Rühl G (2019) Smart contracts und andwenbares Recht. In: Braegelmann TH, Kaulartz M (eds) Rechtshandbuch smart contracts. CH Beck, Munich, K. 12
Ryan P (2017) Smart contract relations in e-Commerce: legal implications of exchanges conducted on the blockchain. Technol Innov Manag Rev 7:14–21
Savelyev A (2017) Contract law 2.0: 'Smart' contracts as the beginning of the end of classic contract law. Inf Commun Technol Law 26:116–134
Scholz LH (2017) Algorithmic contracts. Stanf Technol Law Rev 20:101–169
Schrey FJ, Thalhofer T (2017) Rechtliche Aspekte der Blockchain. Neue Juristische Wochenschrift 70:1431–1436
Segrave K (2012) Vending machines: an American social history. McFarland, Jefferson
Sklaroff JM (2017) Smart contracts and the cost of inflexibility. Univ Pa Law Rev 166:263–303
Sokolov M (2018) Smart legal contract as a future of contracts enforcement. https://papers.ssrn.com/sol3/papers.cfm?abstract_id=3208292
Splinder G, Woebbeking MK (2019) Smart contracts und Verbraucherschutz. In: Braegelmann TH, Kaulartz M (eds) Rechtshandbuch smart contracts. CH Beck, Munich, K. 11
Stazi A (2004) La pubblicita commerciale on line. Giuffrè, Milan
Stazi A (2019) Automazione contrattuale e "contratti intelligenti". Gli smart contracts nel diritto comparato. Giappichelli, Turin
Stazi A (2020) Genetically modified organisms and sustainable development: regulatory approaches, access to resources and traceability. BioLaw J, 127–149
Steinmetz F (2017) Blockchain technology and the future of temporary employment. Medium, March 2017. https://blog.hacking.law/Blockchain-technology-and-the-future-of-temporary-employment-51ff7062b6
Surden H (2012) Computable contracts. UC Davis Law Rev 46:629–700

Svikhart RT (2017) Blockchain's big hurdle. Stanf Law Rev Online, 70:100–111. https://review.law.stanford.edu/wp-content/uploads/sites/3/2017/11/70-Stan.-L.-Rev.-Online-100-Svikhart.pdf

Szabo N (1994) Smart contracts. http://www.fon.hum.uva.nl/rob/Courses/InformationInSpeech/CDROM/Literature/LOTwinterschool2006/szabo.best.vwh.net/smart.contracts.html

Szabo N (1996) Smart contracts: building blocks for digital markets. www.fon.hum.uva.nl/rob/Courses/InformationInSpeech/CDROM/Literature/LOTwinterschool2006/szabo.best.vwh.net/smart_contracts_2.html

Szabo N (1997) Formalizing and securing relationships on public networks. First Monday. http://firstmonday.org/ojs/index.php/fm/article/view/548/469

Szostek D (2019) Blockchain and the law. Nomos, Baden-Baden

UK Government Chief Scientific Adviser (2016) Distributed ledger technology: beyond blockchain. https://assets.publishing.service.gov.uk/government/uploads/system/uploads/attachment_data/file/492972/gs-16-1-distributed-ledger-technology.pdf

Unsworth R (2019) Smart contract this! An assessment of the contractual landscape and the Herculean challenges it currently presents for "Self-executing" contracts. In: Corrales M, Fenwick M, Haapio H (eds) Legal tech, smart contracts and blockchain. Perspectives in law, business and innovation. Springer, Berlin, pp 17–61

Wallach DA (2014) Bitcoin for rockstars: how cryptocurrency can revolutionize the music industry. Medium, December 2014. https://medium.com/backchannel/bitcoin-for-rockstarsca8366802f9

Wang J, Lei C (2019) Will innovative technology result in innovative legal frameworks? Smart contracts in China. Eur Rev Priv Law 26:921–942

Weber R (2019) Smart contracts: do we need new legal rules? In: De Franceschi A et al (eds) Digital revolution – new challenges for law. CH Beck, Munich, pp 299–312

Wendehorst C (2016) Consumer contracts and the internet of things. In: Schulze R, Staudenmayer D (eds) Digital revolution: challenges for contract law in practice. Hart-Nomos, Baden-Baden, pp 189–224

Werbach K (2018a) Trust, but verify: why the blockchain needs the law. Berkeley Technol Law J 33:489–550

Werbach K (2018b) The blockchain and the new architecture of trust. MIT Press, Cambridge-London

Werbach KD, Cornell N (2017) Contracts Ex Machina. Duke Law J 67:313–382

Williamson OE (2002) The theory of the firm as governance structure: from choice to contract. J Econ Perspect 16:171–195

Woebbeking MK (2019) The impact of smart contracts on traditional concepts of contract law. JIPITEC 10:106–113

Zeno-Zencovich V (2021) "Smart contracts", "granular norms" and non discrimination. In: Busch C, De Franceschi A (eds) Algorithmic regulation and personalized law. CH Beck/Hart/Nomos, Munich/Oxford/Baden-Baden, p 264-278

Zhan F (2016) Town crier: an authenticated data feed for smart contracts. In: Weippl E (ed) Proceedings of the 2016 ACM SIGSAC conference on computer and communications security. ACM, New York, pp 270–282

Zou M, Cheng G, Soria Heredia M (2019) In code we trust? Trustlessness and smart contracts. Soc Comput Law J, April 2019. https://www.scl.org/articles/10493-in-code-we-trust-trustlessness-and-smart-contracts

Chapter 5
Elements, Pathologies, and Remedies of Smart Contracts

5.1 Identity and Capacity of Contracting Parties

With reference to the identity of the contracting parties of a smart contract, it should first be noted that they are generally not required to be identified.[1] They are represented by an online address, which creates difficulties in identifying the counterparty, indicated merely by means of a progressive number.

This is problematic because a contract in a legal sense requires that the parties have the ability to contract, or can request a legal representative, for example of a company.

Moreover, the human counterparty could be very remote in a chain of smart contracts. Consequently, the party may not recognize or know its counterpart.[2]

Therefore, smart (legal) contracts should obligatorily contain the name of the counterpart and/or the platforms should allow effective identification processes. In this perspective, then, the smart contract should be considered validly concluded as long as it is possible to trace the counterpart to a specific natural or legal person.[3]

Since smart contracts have no means of testing capacity, they can be entered into by minors, drunks, or any other incapable person. So, people who in the real world lack the ability to sign a contract, could potentially do so through a smart contract.

However, in the absence of capacity, the counterparty could invalidate the execution and/or transfer through the legal remedy of the action of unjustified enrichment and technically through an inverse transaction. On the other hand, in practice these solutions meet the obstacle mentioned above of the difficulties of

[1] In practice, Ethereum and most of the Blockchain platforms for smart contracts currently available do not verify identity and ability to contract. Therefore, anyone could open an account and enter into contracts without having sufficient capacity to do so.

[2] See: Durovic and Janssen (2019), p. 768; Sokolov (2018), p. 27; Jaccard (2017), p. 21; Wagner and Weber (2017), p. 69.

[3] In this sense, see: Jaccard (2017), p. 22.

A. Stazi, *Smart Contracts and Comparative Law*,
https://doi.org/10.1007/978-3-030-83240-7_5

identification of the counterparty to be sued, due to the fact that mostly users are identified through mere cryptographic strings of letters and random numbers.[4]

From a comparative point of view, in general, both in civil law, for example in France[5] and Italy,[6] but also in common law, such as in the US,[7] England,[8] Australia, etc., a minor cannot enter into a contract because she has no capacity.

In common law, for example in English and Australian systems, limited exceptions are made to the rule that a minor cannot contract, for example in the case of "necessity" of goods or services to keep the minor in her status or condition.[9]

In all other cases, as in the US,[10] or in France and Italy,[11] the contract can generally be voidable at the request of the minor.

Since the parties of a smart contract can be, and indeed often will be, unknown to each other, there is a very real risk that a party may inadvertently contract with a minor. In this regard, elaborate verification procedures may be necessary to determine the age before entering a transaction on a Blockchain, although these may be difficult to carry out given the complexity of the checks necessary to ascertain the age of the contracting party.[12]

Moreover, the assessment of the binding nature of such a contract would depend on the jurisdiction or the jurisdictions in which it was formed, that is, for example, in the common law systems, if the contract fell within one of the foreseen exceptions.[13]

A related problem occurs when one party contracts with another party on the assumption that the counterparty is who she claims to be, while in reality she is someone else who has appropriated her digital identity and possibly her amount of cryptocurrency.

---

[4] In this regard, see: Durovic and Janssen (2019), p. 768, who inter alia reply to the observation that the contracting parties of a smart contract are technically not even the people but only the cryptographic private keys that represent the same; Werbach and Cornell (2017), p. 371, highlighting that private keys do not act alone but on the basis of instructions from human beings; Jünemann and Kast (2017); Schrey and Thalhofer (2017).

[5] See Arts. 1123–1124 *Code Civil.*

[6] See Art. 2 of the Civil Code.

[7] All but the United States establish 18 as the age of majority, except Alabama (19), Nebraska (19), and Mississippi (21).

[8] Following the ratification of the United Nations Convention on the Rights of the Child, approved by the United Nations General Assembly on 20 November 1989 and ratified by Italy with law of 27 May 1991, n. 176.

[9] In this regard, see: Chapple v Cooper (1844) 13 M & W 252; 153 ER 105.

[10] See: Restatement (Second) of Contracts (1981) art 14; Casey v Kastel 237 NY 305 (1924).

[11] See respectively: Art. 1146 ff. of the French *Code Civil* and Arts. 1425–1426 of the Italian Civil Code, on which see e.g.: Franzoni (2005); Bell et al. (1988), pp. 425 ff.

[12] See: Sokolov (2018), p. 27; Werbach and Cornell (2017), pp. 48 f.

[13] On this point, for example, it was argued that it would be questionable to suggest that a purchase of a cryptocurrency, for example, could be considered "necessary", since, at first glance, it is not vital for the subsistence of the minor; see.: Giancaspro (2017), p. 834.

According to the doctrine of error in the Italian and French legal systems, for example, an error can void an agreement in which it influences the very essence of the same.[14]

In the United States, a contract can generally be voided at the discretion of the misled party, if the other party was aware of it—as in the case of identity theft—and the execution of the contract would be unreasonable.[15]

Under English and Australian law, in cases where the parties do not contract in attendance and one of them is mistaken about the identity of the other at the time of signing the agreement, the contract is void under common law.[16]

Thus, the potential ease with which identity theft and/or financial fraud can be committed through digital technologies gives rise to the risk that many transactions through smart contracts may be voidable.

Furthermore, the potentially transnational dimension of smart contracts, with parts and effects in different jurisdictions, makes difficult the compensation process for damaged parts and sanctions for defaulting ones.[17]

5.2 Contract Formation and Meeting of the Minds

In relation to smart contracts, consent is manifested by signing the transaction in a cryptographic way. In this regard, more than in the form of consent,[18] the main question lies in the fact that the computer code represents an obscure language for most human beings.[19]

From a legal point of view, as noted above, the question of understanding computer language is often filled with the form of consent expressed through so-called click-wrap agreements. However, the assessments regarding their validity in court are not yet unambiguous.[20]

In this perspective, we can distinguish between situations, depending on whether the smart contract on the Blockchain is the only existing contract as the parties have never reached an oral agreement or entered into a written document, or there is an oral or written agreement next to or that includes the smart contract.

In the first case, the computer code represents the only proof of a legal relationship between the parties. Therefore, it is not clear whether the contract and/or its

[14] See: Art. 1130 ff. of the French *Code Civil*; Art. 1429 ff. of the Italian Civil Code.

[15] In this sense, see: Restatement (Second) of Contracts (1981) art 153; Gethsemane Lutheran Church v Zacho 258 Minn 438 (1960); Maryland Casualty Co v Krasnek 174 So 2d 541 (1965).

[16] See: Cundy v Lindsay (1878) 3 App Cas 459; Shogun Finance Ltd v Hudson (2003) UKHL 62. This is the case known as "unilateral mistake".

[17] In this regard, see: Giancaspro (2017), p. 835.

[18] See, among others: Xoudis (2012).

[19] In this regard, in addition to referring below, see again: Giancaspro (2017), pp. 830 ff.

[20] In this sense, in addition to referring above to Sect. 3.2, see: Jaccard (2017), p. 22.

clauses have been well understood by them, but based on both the principle of freedom of form and the ever wider regulatory acknowledgments,[21] the contract can still be considered valid.[22]

In this context, the entire process of proposal or offer, acceptance and existence of consent takes place only on the Blockchain. In case of uncertainty on the content, the rules that require to interpret the will of the parties must be applied, and in the event of non-compliance, declare the nullity of the contract or clauses without consent.[23]

In the second case, in which there is an oral or paper version alongside or that includes the smart contract, the first can be considered hierarchically higher than that expressed in the computer code, similarly to what is considered for the interpretation of the click-wrap agreement in relation to the main contract.[24]

Some scholars believe that coexistence with an off-chain contract should become a good practice whenever the contract is of some relevance.

In fact, the automatic compilation of a smart contract in human-readable language is quite easy. In this way, the parties can verify that consent has been given on the specific content of the contract.[25] On the other hand, this practice—especially if applied for simpler transactions—could risk reducing the advantages of using smart contracts in terms of speed and saving of transaction costs.

As regards the requirement of meeting of wills, the cryptographic signature of both parties appears sufficient to satisfy it, while in the absence of both signatures a bilateral contract, but possibly unilateral, should not be considered concluded.[26]

The conclusion of the contract, therefore, can be considered to have occurred when the smart contract has been signed cryptographically by both parties (and not when it is registered on the Blockchain).[27]

The initial phase of a contractual agreement relating to a smart contract can therefore be similar to that of traditional contracts, with the parties that must agree on a series of contractual terms, or closer to standard contracts in the case of a smart contract unilaterally prepared by one of the contracting parties.[28]

The rules on proposal/offer and acceptance do not in themselves represent an obstacle to the recognition of smart contracts as legally binding.

First, in view of the objective evaluation of the offer and acceptance, as well as the behavior of the parties,[29] the sending of the cryptographic private keys of the

---

[21] With regard to which see above in Sect. 4.5.

[22] See, for example: Swiss Federal Council, Rapport du Conseil fédéral sur les monnaies virtuelles en réponse aux postulats Schwaab (13.3687) et Weibel (13.4070) du 25 juin 2014, p. 11.

[23] See: Jaccard (2017), pp. 22–23; Eggen (2017), p. 8.

[24] In this sense, see: Giancaspro (2017), p. 834; Winiger (2012).

[25] See: Hazard and Haapio (2017), pp. 2 ff.

[26] In these terms, see: Eggen (2017), p. 7.

[27] Thus: Jaccard (2017), p. 23.

[28] See: Raskin (2017), p. 322.

[29] See, among others: Kaulartz and Heckmann (2016), p. 621. In case law, see: Smit v. Hughes (1871) LR 6 QB 597, 607.

contracting parties to commit resources in a smart contract based on Blockchain is the proof of a commitment.[30]

The publication of the contract on the chosen Blockchain platform appears configurable as a proposal/offer, and the acceptance of the other party by means of its own cryptographic key will therefore configure an acceptance.[31]

Similarly to what happens in the context of electronic bargaining *tout court*, depending on the circumstances, the publication of the message by the proposing party on the Blockchain can be considered similar to an advertisement and therefore a mere invitation to treat,[32] or otherwise, where the terms of the transaction are specified, configure a real contractual proposal/offer.[33]

Furthermore, the publication may, depending on the preferences of the proposer/offerer and the permissioned or permissionless characteristics of the Blockchain, constitute a proposal to a specific recipient or an offer to the public.[34]

The contractual proposal or offer to the public is followed by the acceptance of a counterparty,[35] which can also occur—very frequently—through conclusive behavior, especially by uploading a digital asset to the smart contract,[36] such as a sum of a cryptocurrency or a digital representation[37] of an offline asset, which provides an unequivocal communication of acceptance of the proposal or the offer.[38]

---

[30]Thus: Werbach and Cornell (2017), p. 368; Sokolov (2018), pp. 23–24.

[31]In this sense, see: Finocchiaro and Bomprezzi (2020), pp. 117–119; Durovic and Janssen (2019), p. 762.

[32]United Nations Convention on the Use of Electronic Communications in International Contracts. New York, November 23, 2005, Art. 11. See: Kaulartz and Heckmann (2016), p. 621.

[33]See: Durovic and Janssen (2019), p. 762. In the same perspective regarding telematic commercial communication, one may see: Gambino et al. (2019), pp. 157 ff.; Stazi (2004), pp. 16 ff. and 173 ff.

[34]For a comparative framework, with particular regard to the English, US, and Australian common law, see: Madir (2018), pp. 7 ff.; Chamber of Digital Commerce – Smart Contracts Alliance (2018), pp. 15 ff.; R3, Norton Rose Fullbright (2016), pp. 27 ff. For an analysis of the issues posed by smart contracts in the Chinese system, see: Wang and Lei (2019).

[35]On this point, critically speaking, especially on the accepting party's understanding of the content of the proposal/offer, see: Wang and Lei (2019), p. 930; Söbbing (2018), p. 46.

[36]In this regard, see among others: Hojnik (2017); Quah (2003).

[37]Through a so-called token (about which, one may see above in Sect. 4.1).

[38]Provided that according to the procedure and terms requested by the bidder; in this sense, see for example in US law: UCC §2-206 (1) (a) (1); in the French system: Cass. 1re civ., July 1, 2015, No. 14-19,781, Court of Appeal of Paris, February 4, 2016, No. 13-21057. Among scholars, see: Madir (2018), pp. 7–8; Catchlove (2017), p. 11; Durovic and Janssen (2019), pp. 762–3, who propose the example of a proposer/offerer of a smart contract which states that she will transfer ownership of a car for the sum of ten Ethereum. The proposer/offerer prepares the contract, uploads it to the Blockchain together with the digital token that represents the car and the cd. gas with which the payment is made for the loading of the contract. This upload constitutes a proposal or offer. Subsequently, a subject that is willing to accept will upload the ten Ethereums to the smart contract, thereby expressing their acceptance/adhesion. The smart contract will detect the loading of the sum and will automatically transfer it to the proposer's/offerer's wallet, while at the same time transferring the token to the counterparty that loaded the ten Ethereums. The proposer/offerer will not

Therefore, acceptance can take place either through the execution of a specific service, or through authorization to transfer a consideration or digital asset by entering a cryptographic key. In both cases, there is a clear act of acceptance, which can be an execution of the terms in a unilateral contract or a signature by entering the personal cryptographic key.[39]

From what has been highlighted so far, it is clear that currently smart contracts are sometimes unilateral contracts, which promise that a certain fee will be paid for a certain performance/service, or vice versa a payment will be made for the latter.

Therefore, the acceptance is substantiated in the fulfillment of the performance/service or in the payment of the consideration provided in the smart contract.[40]

The offer and the contractual acceptance, then, can be considered expressed, in the light of the regulations in force at transnational level, by data messages stored in a Blockchain.[41]

These are defined in the UNCITRAL Model Electronic Commerce Act as information generated, sent, received, or stored by electronic, optical, or "similar" means. This definition sembra applicable to both traditional communication techniques and digital communications, including smart contracts.[42]

The United Nations Convention on the Use of Electronic Communications in International Contracts, then, with regard to the formation of a contract, provides the principle of functional equivalence, under which the execution of a contract by an automated system cannot be denied for the only reason that no natural person intervened in each of the actions carried out by the system itself.[43]

A smart contract satisfies the contractual principles of being a "writing" if the information it contains is accessible for later reference. The signature requirement is met if: (a) it is obtained by a method that identifies the person who approved the

---

have to confirm that she has received the sum, the token will be transferred automatically without any verification or discretion by the proposer/offerer.

[39] See: Jaccard (2017), p. 22; Szczerbowski (2018), p. 336. See also: Carlill v. Carbolic Smoke Ball Co Ltd (1892) *1 QB 256*, 262. Finocchiaro and Bomprezzi (2020), pp. 118–119 points out that if the declaration of the offeree does not refer to all the terms of the offer or does not consent to the precise terms of the offer, it is not an acceptance but rather a counteroffer. Consequently, the offeree would need to upload a new smart contract and upload it to the blockchain (thus becoming the offerer).

[40] In this sense, see: Durovic and Janssen (2019), p. 763, who notes that on the whole the rules on the offer and acceptance will not pose fundamental problems for the formation of smart contracts, since the procedure for the formation of these agreements includes the elements of the offer and acceptance.

[41] See e.g.: Finocchiaro and Bomprezzi (2020), pp. 120–121; R3, Norton Rose Fullbright (2016), p. 22.

[42] UNCITRAL Model Law of Electronic Commerce with Guide to Enactment, 1996, Arts. 2 (a) and 11 and par. 31.

[43] United Nations Convention on the Use of Electronic Communications in International Contracts. New York, cit., Arts. 8 and 12. On the topic, on top of what has been said above in Sect. 2.3, see: Ooi (2019).

information contained in the data message; (b) the method adopted is reliable and reasonable in the light of the circumstances and of any relevant agreement.[44]

The subscription requirement can be difficult to fulfill for smart contracts since the "signature" could only be a code entered into the software by one of the contracting parties.

Moreover, the purpose of a signature is to ensure that the signatory party intended to contract,[45] while a fully electronic environment without any human intervention can make it extremely difficult to establish an intent according to traditional rules.[46]

On the other hand, the smart contracts meet the originality and integrity requirements of the data messages provided for in the Model Law on electronic commerce,[47] given the characteristics of tamper resistance and tendential unchangeability of the Blockchain.[48]

The Model Law on Electronic Transferable Records, which allows the use of these registers[49] for transferable instruments, including bills of lading, bills of exchange, and receipts of deposit, provided that the electronic record meets the purposes and functions of the transferable instrument,[50] requires the guarantee of the singularity of the document and the use of a reliable method for identifying and checking the record.[51]

In the case of smart contracts, on the one hand, providing an absolute guarantee of non-replicability may not be technically possible since the data is stored on multiple nodes on the Blockchain scattered in various jurisdictions.

On the other hand, this technology appears to be able to replace the registry administrator with an algorithm that guarantees that the tokens registered in it are subject to the exclusive control of the holders of the relative private keys.[52]

As always in the case of electronic signatures, it is possible that a private key may be intentionally or accidentally disclosed and, given the absence of a physical monitoring mechanism, an algorithm will be able to monitor only the insertion of the private key and not by whom it is used.[53]

---

[44] See: UNCITRAL Model Law of Electronic Commerce with Guide to Enactment, cit., Arts. 6–7.

[45] See UNCITRAL Model Law of Electronic Commerce with Guide to Enactment, cit., par. 56.

[46] Thus: Mukherjee (2018).

[47] See again: UNCITRAL Model Law of Electronic Commerce with Guide to Enactment, cit., Arts. 8–10.

[48] In this sense, see: Mukherjee (2018).

[49] A transferable register is a document that authorizes the holder to claim fulfillment of the obligation indicated in the document and to transfer the right to execute. See: UNCITRAL, Model Law on Electronic Transferable Records, 2017, Art. 2.

[50] Thus: UNCITRAL, Model Law on Electronic Transferable Records, cit., Art. 1 (1).

[51] UNCITRAL, Model Law on Electronic Transferable Records, cit., Arts. 10–11 and par. 189–190 of the Explanatory Note. Since it embodies the right to claim the execution of one obligation by another, it is essential to prevent multiple complaints about the same obligation.

[52] See: Takahashi (2016), p. 209.

[53] On this point, see: Mukherjee (2018).

Even in the case of smart contracts signed with electronic signature, the remedies of procedural law aimed at the eventual disavowal of private writing remain unaffected.

This, also with specific regard to the existence of a mandate to sign in the sense of legitimacy for use of the signature device, which is decisive for the authenticity of the subscription and its compliance with the declaratory will of the mandator-holder of the device.[54]

In disregarding the subscription, the party against whom the computerized writing was produced will be invested with the burden of proof to the contrary. In this regard, she will have to use the computer verification procedure, to demonstrate that the signing by a third party is occurred outside the control sphere of the device owner.[55]

The Electronic Records Model Law also requires a reliable method to be used to identify the signatory person to meet the signature requirement.[56]

A signer can use a pseudonym, but the distributed registry system must have the ability to link it to a real name to meet the signer identification requirement, since some reports or actions require mandatory links to real names.[57]

In civil law, for example in Italian and French law, it is essential to establish consent to the contract through a meeting of wills, identifying a proposal/offer by a party to do or not to do something, as well as a corresponding acceptance.[58]

The United States Uniform Commercial Code provides that an offer to enter into a contract must be interpreted as an invitation to accept in any way and by any reasonable means in the circumstances.[59]

Pursuant to English and Australian regulations, an offer is similarly characterized by an indication of the willingness of one party to be bound by the terms of a promise it made to another party, with a choice for the latter between acceptance and rejection of the proposal.[60]

[54] See e.g.: Ricci (2003), pp. 230 ff. and 282 ff.

[55] As for example in the case of the innocent loss of the device with production in court of the theft or loss report and the timely notification to the service provider for the revocation of the certificate. This, however, without prejudice to the obligation of compensation of damages by the apparent author against the third party for fault in violation of the obligations of safekeeping and personal use of the signature device.

[56] See: UNCITRAL, Model Law on Electronic Transferable Records, cit., Art. 9.

[57] UNCITRAL Model Law on Electronic Signatures with Guide to Enactment, 2001, par. 29. For example, pseudonyms shall be linked to real names to appeal against a promissory note. The explanatory notes also suggest that to link pseudonyms to a real name, it is possible to rely on factual elements outside the distributed registry system.

[58] See e.g., Art. 1321 ff. of the Italian Civil Code and Art. 1101 ff. of the French Code Civil.

[59] Thus: Uniform Commercial Code, art 2-206.

[60] See Stover v Manchester City Council (1974) 1 WLR 1403; Brambles Holdings Ltd v Bathurst City Council (2001) 53 NSWLR 153.

The unequivocal consent to the offer, therefore, confirms that it has been formally accepted and that a "meeting of minds" has occurred.[61]

In identifying the moment when a contractual proposal/offer was submitted to and accepted by the counterparty, it should be considered that smart contracts are generally initiated through messages sent using the public key infrastructure via an Internet connection, similarly to emails.[62]

Thus, it is necessary to determine whether a proposal/offer has been validly presented and accepted. The main question that arises is whether acceptance occurs when the party trying to purchase the goods transmits its proposal/offer, once it has been received and authenticated through the consent of the network users, or once it has been coded and added to the Blockchain.[63]

The answer may lie, according to the legal system, in a broad interpretation of the rules of the dispatch or of the receipt of acceptance previously recalled regarding telematic contracts.[64]

Although these rules do not refer to the concept of smart contracts, it can be assumed that the rules remain valid and applicable also in this context. So, according to the dispatch rule, the contract is concluded when the offeree sends the acceptance after having signed it with her private key. According to the receipt rule, the contract is concluded when the transaction of acceptance reaches the offerer's node.[65]

In fact, the authentication through consent by users and the insertion on the Blockchain are logically subsequent steps to the transmission of the proposal/offer and acceptance, which must be considered legally binding regardless of their validation events on the adopted platform.

The moment of the contractual obligation will arise when the wills meet in a legal sense through the exchange of proposal/offer and acceptance, and not that of the execution of the program in a technical sense.

The reference to the effects predefined by the parties, then, must not be understood in the literal sense as jointly set by them, but, always in compliance with the provisions of the legal system, can be traced, as appropriate, to both the bilateral or plurilateral contract scheme, or to that of the contract unilaterally prepared by one of the parties and accepted by the other or by the other.[66]

Furthermore, on the Blockchain platform, the possibility of a promise of a donation would be carried out irrevocably in the same way as other smart

[61] See: Scriven Bros & Co v. Hindley (1919) 3 KB 564; in doctrine, see: Giancaspro (2017), p. 832.

[62] See: R3, Norton Rose Fullbright (2016), p. 22.

[63] See again: Giancaspro (2017), p. 833.

[64] In this regard, see above, in Sect. 3.1.

[65] See: Finocchiaro and Bomprezzi (2020), p. 121.

[66] The latter hypothesis, however, in common law facilitates the solution of the issues relating to consideration, which can be identified in re ipsa in the service performed by the accepting counterpart; on the point, see: Carlill v. Carbolic Smoke Ball Co Ltd (1892) 1 QB 256, 265.

contracts.[67] This does not mean, however, that such contracts make gifts legally enforceable.

As noted above, not all smart contracts are contracts, and the fact that a gift through such an instrument is irrevocable does not mean that it is legally valid. A donor who has changed her mind could invoke the refund pursuant to the unjustified enrichment remedies, even if the liberal payment would make the recovery substantially more complex.[68]

5.3 Intention to Create Legal Relations, Exchange of Promises, and Form of Contract

In commercial relations, the intention to create legally binding relationships is presumed following the meeting of wills in both civil and common law,[69] and must eventually be denied by the party claiming that there is no such intention.[70]

Therefore, for any smart contract entered into in commercial contexts, the intention to create a legal constraint can be presumed, regardless of whether it is a transaction between businesses or between businesses and consumers.

On the other hand, some scholars believe that by entering into a smart contract the contracting parties opt for an alternative regulation system to contract law,[71] so there may not be a real intent to create legal relationships.

However, they also admit that if the result the parties achieve is substantially the same as that governed by traditional contracts, the nature of the relationships can be considered the same.[72]

Even if the parties believe that court intervention will not be necessary since the execution of the smart contract is guaranteed by its technology, this does not exclude[73] the intention of a legal relationship, which justifies the fulfillment of the contractual performance and prohibits the request for the return of what has been carried out as undue payment or unjustified enrichment.[74]

---

[67] See: Werbach and Cornell (2017), p. 370.

[68] In this sense, see: Durovic and Janssen (2019), pp. 766–767.

[69] Referring to objective criteria; see for example, in English case law: RTS Flexible Systems Ltd v Molkerei Alois Müller GmbH & Co KG (2010) UKSC 14, ¶45; Empro Mfg. Co. v Ball-Co Mfg., Inc, 870 F.2d 423, at 425 (7th Cir. 1989); Taylor v Johnson (1983) 151 CLR 422. Among scholars, see e.g.: Madir (2018), pp. 9–10; Sokolov (2018), pp. 21–22.; R3, Norton Rose Fullbright (2016), pp. 27 ff.

[70] See, for example: Esso Petroleum Limited v. Commissioners of Customs and Excise (1975) UKHL 4.

[71] In this regard, see: Werbach (2018), pp. 507 ff.

[72] In this sense, see: Savelyev (2017), pp. 128 ff.

[73] Although with some effects limited in practice.

[74] Thus: Durovic and Janssen (2019), p. 767.

Furthermore, the fact that the parties do not wish to enforce their smart contracts in court does not amount to wishing that if they end up before a court, they will not be confirmed by it.

In the practice of concluding a smart contract, however, usually if the proposal/offer has been accepted it has also started to be executed. So, it is very unlikely that a reasonable party would not consider it a binding and applicable agreement.[75]

In any case, a party that wants to ensure the formalization of an intention to create a legal relationship can do so through the stipulation of a contract in traditional language that accompanies the one drafted, or in which the part drafted in computer code is inserted, even by limiting itself to declare its legal validity.[76]

In common law, while some scholars acknowledge that the smart contracts in the meaning accepted here imply a sort of mutual promise and consideration,[77] others affirm that they do not contain an exchange of promises, as usually happens in traditional contracts, and is required for valid consideration.[78]

Moreover, this finding—which can be shared to the extent that it is not generalized to all smart contracts, which, as mentioned above, can also expressly include the exchange of promises—does not prevent the scholars themselves from reaching the conclusion that smart contracts are legally valid contracts.

Those scholars, in fact, acknowledge that smart contracts, even if they do not contain promises in themselves, are aimed at modifying the rights and obligations of the contracting parties, and that an agreement can be considered a contract even if it does not include specific promises to be made.[79]

As is known, the parties express their will through the act of entering into a contract, and are therefore bound by the modifications of rights and obligations resulting from it. Moreover, contract law recognizes immediate execution contracts, which are executed immediately upon conclusion.[80]

In general, contractual freedom allows contracting parties to draw up the contract in any form and language they wish, including the computer code.[81]

---

[75] See: Catchlove (2017), p. 11.

[76] In this regard, see: Durovic and Janssen (2019), pp. 767–768.

[77] See: Sokolov (2018), pp. 20–21.; Raskin (2017), pp. 322–323.

[78] In this perspective, see: Werbach and Cornell (2017), p. 340.

[79] In this sense, again: Werbach and Cornell (2017), pp. 341 and 370. Regarding the existence of the consideration in similar cases, see: Currie v. Misa (1876) LR 1 App Cas 554, in which it was stated that: "A valuable consideration, in the sense of the law, may consist either in some right, interest, profit, or benefit accruing to the one party, or some forbearance, detriment, loss or responsibility, given, suffered, or undertaken by the other".

[80] See: Savelyev (2017), p. 129, who concludes—in a less convincing way—that it is probably more correct to say that the main consequence of the conclusion of a smart contract is not the establishment of obligations but the self-limitation of certain rights by technical means.

[81] See, among others: Szczerbowski (2018), p. 335; Jünemann and Kast (2017), p. 533; Kaulartz and Heckmann (2016), p. 622; Kaulartz (2016), p. 204. This, except in the case of relations between professionals and consumers, as to which, see below in Sect. 5.5.

Similarly to what happened in the past with the progressive adaptation of contract law to the new communication methods and technologies, it was noted earlier that a similar adaptation to smart contracts is underway, in some systems through regulatory interventions *ad hoc*.[82]

As in the case of the vending machine, in which a contract is formed when the coins are inserted into the machine, the fact that the subsequent execution process occurs without human intervention does not preclude the formation and existence of a legally binding contract.[83]

Regarding the question of the intelligibility of the contractual content,[84] except for the hypothesis in which both parties participate in the drafting and/or understand the terms written in the computer code, problems arise if at least one of the contracting parties does not understand the computer code but concludes the smart contract.[85]

In this case, the party itself could try to support *ex post* the existence of an error and request the cancellation of the contract.

Some scholars believe that in contracts drawn up by one of the contracting parties it is reasonable to attribute to the same the burden of proof of understanding of the computer code by the other.[86]

However, this option has so far been rejected, for example in German law pursuant to § 119 (1) BGB, or in Italian law pursuant to Art. 1429 of the Civil Code, believing that the risk of the conclusion of a contract without knowing the underlying computer code lies with the parties, according to the principles of self-responsibility and entrustment.[87]

The rules governing contract law both in civil and common law refer to the form of the contract, sometimes providing for legal requirements relating to the need for a specific form *ad substantiam* or to ensure particular guarantees.

In common law and in the civil law codes inspired by the French *Code Civil*, the rules of form belong to contract law, while the Civil Codes inspired by the German BGB regulate the form in the general part of the code.

---

[82] More or less necessary, as also highlighted above in Sect. 4.5. For a reconstruction of the various approaches adopted so far in different legal systems, see: R3, Norton Rose Fullbright (2016), pp. 22 ff.

[83] In this sense, see: Durovic and Janssen (2019), pp. 764–765, who recall what has been established in this regard in Thornton v. Shoe Lane Parking (1978) 2 QB 163 (Lord Denning MR), and R (Software Solutions Partners Ltd) v. HM Customs & Excise (2007) EWHC 971, par. 67.

[84] From which, moreover, as is known, contracts drawn up in natural language are not exempt; see: Madir (2018), pp. 10–11, who also notes that, for example, in the German legal system the validity and binding nature of a contract is not affected by the lack of understanding of the German language (see: Bundesarbeitsgericht, 5 AZR 252/12 (B), 19 March 2014); International Swaps and Derivatives Association, Linklaters (2017), p. 17.

[85] See again: Durovic and Janssen (2019), pp. 764–765.

[86] Thus: Szczerbowski (2018), pp. 336–337.

[87] In this regard, see: Gambino (1997), pp. 83 ff.; Jünemann and Kast (2017), p. 533; Kaulartz and Heckmann (2016), p. 622. In common law, for an approach aimed at reconciling the doctrine of error and responsibility, see: Ooi (2019).

Two forms are currently the most used in practice: the written form which requires a material form with the signatures of the parties, and various forms of electronic communication which contain only an identity declaration, the so-called documentary form.[88]

In addition to the written form and the documentary form, there are rules which allow electronic documents if they use special technical solutions provided by third parties certified by the state, such as electronic signatures, to combine the strong evidentiary role of the written form and the ease of transmission allowed by the documentary form.[89]

The smart contracts recorded on the digital support of the Blockchain platforms, as such, do not allow contracting parties to make declarations in writing, but possibly in documentary form where there are two elements: (1) the drafting of the declaration as a document; (2) the identifiability of the author of the declaration.

The first requirement, according to the above-mentioned UNCITRAL principle of functional equivalence, appears satisfied by the smart contracts since the declarations are recorded in a distributed ledger, which constitutes an informative support that allows the dispatch, receipt, reading and signature of the content.

In smart contracts, the offerer and the offeree link some data, that is, the private keys, to the transaction data and approve the information included in the latter data, giving rise to a proposal/offer and an acceptance.[90]

Regarding the identification requirement, the declarations registered on Blockchain are labelled by the addresses of the accounts, a series of numbers and letters that does not indicate a specific person, but allows their identification.[91]

As is known, to be effective, contracts must be legally certain, and as mentioned above, this raises important questions in the context of smart contracts.[92]

The more complex the context in which the contract and the intent of the parties fit, the more probable the contractual conditions will be ambiguous or imprecise, and they will therefore generate a greater need for interpretation in the event of a dispute.

---

[88] In this regard, see among others: Szczerbowski (2018), p. 335, who highlights that the written form is usually preferred by the parties in contracts of considerable economic value, while they opt for the documentary form in contracts where it is important to reduce transaction costs; moreover, the written form is generally considered to be a better proof than the documentary form, although in fact the courts evaluate the evidence on a case-by-case basis.

[89] On electronic documents and electronic signatures, in addition to what was noted above in Sect. 3.2, one may see: Gambino et al. (2019), pp. 26 ff.

[90] According to the EU e-IDAS Regulation, for example, such signatures can be considered simple, advanced, or qualified electronic signatures, depending on whether the data that they include are uploaded/signed according to the requirements of simple, advanced, or qualified signatures. Finocchiaro and Bomprezzi (2020), pp. 130–133.

[91] In this sense, see: Szczerbowski (2018), p. 336.

[92] See, in particular: Giancaspro (2017), pp. 830 ff.

In such cases, reliance on contracts drawn up in computer code will prove to be rather difficult and natural language will be more efficient in formulating and describing the intent of the parties and their respective obligations.[93]

Moreover, as noted above, it must be considered that in practice there is a tendency to adopt the approach of split contracting or hybrid agreement, with the contextual drafting of a natural language contract together with a copy in computer code, or with the inclusion in the contractual text of some codified and self-executable parts.[94]

In fact, the drafting of the contract generally takes place through a web interface, that is, a module which contains, on the one hand, the text in natural language, on the other, the parameters that can be programmed in computer code, relating to any information to be collected from external sources, any conditions to which execution or modification is subject, and the automatic execution mechanism.[95]

The latter is aimed at ensuring that execution takes place according to the encoded data, based on the information entered in the contractual form by the will expressed by the contracting parties, or through a *sui generis* negotiation expressed with the legal and/or technical support of the respective consultants, or unilaterally prepared by one of the contracting parties and accepted by the other through electronic signature.[96]

Furthermore, in European Union this method of concluding the smart contract, together with its tracing back to the *genus* of telematic contracts, makes it possible that the smart contract complies with the rule of Art. 11 of Directive 2000/31/EC

---

[93] In this regard, see: Finocchiaro and Bomprezzi (2020), p. 123; Cannarsa (2019), p. 779; Run and Ying (2018), p. 95; Sklaroff (2017), pp. 291 ff.; Catchlove (2017), p. 16. In particular, the other party should have the opportunity to understand the moment in which she is going to enter into a contract; see: McKinney et al. (2018), p. 326, who propose an "execute" button; O'Shields (2017), p. 186, for an "I agree" button. On the problems of interpretation and costs that would result in the translation into natural language of smart contracts written in computer code, see: Wang and Lei (2019), p. 930; Grundmann and Hacker (2017), p. 279; Xiaojing (2018), p. 4.

[94] In this regard, in addition referring above to Sect. 4.2, see in particular: De Filippi and Wright (2018), pp. 76–78; Madir (2018), p. 12; Dutch Blockchain Coalition (2017), p. 23. One may also see: Gambino and Stazi (2021).

[95] Often referred to in technical jargon as a smart contract, but which from a legal point of view actually constitutes only the part relating to the automatic execution.

[96] For an example, one may see the smart contract form proposed by the start-up Trakti—of which for this book, the author interviewed the CEO to deepen the functioning of smart contracts in practice—available on: https://www.trakti.com. Another hypothesis that could appear similar but falls within the unilateral acts is that of the so-called time stamping, hypothesis of use of the Blockchain aimed at attributing temporal certainty to a specific act or fact; for an example, it can be seen: https://www.bernstein.io. Furthermore, the improperly called smart contract execution mechanism can also be used to execute individual clauses and not an entire negotiating facility, for example for hypotheses of termination or resolution, criminal clauses, etc.; see: Smedlund et al. (2018), p. 82.

regarding the obligation of the service provider to make available to the recipient with an order receipt with essential contractual information.[97]

5.4 Interpretation, Integration, and Subsequent Modification

As regards the interpretation of the smart contract, where reference is made to it having regard exclusively to the codified part, it can be considered inflexible and interpretable in one way only: based on the computer code, precisely.[98]

In this sense, smart contracts could therefore be considered inflexible and unable to adapt to changing circumstances or the preferences of the parties.[99]

On the other hand, computer code is a universal language which may facilitate mutual understanding in contractual relations compared to the variety of national languages.[100]

Unlike natural language, computer code does not leave much room for interpretation, so the use of smart contracts could, at least for the part or version of the contract drawn up in codified form, reduce the use of the intervention of the courts in interpretative function.[101]

[97] Directive 2000/31/EC of the European Parliament and of the Council of 8 June 2000 on certain legal aspects of information society services, in particular electronic commerce, in the Internal Market, OJ L 178, 17.7.2000, Art. 11, par. 1–2, pursuant to which: “1. Member States shall ensure, except when otherwise agreed by parties who are not consumers, that in cases where the recipient of the service places his order through technological means, the following principles apply: – the service provider has to acknowledge the receipt of the recipient’s order without undue delay and by electronic means, – the order and the acknowledgement of receipt are deemed to be received when the parties to whom they are addressed are able to access them. 2. Member States shall ensure that, except when otherwise agreed by parties who are not consumers, the service provider makes available to the recipient of the service appropriate, effective and accessible technical means allowing him to identify and correct input errors, prior to the placing of the order”.

[98] In this regard, see: De Filippi and Wright (2018), p. 82.

[99] These characteristics, which can also be considered an advantage as instruments of guarantee of execution, could also be altered through provisions that allow modification of some parts of the contract, for example through information from the oracles or interventions of the parties; see again: De Filippi and Wright (2018), pp. 75 ff.

[100] In this regard, see: Cannarsa (2019), p. 781, according to whom the computer code could progressively replace legal English as a common legal language, drastically reducing the issues related to legal translation.

[101] In this sense, see: Savelyev (2017), pp. 13–14; De Filippi and Wright (2018), p. 78. In view of the economic operation pursued by the parties, particularly the expression of the contractual terms through the computer code can be considered as more suitable for expressing the economic programs that the parties aim to carry out, since it forces them to clearly represent only the objective economic operation they want to implement by translating their common will into specific instructions.

In this perspective, smart contracts appear similar to standard contracts, in the sense that through the codification of information into data they make the interpretation easier and more systematic, with relative advantages in terms of reducing editorial costs.[102]

From a comparative point of view, the interpretation of smart contracts is also relevant from the point of view of the relationship between civil law and common law contracts.

Common law contracts are drawn up in detail and tend to prevent judicial interpretative intervention, while in civil law contracts are generally shorter and based on general legal concepts, leaving the courts an important role in interpretation.

The smart contract stimulates a precise and detailed preparation, so they can bring the patterns of presentation and interpretation towards an approach closer to the common law.[103]

In civil law, questions on the certainty of contractual conditions, for example in Italy and France, have tended to focus on price, goods or services and other essential profiles of the agreement.[104]

In the Italian and French legal systems, a contract must have a specific or determinable object.[105] The Italian and French laws provide the courts with extensive tools in the interpretation of contracts, in which the objective of the coherence of the contract as a whole appears central.[106]

Under US common law, contracts that are indefinite or vague as to their essential terms are generally considered inapplicable.[107] The Uniform Commercial Code, however, provides that sales contracts are applicable even when "one or more terms are left open" on condition that the parties intend to enter into a contract and there is a "reasonably certain basis for providing an adequate remedy".[108]

---

[102] See: De Filippi and Wright (2018), pp. 74–82; on the advantages of data-oriented and computable contracts, see also: Surden (2012). In the same direction, the creation of automated tools for the setting of interpretative rules was also hypothesized, in line with trends already existing in contract law such as the so-called "entire agreement", "four-corner" or "merger" clauses, according to which the entire agreement between the parties can be found within the contract, and any other previous agreement entered into between the parties has no effect. This, moreover, would presuppose the contractual strength, the legal competence and the technical ability of the parties and their consultants to codify their own rules of interpretation. In this regard, see: Cannarsa (2019), pp. 782–783; Werbach and Cornell (2017), pp. 360 ff.; Tjong Tjin Tai (2017a), pp. 4 ff.

[103] So again: Cannarsa (2019), pp. 781–782.

[104] For example, see in the context of sales contracts: Art. 1583 ff. of the French *Code Civil*; Art. 1470 ff. of the Italian Civil Code.

[105] In this sense, see: Arts. 1128 and 1163 ff. of the French *Code Civil*; Arts. 1325 and 1346 ff. of the Italian Civil Code.

[106] See: Art. 1188 ff. of the French *Code Civil*; Art. 1362 ff. of the Italian Civil Code.

[107] See, for example: Laseter v Pet Dairy Products Co 246 F.2d 747 (4th Circ. 1957); Robinson v Wilson, Inc. v Stone 35 Cal. App. 3d 396 (1973); Rosenthal v National Produce Co 573 A.2d 365 (DC App. 1990).

[108] Uniform Commercial Code, Arts. 2-204 (3).

US courts prefer to interpret contracts in a way that gives them meaning and establishes validity, rather than judging them inapplicable due to uncertainty of terms.[109]

In English law, to be binding, the contract must be sufficiently certain in terms of intrinsic clarity and completeness.[110]

Australian courts take a liberal approach and strive to attach meaning to obscure contract terms, deeming the contract inapplicable only where that meaning cannot be clarified.[111]

Other problems of certainty of terms and interpretation may derive from the algorithmic application of clauses that refer to regulatory standards, such as good faith, correctness, reasonableness, etc., or that contain a variation mechanism, which is a common feature in many commercial agreements.

These notions are rather vague and broad, and in any case, they do not perfectly fit the "binary" approach of the computer code. It is not clear, at least so far, how it is possible to code a smart contract to identify the content of these terms in the specific case.[112]

Except for the hypothesis of recourse to an external oracle, the need to insert similar clauses would therefore seem at the moment to make inappropriate the use of smart contracts, which as mentioned are more suitable for the regulation of simple relationships, or possibly to be determined from an economic-quantitative point of view or through objective data also coming from outside.

Smart contracts appear, instead, not so suitable with respect to the general clauses of the legal system, which require discernment and application of the laws which—even in a context that sees the emerging role of computer programmers—are still distinctive features of the human jurist.[113]

In a smart contract, the terms are translated into a computer code that is usually incomprehensible to the lawyer or the average judge.

The reference to the terms in a readable linguistic form in external materials[114]—even where as in common law would be prohibited by the so-called parol evidence

[109] See, among others: American Sugar Refining Co v Newman Grocery Co 284 F. 835 (5th Circ. 1922).

[110] In this regard, see e.g.: G Scammell & Nephew Ltd v HC & JG Ouston (1941) AC 251.

[111] See: Upper Hunter County District Council v Australian Chilling & Freezing Co Ltd (1969) 118 CLR 429.

[112] On this point, see: Cannarsa (2019), p. 780; Giancaspro (2017), pp. 830–831; Farrell et al. (2016), who point out how trying to program similar clauses so that they can be performed computationally is currently science fiction (without the use of a huge amount of code or computing power).

[113] In this perspective, see: Zeno-Zencovich (2019), pp. 7–8; one may also see: Stazi (2019), pp. 119 ff.

[114] As original terms of reference, negotiation notes, email, etc.

rule[115]—is allowed if the terms of the smart contract are completely ambiguous and incomprehensible without reference to these extrinsic materials.[116]

It is also possible to have recourse to reports from external experts, such as qualified programmers, able to decipher the code of the smart contract.

In any case, it is probable that the process of reconstruction of the contractual meaning will be slowed down due to the need to consider both the contractual conditions encoded in the smart contract, and any contextual text in the same in natural language, or the original text containing the contract terms previously drawn up by the parties.[117]

A further example of a factor that can influence the interpretation of the content of a smart contract is that in which it depends on external sources of information, the so-called oracles, for the application of its terms.[118]

In such cases, if external sources do not function properly or become inactive at any stage, the execution of the smart contract may be compromised.[119]

While a non-fulfillment or non-execution of a traditional contract can be corrected in various ways, from self-help to legal action, the guarantee of the correct fulfillment of a smart contract in similar hypotheses can be particularly complex, given the peculiarities of automatic execution and tamper resistance described above.[120]

[115] According to which extrinsic evidence is inadmissible to change a written contract. See, in US law: Restatement (Second) of Contracts (1981) art 213; Uniform Commercial Code (UCC) art 2-202; in English and Australian case law: Goss v Nugent (1833) 110 ER 713; Mercantile Bank of Sydney v Taylor (1891) 12 LR (NSW) 252. In civil law, see also for example Art. 1359 of the French *Code Civil*, although other provisions affect the way in which the evidence can be used towards the parties involved in the relationship.

[116] See in this regard: Reardon Smith Line Ltd v Yngvar Hansen-Tangen and Sanko SS & Co Ltd (1976) 1 WLR 989; Codelfa Construction Pty Ltd v State Railway Authority of New South Wales (1982) 149 CLR 337.

[117] See: Giancaspro (2017), p. 833. It is evident that in the latter case, as noted by the scholars mentioned in Sect. 4.3, the contractual agreement would be found in that original text.

[118] Suppose, for example, that a smart contract of insurance is created to indemnify a homeowner against bad weather damage. The contract could then be scheduled to obtain information related to rainfall, temperature, or other factors from a meteorological agency's website to determine whether the condition for the reimbursement has occurred. See: Werbach (2018), pp. 547 ff.

[119] On this point, see again: Giancaspro (2017), p. 833.

[120] In this regard, see above in Sect. 4.2.

Possible remedies for such hypotheses could be found, for example, in the rectification or modification of the contract,[121] or in common law in the doctrine of frustration.[122]

However, such remedies, on the one hand, could risk leading to the same unsatisfactory conclusion of the contract that was completely vitiated.[123] On the other hand, they could be inapplicable where the risk of technical error is foreseeable and therefore implicitly assumed by the parties as a "serious possibility".[124]

These considerations could lead to setting a slightly higher threshold of self-responsibility than that configurable in traditional contractual relationships.

Nonetheless, given the immaturity of Blockchain technology and the vulnerabilities of smart contracts, it is still questionable that the content of the latter influenced by programming errors is fully understood in most cases.[125]

Another complex issue relates to the profiles of responsibility if a smart contract does not conform to the will of the parties by mistake or simplification of the programmer,[126] or undergoes a spontaneous modification of the code with consequent losses for one or more parties.

Unlike traditional contracts, the code of a smart contract could spontaneously change during its execution and therefore influence the outcome of the transaction.[127]

In this case, or in those in which the error was caused by a third party such as the programmer who incorrectly codes the terms agreed by the parties or an external source of information so-called oracle, liability may not be imputed to any of the parties, or an application of the principles of self-responsibility and entrustment could be chosen.[128]

This, especially in the case of a contract unilaterally prepared by one of the parties, or also for the responsibility of the platform that has made available the smart contract.

---

[121] For instance, in the Italian legal system, see Arts. 1432 and 1450 of the Civil Code. Herian (2020), pp. 27–29, highlights the criticism of cases in which a mistake or bug in the code of a genesis smart contract produces a variety of unintended outcomes in the subsequent agreements performed semi– or fully autonomously, such as those fulfilled machine-to-machine for example as part of a DAO. In such cases, rectification will be incapable of erasing any former version or versions of a disputed instrument, and there can be no choice but to code and execute a new version to overwrite a mistaken smart contract.

[122] Regarding which see e.g.: Macdonald and Atkins (2014), pp. 467 ff.; Chen-Wishart (2010), pp. 307 ff.

[123] Except for what will be said below, in Sect. 5.6–5.7, regarding the remedies applicable to the various hypotheses of contractual pathologies.

[124] For which they could therefore have included provisions covering the event in the contract. In this sense, see: Carter (2013), pp. 774–775. In case law, see: Simmons Ltd v Hay (1964) 81 WN (Pt 1) (NSW) 358.

[125] In this regard, see: Giancaspro (2017), p. 833.

[126] See: Citron (2008), pp. 1249 ff.

[127] On this point, see: DiMatteo and Poncibò (2019), p. 815; Werbach and Cornell (2017), pp. 42 ff.

[128] See e.g.: Madir (2018), pp. 13–14.

One solution would be to believe that execution of the smart contract has become impossible without the fault of either party.[129] In such a case, the contract would be void in its entirety and the parties would be relieved of any future obligations.[130]

5.5 Contract Modularization and Consumer Protection

In commercial relations practice, most contracts consist essentially of modules that legal advisors or contracting parties themselves assemble and customize based on their needs.

Some sections describe trade terms and what is expected to happen in certain circumstances. These operational aspects are those that can be more easily automated in smart contracts.[131]

Other parts of the contract are more strictly legal terms, such as limitations of damages, indemnities, confidentiality and choice of applicable law or forum. In practice, legal advisers often use standard clauses, but adapt and negotiate them for the specific transaction in question.

Looking ahead, these modules could lead to the creation of smart contracts models of reference for certain contractual objectives and contents.[132] In any case, the legal consultants seem destined to maintain an essential role in the customization of the modules or models, in the choice between the options to be used and in the negotiation of controversial terms.[133]

The negotiation and preparation of smart contracts will necessarily require the intervention and collaboration of subjects who, on the one hand, are able to

---

[129] This is the fundamental logic behind the doctrine of the impossibility that occurred in civil law and frustration in common law. See, for example: in Italy, Art. 1463 ff. of the Civil Code; in France, Art. 1231 ff. of the *Code Civil*. In the United States: Restatement (Second) of Contracts (1981) Art. 265; Uniform Commercial Code Articles 2-613-2-615. In England and Australia: Codelfa Construction Pty Ltd v State Railway Authority of New South Wales (1982) 149 CLR 337; David Contractors Ltd v Fareham Urban District Council (1956) AC 696.

[130] In this sense, see: Giancaspro (2017), p. 830.

[131] In this regard, see: Clack et al. (2016), p. 5.

[132] See: Borgogno (2019a), pp. 891–892, who highlights the benefits in terms of cost savings and reliability. Regarding the possible critical issues deriving from the relationship between standard contracts and the limitations of the computer code, see: Cornelius (2018), pp. 1 ff. For an analysis of the protection of weak contractors in standard contracts in the platform economy scenario, see: Smorto (2018).

[133] See: Werbach (2018), pp. 543 ff., who notes that as a consequence the skills required of lawyers should change more and more towards a "legal engineering" perspective, and there are already several initiatives aimed at developing controls of the computer code which expresses legal terms to ensure that the contracts correspond to the intentions of the parties, similarly to the security controls used by the companies engaged in the development of smart contracts (giving several examples of both phenomena).

understand the legal implications of the contractual clauses, on the other, are capable of writing and reading computer code.

Law professionals and IT programmers, therefore, will find themselves collaborating and/or integrating their preparation and professionalism with a notion of the other knowledge, to obtain contracts that are both at the same time smart and legally binding, so to actually respond to the interests of the parties.[134]

In today's practice of smart contracts inserted on permissionless public Blockchain platforms, therefore, there is a significant trend towards the modularization of contractual relationships.

At least not so far, however, there is a push toward their further widespread standardization since, unlike what some scholars have envisioned,[135] in this context the lack of pre-contractual negotiation, the unilateral preparation of the contractual conditions by the proposer/offerer and the formation of the contract through an offer to the public do not represent to date the rule.

Conversely, numerous projects have been developed with the aim of facilitating the creation of smart contracts which are concluded on the basis of the traditional offer and acceptance rules, and modeled on the specific needs of the parties to the individual contractual relationships.[136]

On the other hand, there are also cases of smart contracts relating to unilaterally prepared offers addressed to unspecified recipients and without pre-contractual negotiation, so-called offers to the public.[137] This phenomenon, as mentioned, in perspective could develop increasingly because of the spread of the use of smart contracts in economic relations.

Regardless of the method of conclusion of the contract, for the relations between professionals and weak contracting parties, smart contracts, on the one hand, have the potential to facilitate the protection of the latter as they can automate that by

---

[134] In this regard, see: Ellul et al. (2019); Mik (2017).

[135] See: Durovic and Janssen (2019), p. 768; Tjong Tjin Tai (2017b), p. 182.

[136] In addition to the model previously mentioned proposed by the start-up Trakti, another example is that of LegalThings, available on: https://legalthings.io, aimed at providing a platform for smart contracts in the real estate sector, for which any real estate company can automate and digitize the entire contract lifecycle process. Through a technology called Live Contract, contracts and processes are transformed into company rules and data that allow automation in a decentralized way. Even if the Live Contracts are based on a series of predefined static digital data corresponding to certain contractual clauses and machine instructions, new datasets can be added by the parties that interact with the contract through their public keys, thus providing some margin for pre-contractual negotiation. The contract is considered concluded once all the parties have digitally signed the final version of the agreement, according to the procedure which is itself defined by the parties.

[137] The best-known example of which is currently represented by the marketplace OpenBazaar. This open-source platform is based on a protocol for e-commerce transactions in a completely decentralized market, which allows users to connect directly to the rest of the peer-to-peer network after downloading the software, and participate in transactions such as sellers or buyers, with payments made in a pre-selected cryptocurrency, without intermediaries and therefore without commissions (see: https://openbazaar.org).

eliminating the possibility for professionals to rely on their inertia and the relative failure to activate the rights.[138]

On the other hand, smart contracts also pose relevant questions because of their rigidity and complexity.[139]

Therefore, although doubts have been expressed regarding the compatibility between the general structure of smart contracts and consumer protection,[140] the regulation in force to protect them is in principle applicable, where the requirements for its applicability are met.[141]

Under European contract law, in particular, standard terms are subject to restrictions which may also apply to smart contracts. Some scholars have argued that consumer legislation in principle applies to smart contracts, but have expressed doubts about the applicability of Directive 93/13/EEC on unfair terms, as it would imply an unfair contractual clause in text form that does not would exist in the case of an algorithm.[142]

This objection is not acceptable either because the Unfair Contract Terms Directive and subsequent EU rules to protect consumers require for their application a text document, and because it would be counterproductive if the protection afforded therein could easily be circumvented by converting unfair terms etc. in the computer code of a smart contract.[143]

---

[138] In this regard, in addition to referring to Sect. 4.2, see: Borgogno (2019a), pp. 892 ff.; Id. (2019b), pp. 8 ff., who notes that in this way consumers should not spend resources to ascertain whether they are entitled to compensation, or to incur often excessive expenses with respect to the injury suffered resulting from the dispute resolution procedure. This, highlighting how instead consumers so far have not adequately asserted the rights recognized by the legal systems, especially in the European context, because they are either unaware of it or have difficulty in enforcing it—also due to the amount of information they receive highlighted above in Sect. 3.6—so even if the standardized contracts between businesses and consumers usually contain many mandatory terms in favor of the latter, in practice they are often difficult to exercise given the costs and complexity or criticality of the remedies envisaged. The author also appropriately specifies how, in order to assess when consumer rights can be adequately optimized through smart contracts, a preliminary assessment of the fulfillment of three conditions is required. First, only consumer rights that are not based on ambiguous or abstract terms can be translated into computer code. Second, they must be independent of relational expectations between the parties. Finally, they must be activated on a large scale and in an identical or at least standardized form. For an example that supplements these conditions, therefore, he cites the rights of passengers, also mentioning the need for coordination with external information sources. In a similar perspective, see also: Fries (2018), p. 88; Fairfield (2014). Regarding the issues of individual and collective consumer protection in Europe and the United States, see among others: Di Porto and Zuppetta (2020); Geradin (2015); Ben-Shahar and Schneider (2014); Id. (2011); Bar-Gill and Ben-Shahar (2013).

[139] In this regard, see: Durovic and Janssen (2019), pp. 768 ff.; De Filippi and Wright (2015), p. 26.

[140] In this sense, see: Savelyev (2017), p. 20.

[141] Thus: Durovic and Janssen (2019), p. 769; see also: Buchleitner and Rabl (2017), pp. 12 ff.; Kaulartz (2016), pp. 204 ff.

[142] In this sense, see: Söbbing (2018), p. 46.

[143] In this regard, see: Durovic and Janssen (2019), p. 769.

Others raised the question of the applicability of the same Directive on unfair terms with reference to the fact that not the entire content of the smart contract could be pre-formulated, but some terms could be negotiated individually.[144]

As is known, in contracts with consumers a clause is considered abusive if, despite the requirement of good faith, it causes a significant imbalance in the rights and obligations deriving from the contract to the detriment of the consumer.

However, the fact that certain aspects of a clause or a specific clause have been individually negotiated does not exclude the application of the regulation on unfair terms to the rest of the contract, if a global evaluation of the same indicates that it is still a pre-formulated standard contract.[145]

This regulation seems fully applicable also in the cases in which the clauses of the smart contracts act as standard contractual terms, or the contracts themselves have been unilaterally prepared by one of the contracting parties.

For both cases, the professional has the burden of proving that a standardized clause, or the entire contract prepared by her, have been the subject of individual negotiations with the consumer.[146]

Vice versa where, as it occurs frequently in commercial practice, the use of modules, possibly also prepared by platforms for smart contracts,[147] which have been assembled and customized according to their needs by the contracting parties themselves or by their respective consultants, can be deemed to be outside the scope of the regulation on unfair terms.

Furthermore, Directive 2000/31/EC on electronic commerce[148] and especially Directive 2011/83/EU on consumer rights provide for various rights and related information obligations,[149] for the exercise and respect of which, on the one hand, it appears necessary to use a text written in natural language.[150]

On the other hand, at least in current practice, any contractual forms are usually not drawn up in advance by a party for a multitude of contracts, but are prepared by the suppliers of platforms for smart contracts.

---

[144] See: Kaulartz and Heckmann (2016), p. 622, who also conclude on the applicability of the provisions of the Directive.

[145] See: Directive 93/13/EEC, Art. 3, par. 1–2. In this regard, see: Möslein (2019), p. 15; Id. (2012).

[146] This can be done by producing representative documents of the negotiation signed by them with electronic signatures, or even emails exchanged before the conclusion of the contract if their compliance with the facts represented is not denied. See again: Durovic and Janssen (2019), p. 769.

[147] In this regard, the examples mentioned above in Sect. 5.3.

[148] See: Directive 2000/31/EC, Arts. 5 and 10.

[149] Extended beyond contracts negotiated away from business premises and remotely (see the considerations proposed above in Sects. 2.4 and 3.6). In this regard, see Art. 5 ff. of Directive 2011/83/EU; see: Finocchiaro and Bomprezzi (2020), pp. 124–127; Srivastava (2017); Helberger et al. (2013).

[150] Through the so-called split contracting or hybrid agreement approaches referred to above in Sects. 4.2 and 5.3, or possibly through the provision *ad hoc* in natural language of the information required by the regulation.

Therefore, the professional must verify that the information required by the consumer regulation is entered or adapt the smart contract and/or provide the missing information.[151]

If smart contracts are not individually negotiated, their clauses will be subject to the obligation of good faith provided for in the directive on unfair terms and to the prohibition of giving rise to significant imbalances in the rights and obligations of the parties.[152]

A provision of particular importance for smart contracts is the one in letter q) of the Annex of the Directive,[153] as, due to their self-executive nature, they could limit consumers' right to take actions or appeals or to exercise legal remedies.[154]

Similarly, depending on the specific method in which the computer code is drawn up, further hypotheses listed in the Annex itself may also be highlighted, including those of (1) the exclusion or limitation of the consumer's legal rights against the professional or another party, (2) the provision of a definitive commitment of the consumer while the performance of the professional's services is subject to a condition that depends solely on her will, (3) the obligation of the consumer to fulfill her obligations even in the event of a non-fulfillment of the professional,[155] etc.

The provisions of Art. 5 of the Directive on unfair terms and Articles 7 and 8 of the Consumer Rights Directive, then, require that the pre-formulated terms must always be drafted in simple and understandable language and the professional must provide the consumer with the mandatory information in an appropriate manner to the means of distance communication used in simple and understandable language.

If on the one hand the parties are in principle free to choose any language for the stipulation of the contract, including computer language, in the context of relations between professionals and consumers autonomy in this sense appears to be considerably limited by the rules, as it is difficult to maintain that the computer code is a simple and comprehensible language for consumers.

This, therefore, implies an obligation for professionals to provide consumers with translations of the computer code that are clear and understandable for them, that is usually in natural language.[156]

---

[151] On this point, see: Möslein (2019), p. 15; Heckelmann (2018), p. 507.

[152] See: Fries (2018); Kaulartz and Heckmann (2016), p. 622. Similar considerations can be made, mutatis mutandis, regarding the provisions of EU Regulation 2019/1150 on promoting fairness and transparency for business users of online intermediation services, with the related obligations placed on operators that provide them with transparency on distribution channels and related affiliate programs, as well as ownership, control of intellectual property rights and the parameters that determine positioning.

[153] Which, pursuant to Art. 3, par. 3 of the Directive contains an indicative and non-exhaustive list of clauses that can be declared unfair.

[154] In this sense, see again: Möslein (2019), p. 15.

[155] See: Annex to Directive 93/13/EEC, respectively lett. b), c), o).

[156] In this sense, see again: Durovic and Janssen (2019), p. 770; Söbbing (2018), p. 46; Kaulartz and Heckmann (2016), p. 622; Kaulartz (2016), p. 204.

On the right of withdrawal, to be exercised within 14 working days,[157] in the smart contract it can be implemented by programming the same so that its execution remains suspended within the first 14 days of the conclusion of the contract.

At the end of this period, the smart contract will check whether the condition for exercising the withdrawal exists, and if not, it will give rise to automatic execution.

In this context, the withdrawal becomes a pre-set option within the smart contract, which is provided on the web interface through which the contract with the consumer is concluded and it takes place automatically and without the need for actions aimed at its exercise.[158]

Other recent additional regulations relevant for smart contracts at European level are represented by EU Directives 2019/770 and 2019/771, respectively, on contracts for the supply of digital content and services and for the sale of goods in which such content is incorporated or interconnected and services.[159]

Such Directives provide that the digital content or service or the support good must correspond to the description, quantity and quality provided for in the contract, presenting the functionality, compatibility, interoperability, and other characteristics provided for by the contract, and be adequate for the purposes for which similar digital content or services would normally be used.

This, taking into account any EU and national law and existing technical standards, or in the absence of them the industry specific codes of conduct applicable to the sector.[160]

These provisions, therefore, subject the terms of smart contracts to a correspondence check with respect to what was agreed and of adequacy to the use of the content or service provided, characteristics that must be evaluated, unlike the regulation on unfair terms, not only with respect to regulatory parameters but also to best market practices.[161]

5.6 Automatic Execution, Modifications, and Fulfillment

In many cases, traditional contracts contain provisions that allow respect of the rights deriving from the contract towards a defaulting party. The choice to use these provisions is critically informed by human judgment. Automatic application may

[157] Pursuant to Articles 9 ff. of Directive 2011/83/EU.

[158] Therefore, it will no longer be necessary to send any registered letter, email, or fax.

[159] With regard to which, one may refer to what was noted above in Sect. 2.4.

[160] EU Directive 2019/770, Article 7, lett. a) and Art. 8, par. 1, lett. a); EU Directive 2019/771, Art. 6, lett. a) and Art. 7, par. 1, lett. to).

[161] With respect to the original proposal for a Directive on contracts for the supply of digital content, see: Möslein (2019), pp. 15–16; Giliker (2017), pp. 110 ff.

not be the best course of action, but the smart contract would have no other options.[162]

By virtue of their nature, smart contracts are self-executable, resistant to tampering and tend to be unchangeable. Once entered on the Blockchain, it can be extremely difficult or impossible to access a smart contract and change its code.[163]

These characteristics are considered significant advantages, as they allow to eliminate human error in execution and obtain the guarantee that the data in the Blockchain are valid according to certain predefined system rules.[164]

On the other hand, by virtue of the characteristics themselves, smart contracts present the risk of programming errors and/or incorrect representation of the will of the parties.

These actions may not be reversible, or may require significant efforts to this end, as well as, given the possibility of spontaneous alteration of the computer code, they may give rise to the risk of complex disputes over liability for technical error.[165]

As regards the ancillary elements of the contract such as conditions or terms, vice versa, there are no particular obstacles to their inclusion originally in the smart contract.

Some questions arise regarding specific profiles, such as the retroactive effectiveness of the fulfillment of the condition,[166] which could contrast with the characteristics of smart contracts.

In practice, in the event of a suspensive condition, the contract can only be entered in the Blockchain when the condition is fulfilled, while for the resolutive condition a subsequent restitutive bargain must be accompanied by an *ex nunc* dissolution of the previous contract.

Even the length of the term, relating to a future and certain event, will be usable in the context of smart contracts through a specific provision in the computer code that links the relative legal effect upon its expiry.

---

[162] In a critical view of this rigidity in the case of more complex, relational and/or incomplete contracts, see: Herian (2020); Giancaspro (2017), p. 830; Wang and Lei (2019), pp. 931 ff.; Sklaroff (2017), pp. 291 ff.; Levy (2017); Xiaojing (2018), pp. 3–4.

[163] In this regard, see again: Giancaspro (2017), p. 830.

[164] See: Sklaroff (2017), pp. 279 ff.; Delmolino et al. (2016).

[165] In this sense, see: Giancaspro (2017), pp. 830–831, who reports examples of the significant economic consequences that occurred on the Ethereum platform; Luu et al. (2016), pp. 254 ff.

[166] Wanted by the parties or imposed by law (so-called *condicio iuris*). For example, in the Italian legal system, the retroactivity mechanism on the one hand may not exist due to the will of the parties or to the nature of the relationship, on the other hand it is without prejudice to the acts of ordinary administration carried out in the meantime by the entitled person and the executed performance in contracts with continuous or periodic execution (see Art. 1360-1 of the Italian Civil Code). In the French legal system, see Art. 1304-6 and 1304-7 of the *Code Civil*, which following the 2016 reform eliminated the retroactivity for the suspension condition and not for the resolutive one, except for leaving both parties the right to predict or eliminate it respectively, and in any case maintaining the risk for the debtor and the effectiveness of the conservative and administrative documents.

In verifying the fulfillment of both the condition and the expiration of the term, it may be useful to acquire objective data from the outside through the oracles.[167]

The rigidity of smart contracts can constitute a significant limit for any interventions by public authorities, with a view to guaranteeing compliance with legislative or regulatory provisions, or judicial interventions *ex post* in application of contract law institutions such as, for example, withdrawal or nullity.[168]

The immutability of smart contracts appears to be particularly problematic as regards the system of legal protection with respect to invalid or illegal contracts.[169]

The problem is that a smart contract can enforce an illegal obligation, without the possibility for a judge or anyone to disable it. Therefore, the absence of cancellation or withdrawal mechanisms in the contract code could be potentially harmful, since the smart contract would still be performed although legally non-binding.[170]

However, as mentioned above, there are some technical solutions to prevent similar situations. The first is the destruction of the smart contract through the so-called self-destruction function. This allows parties to eliminate the contract. However, such a remedy could be excessive compared to the problems encountered.

Therefore, other functions have been developed, such as the so-called callcode, enum or other, which can modify the content of the computer code in a more specific way. The use of these functions by the courts could provide an effective tool in resolving the legal issues that arise during or as a consequence of the execution of the contract.[171]

If the smart contracts appear particularly useful because they can guarantee that the contract will be executed, then the creditor's right to the performance is not absolute, and each legal system recognizes that the execution of the contract can be prevented by several external factors.[172]

Civil law systems adopt an approach to contractual contingencies—in line with that envisaged in the Draft Common Frame of Reference[173]—based on the notion of an impediment, force majeure, or impossibility, which causes non-compliance.

German law uses a general notion of liability to delimit force majeure from impediments that arise at the risk of the debtor.[174] Italian and French laws provide

---

[167] Regarding the relevance of oracles to mitigate the rigidity of smart contracts, introduce conditions or terms, etc., but also on any risks in terms of trust and security, see: Mik (2017), pp. 292–293; Wang and Lei (2019), pp. 937–938; Ortolani (2016).

[168] See: Giancaspro (2017), p. 831, who mentions the example of the injunction with the relative complexity of interrupting the execution of the smart contract.

[169] For example, whenever a smart contract has an illegal object, or does not include all the essential elements of the relationship, or does not comply with the formal requirements, or a clause occurs *rebus sic stantibus*.

[170] In this regard, see: Jaccard (2017), p. 24.

[171] On this point, see e.g.: Juels and Marino (2016), p. 158.

[172] See: Tjong Tjin Tai (2018), p. 5.

[173] On which, see: Kotz (2017), pp. 245 ff., along with seeing above in Sect. 3.5.

[174] See the provisions dictated regarding various hypotheses of occurrence to §§ 275–323 BGB. Among scholars, see: Markesinis et al. (2006), pp. 406 ff.; Grundmann (2005).

for more detailed descriptions of the notion of imputation close to what is provided for in the DCFR.[175]

Although at first glance the approach of the English common law seems to differ radically from the DCFR,[176] a more specific evaluation leads in fact to identify a similar basic structure.

While the common law does not recognize a general requirement according to which an impediment must be imputable, opting instead for strict liability, several exceptions to liability are recognized, such as the impossibility or the illegality that occurred. Furthermore, in practice the parties may contractually agree that certain causes are not at the debtor's risk.

Thus, a considerable number of causes of non-fulfillment do not involve liability, producing a result substantially similar to civil law systems.[177] Similarly, US law provides for the changed or unexpected circumstances doctrine, which operates in a similar way.[178]

In smart contracts, some contingencies can be easily foreseeable and programmable in the computer code, where they are part of the smart contract environment, such as in the case of insufficient balance of the cryptocurrency.

Other causes may be more difficult to assess, and possibly require the use of an oracle, such as in the case of ascertainment of the failure of a parcel delivered by a courier, which thus acts as an oracle. Still other causes may be more complex to predict, code and verify, such as strikes, technical failures, etc.

Furthermore, while it is theoretically possible to include long lists of possible contingencies, the determination is further complicated as there may be different relevant causes depending on the type of contract and different ways in which their occurrence can be verified.[179]

A first hypothesis of solution may be the inclusion in the contract of the exception of force majeure, which can be invoked by the debtor and activated by the judgment of an oracle, arbiter, or judge. On the other hand, it has been noted that in this way, in fact, on the one hand an ADR or ODR mechanism is introduced inside the smart contract, on the other such a mechanism interferes with its main advantage, that is, automatic execution.[180]

---

[175] Various rules in this regard are dictated, e.g., in § 280 ff. of the German BGB, 1217 ss. of the French *Code Civil* and Art. 1453 ff. of the Italian Civil Code. See: Tjong Tjin Tai (2018), pp. 8–9.

[176] See, among others: Andrews (2016), pp. 248 ff.; Davies (2016), pp. 170 ff., McKendrick (2016), pp. 702 ff.; Smith (2006), pp. 167 ff.

[177] In this sense, see: Tjong Tjin Tai (2018), p. 11.

[178] See: Fuller and Eisenberg (2006), pp. 510 ff; Kim (2016), pp. 93 ff.; Bix (2012), pp. 81 ff. The general approach to the issue of contingencies is confirmed in international legislation such as Art. 79 of the Vienna Convention on Contracts for the International Sale of Goods, and Arts. 6.2.2, 72.2, and 7.1.7. of the UNIDROIT Principles of international commercial contracts.

[179] In this regard, see: Xiaojing (2018), pp. 3–4; Tjong Tjin Tai (2018), p. 12.

[180] See, also regarding today's ODR difficulties in the international commercial context, see: Wang and Lei (2019), pp. 933 ff.; Kaal and Calcaterra (2018); Tjong Tjin Tai (2018), p. 12. Regarding the usefulness of the provision in smart contracts of dispute resolution mechanisms by courts or

A solution closer to the nature of smart contracts and to the approach adopted as mentioned in most legal systems and contractual practice, may be that of the presumption that the failure is attributable and the possibility of coding a limited set of foreseeable causes of significant contingency.

Any remaining and unforeseen causes would therefore remain the responsibility of the debtor, in accordance with the provisions of most legal systems.[181]

However, it was also highlighted that in the cases of contracts of considerable importance, at least three complications may arise regarding: (1) the determination of the relevant cause, since the breach could derive, for example, from a different previous cause; (2) the distinction of the causes due to the creditor, such as the non-acceptance of the sent package;[182] (3) the adoption of the correct procedure for the notification of the breach, which is not easily programmable in a smart contract.[183]

Therefore, with particular regard to the most relevant and/or complex contracts, an in-depth analysis may be necessary regarding the possible existence of facts that make the imputation of the cause of impediment or justification of the failure to fulfill the obligation configurable or not.

In such cases, however, it is difficult to code all the possibilities of interaction of the causes and to deal with them satisfactorily. Conversely, for simpler contracts or contracts with a low monetary value, the parties could be willing to take on the unknown risks of unexpected causes of violation.[184]

In concrete terms, in smart contracts it seems possible to program: (a) a list of possible causes that are easily identifiable and verifiable through automatic and/or third-party oracles; (b) a presumption that one of these causes, if present in a given period, actually represents the relevant cause of the breach.

Conversely, multiple causality and impediments due to the creditor appear at present to be more complex questions to be addressed.[185]

---

arbitrators whose intervention is programmed in the computer code such as that of external oracles, see: Werbach (2018), pp. 547 ff.; De Filippi and Wright (2015), p. 50.

[181] See again: Tjong Tjin Tai (2018), p. 13, who highlights that the debtor will generally be in the best position to identify the possible risks and causes of non-fulfillment in advance and take precautionary measures or take out insurance against them.

[182] Which, moreover, could be justified for example if the package clearly does not contain the ordered item.

[183] In this regard, see: Tjong Tjin Tai (2017a), pp. 5 ff.

[184] In this sense, see: Tjong Tjin Tai (2018), p. 14.

[185] Thus, again: Tjong Tjin Tai (2018), pp. 14 and 18–19; Id. (2017a), p. 3 ff., who also notes in general that the way in which contractual relationships work in commercial practice—as highlighted in the perspective of the so-called relational theory—is in contrast with the automatic execution and rigidity of smart contracts; on this point, see also: Werbach and Cornell (2017), pp. 367 ff.; Levy (2017). On the other hand, the author adds that in some situations the relational approach may not be valid, such as in the case of remote purchases of low monetary value, related to one-off transactions with little possibility of effective legal protection, so the smart contract with the relative guarantees allows significant advantages.

5.7 Withdrawal, Termination, and Rescission of the Contract

Further peculiarities may arise with reference to the cases of withdrawal attributed by law or contractual clause to one of the contracting parties, which in contracts with continuous or periodic execution can be exercised even after the start of execution,[186] and of the termination as refusal to renewal an automatic duration contract.[187]

In both cases, an *ex-ante* programming of these hypotheses and the related conditions at the time of the conclusion of the smart contract may be considered configurable, possibly against a deposit or promise of a consideration in cryptocurrency.[188]

In this perspective, the withdrawal could therefore be codified subordinating the execution of the smart contract to the moment in which its failure to exercise will be verified,[189] while the termination could be similarly programmed so that, if it has not occurred within the deadline for the renewal, the latter will take place automatically.[190]

The rescission of a contract concluded for example, depending on the civil law or common law system, in a state of need or of danger, misrepresentation, duress or undue influence, which led to unfair conditions, in the context of smart contracts raises the question of how such conditions can be foreseen in the computer code.

In these hypotheses, the imbalance of the synallagma originates from the exploitation of one contracting party to the detriment of the other. Therefore, the aim of the remedy is *restitutio in integrum*.[191]

Since the unfair conditions can be multiple and are not typified, it is generally difficult for a rescission due to a state of danger, duress, or undue influence to be programmed within the smart contract code.[192] However, the technical remedy of self-destruction can help.[193]

---

[186] With regard to services that have not yet been performed or are still in progress.

[187] See, among others: Sacco and De Nova (2016), pp. 1715 ff.

[188] Who will then be automatically transferred to the counterparty at the time of the conclusion of the smart contract or the exercise of the agreed faculty. On the configurability of these hypotheses in smart contracts, see: Sokolov (2018), pp. 31–32, who highlights the relevance of the contextual programming of automatic compensation mechanisms.

[189] Traditionally it is believed that the right of withdrawal is exercised by means of a declaration and not of a behavior that indicates the will not to fulfill; see e.g.: Sacco and De Nova (2016), pp. 1721 ff. On the other hand, in the context of automatic execution, the inclusion of a specific automatic mechanism, possibly following the occurrence of a certain condition, could also be considered configurable for the expression of the withdrawal declaration.

[190] Conversely, if the condition occurs, the program will result in the termination of the contract with the related legal consequences.

[191] See e.g.: Herian (2020), pp. 29–30.

[192] In this regard, see: Tjong Tjin Tai (2018), pp. 12 ff.

[193] See: Herian (2020), pp. 30–31.

In cases of a state of need or misrepresentation, then, such programming can occur in the cases in which the value of the performance can be anchored to precise external parameters, that is, through oracles.

Another question that arises is that of not prejudicing the rights acquired by third parties, a guarantee that is complex if the automatic execution has taken place. In fact, this would leave room only if necessary for an action to repeat the undue and/or to compensate damages.[194]

With regard to the resolution of the contract for non-performance,[195] supervening impossibility or excessive supervening burden, since these constitute objective and therefore verifiable conditions, they can be programmed from the beginning in the smart contract.[196]

In the event of non-fulfillment, the program may provide that if the obligee has not performed his service within a certain date, the contract will automatically be terminated.[197]

On the other hand, because of non-fulfillment, the party may not have an interest in activating the resolution and, if it has not yet fulfilled, want to activate an exception of non-performance,[198] or constitute the debtor in default in the interest of obtaining a late fulfillment.

In the smart contract, this could take place where it is envisaged in the contract form that the creditor of the service will be able to choose which remedy to use.

The impossibility of occurrence, which requires that the performance is absolutely and objectively impossible for reasons not attributable to the debtor or creditor and therefore unpredictable,[199] can be contemplated in the smart contract by acquiring the related information from the oracles.

In the hypothesis of the supervening excessive onerousness,[200] then, the smart contract should first ascertain, by means of oracles, that an extraordinary and

---

[194] On this point, see e.g.: Sacco and De Nova (2016), pp. 1482 and 1506–1507.

[195] Aimed at remedying a subsequent change of the synallagma in the hypotheses of non-fulfillment.

[196] As regards non-fulfillment, for example, think of the provision of an express termination clause or an essential term.

[197] With relative retroactive elimination of the effects of the contract, total or partial in the cases of contracts with continuous or periodic or plurilateral execution, and without prejudice to the rights purchased by third parties (see, e.g., Arts. 1458–1459 of the Italian Civil Code). This elimination, however, in smart contracts will present the difficulty already noted above for termination. The plaintiff may also be entitled to propose further actions for the repetition of the undue and/or for compensation for the damage. Both the French legal system, pursuant to Arts. 1224–1230 *Code Civil*, and the German one, in §§ 325–327 and 346–256 BGB, like the English one, release the case from the necessary judicial ruling.

[198] In French law, see Arts. 1219–1220 *Code Civil* and Court of Appeal of Paris, 28 January 2015, RG n. 10/15692; in the Italian legal system see Art. 1460 of the Civil Code.

[199] See e.g., § 323 BGB, Arts. 1722 and 1790 *Code Civil* and Art. 1463 of the Italian Civil Code, while the major difficulties in admitting the case in English law were remedied by applying the theory of implied conditions.

[200] In implementation of the so-called *rebus sic stantibus* clause, typically in continuous or periodic or deferred execution contracts, even if extended from the case law in several other cases. This,

unpredictable event occurred, and then measure the economic imbalance between the performances.

This can be foreseen from the beginning, for example, at a value higher than a quarter of the value of the consideration, or correspond to a certain quantity or exchange rate.[201]

From the considerations expressed so far, and even more in cases where the contractual pathologies are invalidity and/or non-existence, considering the difficulties of elimination of the effects to which automatic execution gives rise,[202] the smart contracts show their limits related to what are at the same time their main advantages, namely, automatic execution and resistance to tampering.

To resolve or mitigate these critical issues deriving from the automation and rigidity of smart contracts with a view to the application of contractual remedies, first, as previously noted, the technological tools that are being set up, such as the self-destruction or modification through callcode, enum, etc., may help, also allowing the processing of external inputs.[203]

Another possible solution, then, could lie in the use of the permissioned Blockchain platforms, which allow to restrict access to identified users and pre-select nodes that authorize the operations.

In this context, interventions by public authorities, in particular judicial decisions, would have concrete targets. However, in these platforms the main advantages of

however, if the excessive supervening burden—referred to the provision objectively considered and not to the subjective situation of the debtor—does not fall within the normal scope of the contract; see among others: Sacco and De Nova (2016), pp. 1677 ff.; Schönle (1982).

[201] In fact, this hypothesis would be more properly configured as an express termination clause. In fact, through this mechanism, smart contracts could also operate, possibly also with respect to random contracts, in support of the most heavily burdened part, proceeding with a redistribution of risk, a modification of the *quantum debeatur*, or even the dissolution of the contractual obligation, provided that the condition of the offer of *reductio ad aequitatem* has not been met. On the other hand, this saves the provision of renegotiation; regarding which one may refer above to Sect. 3.5 and see e.g.: Pardolesi (1986).

[202] Which, on the other hand, could also be considered a means of carrying out the validation of the contract where the conditions exist. Think in particular of the automatic execution carried out by one of the parties at the same time as acceptance, considering the same—given the peculiarities of smart contracts—as a means of "contextual realization" of the provisions according to which the annulable contract can be validated by the contractor who is entitled to the action of cancellation, through an act containing the mention of the contract and the reason for annulment and the declaration that it is intended to validate it, or if the contractor herself voluntarily executed it, knowing the reason for cancellation; see e.g. Art. 1444 of the Italian Civil Code and: Sacco and De Nova (2016), pp. 1481 and 1545 ff.

[203] In this regard, see: Juels and Marino (2016), pp. 151 ff. Another hypothesis that could be explored is that of the inclusion in the smart contracts, where appropriate, of a reference to external verification—prior to the automatic execution—of clauses or prices of goods or services imposed by law, of which the law provides the inclusion in the contract by law also replacing different clauses agreed by the parties, and which could be referred to as "legal oracles" in smart contracts.

smart contracts—that is, decentralization and automatic execution—are actually missing or diminished.[204]

References

Andrews N (2016) Contract rules: decoding English law. Intersentia, Antwerp

Bar-Gill O, Ben-Shahar O (2013) Regulatory techniques in consumer protection: a critique of European consumer contract law. Common Mark Law Rev 50:109–125

Bell J, Boyron S, Whittaker S (1988) Principles of French law. Oxford University Press, Oxford

Ben-Shahar O, Schneider CE (2011) The failure of mandated disclosure. Univ Pa Law Rev 159: 647–749

Ben-Shahar O, Schneider CE (2014) More than you wanted to know. The failure of mandated disclosure. Princeton University Press, Princeton

Bix BH (2012) Contract law: rules, theory, and context. Cambridge University Press, Cambridge

Borgogno O (2019a) Smart contracts as the (new) power of the powerless? The stakes for consumers. Eur Rev Priv Law 26:885–902

Borgogno O (2019b) Usefulness and dangers of smart contracts in consumer and commercial transactions. In: DiMatteo LA, Cannarsa M, Poncibò C (eds) The Cambridge handbook of smart contracts, blockchain technology and digital platforms. Cambridge University Press, Cambridge. Available at: https://papers.ssrn.com/sol3/papers.cfm?abstract_id=3350128

Buchleitner C, Rabl T (2017) Blockchain und smart contracts. Revolution oder alter Wein im digitalen Schlauch? Ecolex:4–14

Cannarsa M (2019) Interpretation of contracts and smart contracts: smart interpretation or interpretation of smart contracts? Eur Rev Priv Law 26:773–785

Carter W (2013) Contract law in Australia, 6th edn. LexisNexis, New York

Catchlove P (2017) Smart contracts: a new era of contract use. https://papers.ssrn.com/sol3/papers.cfm?abstract_id=3090226

Chamber of Digital Commerce – Smart Contracts Alliance (2018) Smart contracts: is the law ready? https://digitalchamber.org/smart-contracts-whitepaper

Chen-Wishart M (2010) Contract law, 3rd edn. Oxford University Press, Oxford

Citron DK (2008) Technological due process. Washington Univ Law Rev 85:1249–1313

Clack CD, Bakshi VA, Braine L (2016) Smart contract templates: foundations, design landscape and research directions. Cornell University Library. https://arxiv.org/abs/1608.00771

Cornelius KB (2018) Standard form contracts and a smart contract future. Internet Policy Rev 7:1–18

Davies PS (2016) JC Smith's the law of contract, 2nd edn. Oxford University Press, Oxford

De Filippi P, Wright A (2015) Decentralized blockchain technology and the rise of Lex Cryptographia. https://papers.ssrn.com/sol3/papers.cfm?abstract_id=2580664

De Filippi P, Wright A (2018) Blockchain and the law: the rule of code. Harvard University Press, Cambridge

Delmolino K et al (2016) Step by step towards creating a safe smart contract: lessons and insights from a cryptocurrency lab. In: Clark J et al (eds) Financial cryptography and data security. FC 2016 international workshops, BITCOIN, VOTING, and WAHC. Springer, Berlin, pp 79–94

Di Porto F, Zuppetta M (2020) Co-regulating algorithmic disclosure for digital platforms. Policy Soc 40:1–22

DiMatteo LA, Poncibò C (2019) Quandary of smart contracts and remedies: the role of contract law and self-help remedies. Eur Rev Priv Law 26:805–824

[204] On these aspects, one may also see: Stazi (2019), pp. 182 ff.

Durovic M, Janssen A (2019) The formation of blockchain-based smart contracts in the light of contract law. Eur Rev Priv Law 6:753–771
Dutch Blockchain Coalition (2017) Smart contracts as a specific application of blockchain technology. https://www.dutchdigitaldelta.nl/uploads/pdf/Smart-Contracts-ENG-report.pdf
Eggen M (2017) Chain of contracts. Aktuelle juristische Praxis – Pratique juridique Actuelle, pp 3–15
Ellul J, Gauci I, Pace GJ (2019) The truth in the myth of the lawyer-programmer chimera. "DLT Malta: Thoughts From The Blockchain Island". https://papers.ssrn.com/sol3/papers.cfm?abstract_id=3662678
Fairfield JAT (2014) Smart contracts, bitcoin bots and consumer protection. Washington Lee Law Rev Online 71:36–50
Farrell S et al (2016) How to use humans to make "Smart Contracts" truly smart. http://www.kwm.com/en/au/knowledge/insights/smart-contracts-open-source-model-dna-digital-analoguehuman-20160630
Finocchiaro G, Bomprezzi C (2020) A legal analysis of the use of blockchain technology for the formation of smart legal contracts. MediaLaws, 111–135
Franzoni M (2005) Dell'annullabilità del contratto. Art. 1425–1426. In: Il Codice Civile. Commentario founded by Schlesinger P and directed by Busnelli FD, Giuffrè, Milan
Fries M (2018) Smart contracts: Brauchen schlaue Verträge noch Anwälte? Anwaltsblatt, 86–90
Fuller LL, Eisenberg MA (2006) Basic contract law, 8th edn. Thomson West, St. Paul
Gambino AM (1997) L'accordo telematico. Giuffrè, Milan
Gambino AM, Stazi A (2021) Contract automation from telematic agreements to smart contracts. Italian Law J 7:97–115
Gambino AM, Stazi A, Mula D (2019) Diritto dell'informatica e della comunicazione, 3rd edn. Giappichelli, Turin
Geradin D (2015) Collective redress for antitrust damages in the European Union: is this a reality now? George Mason Law Rev 22:1079–1101
Giancaspro M (2017) Is a 'Smart Contract' really a smart idea? Comput Law Secur Rev 33:825–835
Giliker P (2017) Regulating contracts for the supply of digital content: the EU and UK response. In: Synodinou T et al (eds) EU internet law: regulation and enforcement. Springer, Berlin, pp 101–124
Grundmann S (2005) Germany and the Schuldrechtsmodernisierung 2002. Eur Rev Contract Law 1:129–148
Grundmann S, Hacker P (2017) Digital technology as a challenge to European contract law – from the existing to the future architecture. Eur Rev Contract Law 13:255–293
Hazard J, Haapio H (2017) Wise contracts: smart contracts that work for people and machines. In: Schweighofer E et al (eds) Trends und Communities der Rechtsinformatik/Trends and Communities of Legal Informatics, Tagungsband des 20. Internationalen Rechtsinformatik Symposions IRIS 2017. Österreichische Computer, Vienna, pp 2 ff.
Heckelmann M (2018) Zulässigkeit und Handhabung von Smart Contracts. Neue Juristische Wochenschrift 71:504–510
Helberger N et al (2013) Digital content contract for consumers. J Consumer Policy 36:37–57
Herian R (2020) Smart contracts: a remedial analysis. Inf Commun Technol Law 30:17–34
Hojnik J (2017) Technology neutral EU law: digital goods within the traditional goods/services distinction. Int J Law Inf Technol 25:63–84
International Swaps and Derivatives Association, Linklaters (2017) Whitepaper on smart contracts and distributed ledger – a legal perspective. https://www.isda.org/2017/08/03/smart-contracts-and-distributed-ledger-a-legal-perspective
Jaccard GOB (2017) Smart contracts and the role of law. Jusletter IT, November 2017. https://papers.ssrn.com/sol3/papers.cfm?abstract_id=3099885
Juels A, Marino B (2016) Setting standards for altering and undoing smart contracts. In: Alferes JJ et al (eds) Rule technologies. research, tools, and applications – proceedings of the 10th international symposium RuleML 2016. Springer, Cham, pp 151–166

Jünemann M, Kast A (2017) Rechtsfragen beim Einsatz der Blockchain. Kreditwesen:531–536

Kaal W, Calcaterra C (2018) Crypto transaction dispute resolution. Bus Lawyer 73:109–152

Kaulartz M (2016) Herausforderungen bei der Gestaltung von Smart Contracts. Zeitschrift zum Innovations- und Technikrecht:201–206

Kaulartz M, Heckmann J (2016) Smart contracts – Anwendung der Blockchain-Technologie. Computer und Recht 32:618–624

Kim NS (2016) The fundamentals of contract law and clauses. Edward Elgar, Cheltenham

Kotz H (2017) European contract law. Oxford University Press, Oxford

Levy KEC (2017) Book-smart, not street-smart: blockchain-based smart contracts and the social workings of law. Engaging Sci Technol Soc 3:1–15

Luu L et al (2016) Making smart contracts smarter. In: Association for Computing Machinery, CCS '16. Proceedings of the 2016 ACM SIGSAC conference on computer and communications security, ACM, New York, pp 254–269

Macdonald E, Atkins R (2014) Koffman & Macdonald's law of contract, 8th edn. Oxford University Press, Oxford

Madir J (2018) Smart contract: (how) do they fit under existing legal frameworks? https://papers.ssrn.com/sol3/papers.cfm?abstract_id=3301463

Markesinis BS, Unberath H, Johnston A (2006) The German law of contract: a comparative treatise. Hart, Oxford

McKendrick E (2016) Contract law, 7th edn. Oxford University Press, Oxford

McKinney SA, Landy R, Wilka R (2018) Smart contracts, blockchain and the next frontier of transnational law. Washington J Law Technol Arts 13:313–347

Mik E (2017) Smart contracts: terminology, technical limitations and real world complexity. Law Innov Technol 9:269–300

Möslein F (2012) Kontrolle vorformulierter Vertragsklauseln. In: Schmidt-Kessel M (ed) Ein einheitliches europäisches Kaufrecht? Eine Analyze des Vorschlags der Kommission. Sellier, Munich, pp 255–286

Möslein F (2019) Legal boundaries of blockchain technologies: smart contracts as self-help? In: De Franceschi A et al (eds) Digital revolution – new challenges for law. CH Beck, Munich. https://papers.ssrn.com/sol3/papers.cfm?abstract_id=3267852

Mukherjee A (2018) Smart contracts – another feather in UNCITRAL's cap. Cornell Int Law J Online, February 2018. http://cornellilj.org/smart-contracts-another-feather-in-uncitrals-cap

O'Shields R (2017) Smart contracts: legal agreements for the blockchain. N C Bank Inst 21:177–194

Ooi V (2019) Contracts formed by software: an approach from the law of mistake. SMU Center for AI & Data Governance Research Paper No. 2019/02. https://papers.ssrn.com/G3/papers.cfm?abstract_id=3322308

Ortolani P (2016) Self-enforcing online dispute resolution: lessons from Bitcoin. Oxf J Leg Stud 36:595–629

Pardolesi R (1986) Consensual variation of contracts. Italian National Report to the XII International Congress of Comparative Law, Giuffrè, Milan, pp 87 ff.

Quah D (2003) Digital goods and the new economy. CEP discussion paper CEPDP0563, Center for Economic Performance, London School of Economics and Political Science. http://eprints.lse.ac.uk/2236

R3, Norton Rose Fullbright (2016) Can smart contracts be legally binding contracts? https://www.nortonrosefulbright.com/en-it/knowledge/publications/a90a5588/can-smart-contracts-be-legally-binding-contracts

Raskin M (2017) The law and legality of smart contracts. Georgetown Law Technol Rev 1:305–341

Ricci F (2003) Scritture private e firme elettroniche. Giuffrè, Milan

Run Z, Ying L (2018) Impact of smart contracts on Chinese contract system and solutions. South China Financ:93–95

Sacco R, De Nova G (2016) Il contratto, 4th edn. Utet, Turin

Savelyev A (2017) Contract law 2.0: 'Smart' contracts as the beginning of the end of classic contract law. Inf Commun Technol Law 26:116–134
Schönle H (1982) Imprévision de faits futurs lors de la conclusion d'un contrat générateur d'obligations. In: Peter H, Stark EW, Tercier P (eds) Hundert Jahre schweizerisches Obligationenrecht – Le centenaire du code des obligations, Universitätsverlag, Freiburg, pp 413 ff.
Schrey J, Thalhofer T (2017) Rechtliche Aspekte der Blockchain. Neue Juristische Wochenschrift 70:1431–1436
Sklaroff JM (2017) Smart contracts and the cost of inflexibility. Univ Pa Law Rev 166:263–303
Smedlund A, Lindblom A, Mitronen L (2018) Collaborative value co-creation in the platform economy. Springer, Berlin
Smith SA (2006) Atiyah's introduction to the law of contract, 6th edn. Clarendon, Oxford
Smorto G (2018) Protecting the weaker parties in the platform economy. In: Davidson N, Finck M, Infranca J (eds) The Cambridge handbook of the law of the sharing economy. Cambridge University Press, Cambridge, pp 431–446
Söbbing T (2018) Smart contracts und Blockchain-Technologie. IT-Rechts-Berater:43–46
Sokolov M (2018) Smart legal contract as a future of contracts enforcement. https://papers.ssrn.com/sol3/papers.cfm?abstract_id=3208292
Srivastava A (2017) The new EU Consumer Rights Directive: an empirical study on compliance issues by e-tailers. J Bus Law:282–309
Stazi A (2004) La pubblicità commerciale on line. Giuffrè, Milan
Stazi A (2019) Automazione contrattuale e "contratti intelligenti". Gli smart contracts nel diritto comparato. Giappichelli, Turin
Surden H (2012) Computable contracts. UC Davis Law Rev 46:629–700
Szczerbowski JJ (2018) Place of smart contracts in civil law. A few comments on form and interpretation. Proceedings of the 12th annual international scientific conference "New Trends 2017", Private College of Economic Studies Znojmo, pp 333–338
Takahashi K (2016) Blockchain technology and electronic bills of lading. J Int Marit Law 22:202–211
Tjong Tjin Tai E (2017a) Formalizing contract law for smart contracts. ICAIL 2017, Tilburg Private Law Working Paper Series No. 6/2017. https://ssrn.com/abstract=3038800
Tjong Tjin Tai TFE (2017b) Smart contracts en het recht. Nederlands Juristenblad:176–182
Tjong Tjin Tai E (2018) Force majeure and excuses in smart contracts. Eur Rev Priv Law 26:787–904, Tilburg Private Law Working Paper Series No. 10/2018. https://papers.ssrn.com/sol3/papers.cfm?abstract_id=3183637
Wagner AF, Weber RH (2017) Corporate Governance Auf Der Blockchain. Schweizerische Zeitschrift für Wirtschafts– und Finanzmarktrecht 1:59–70
Wang J, Lei C (2019) Will innovative technology result in innovative legal frameworks? Smart contracts in China. Eur Rev Priv Law 26:921–942
Werbach K (2018) Trust, but verify: why the blockchain needs the law. Berkeley Technol Law J 33: 489–550
Werbach KD, Cornell N (2017) Contracts Ex Machina. Duke Law J 67:313–382
Winiger B (2012) Art. 18 n. 1 ss. In: Thévenoz L, Werro F (eds) Commentaire Romand, Code des obligations I, 2nd edn. Helbing Lichten hahn, Basel
Xiaojing Z (2018) Development of smart contracts based on blockchain and their restrictions through the lens of law. Legality Vision (Fazhi Bolan), pp 1 ff.
Xoudis J (2012) Art. 11 n. 78 ff. In: Thévenoz L, Werro F (eds) Commentaire Romand, Code des obligations I, 2nd edn. Helbing Lichten hahn, Basel
Zeno-Zencovich V (2019) Legal epistemology in the age of big data. In: Peruginelli G, Faro S (eds) Knowledge of the law in the big data age. IOS Press, Amsterdam, pp 3–9

Chapter 6
Conclusion

The book analyzed the most relevant evolutions of the relationship between contract and technology, starting from the contract concluded by automatic to focus on today's "smart contracts".

The comparative approach made it possible to focus attention on the main solutions adopted in different legal systems, with particular regard to the circulation of models and ideas, and to the background and peculiarities of their local variations.

In this perspective, the taxonomy of automatic and telematic contracts was first defined, with specific reference to the regulation of online exchanges. The rules adopted respectively in the European Union and in the United States, in particular, were considered as paradigms of the civil law and common law systems.

The regulation of telematic contracts was then reviewed with respect to the main institutions of contract law. Attention was focused on phenomena, such as the evolution of the role of consent in the formation of the contract, the diffusion of contractual incompleteness, the persistent relevance of good faith, the protections in cases of contractual contingencies and standard contracts, and the distinction between technology as an instrument and/or object of the contractual relationship.

Based on these considerations, the analysis focused on the most recent development in this field represented by smart contracts. Through the examination of the characteristics of the distributed ledger technologies, especially the Blockchain technology on which smart contracts are based, the peculiarities of the latter emerged. In particular, the automatic execution and resistance to tampering, give rise at the same time to significant opportunities but and complex legal issues.

A reading was therefore proposed to reconcile smart contracts with comparative contract law, with a view to defining the perimeter and specificities of their legal effectiveness.

To this end, on the one hand, a distinction was made between the case and others potentially related to it. On the other, the first regulatory approaches in comparative law were examined.

Thus, the usefulness of rules that, where necessary, clarify the correct classification of the phenomenon in the different legal systems, was pointed out.

A. Stazi, *Smart Contracts and Comparative Law*,
https://doi.org/10.1007/978-3-030-83240-7_6

The greatest possible coordination or harmonization was highlighted as a key element to allow the full deployment of the potential of smart contracts as a negotiating instrument that is independent of geographical boundaries.

In the same perspective, the feasible options were identified in the current regulatory framework regarding the issues of applicable law and jurisdiction.

Law & Economics considerations were also proposed regarding the potential, risks and protections for various stakeholders, as well as the peculiar attitude of trust, the traditional lintel of contractual relations, in an allegedly trustless context.

With reference to the elements, pathologies, and contractual remedies in smart contracts, the application peculiarities and the main issues that emerge in the regulatory framework of comparative contract law were examined.

The phenomenon of the circulation of algorithms, which is flanked by the circulation of legal models, together with a diffusion of similar ideas regardless of the origin of the authors, require a comparative approach that favors their understanding and application, as harmonized as possible, in line with the transnational nature of the instrument.

With this in mind, first, as regards the identity and capacity profiles of the contracting parties, the opportunity—but also the difficulty—of allowing effective identification processes of the parties to the contract was highlighted. In this perspective, the doctrine of the error and the application complexity of the remedies of voidability and compensation were reviewed.

On the formation of the contract and the meeting of wills, the question of the difficulties of understanding and the risks of error related to the computer code was identified, along with at the same time the practice of drafting a version of the contract in natural language alongside or which includes the smart contract, respectively the so-called split contracting and hybrid agreement.

As for the requirement of meeting of minds, the relevance of the affixing of electronic signatures was highlighted and the possible legal values of the publication of the contract on the Blockchain platform were specified as, depending on the case, an invitation to offer or a contractual offer, to the public or to a specific recipient.

Then, the relationships between smart contracts and their signatures and the traditional concepts of writing and underwriting in international and comparative law were analyzed.

This, considering also, on the one hand, the profiles of procedural relevance, on the other, the criteria for identifying the moment in which the contractual obligation arises.

Regardless of the tendency to reduce the use of the legal system and the debate on the configurability of a real exchange of promises, the existence of the intention to obligate the parties was in any case identified.

In terms of form, in the light of the principle of freedom, the possible configuration of the smart contract as a documentary form was outlined, also recalling the practice of split contracting and the hybrid agreement which provide a contractual text in natural language.

This practice is also relevant for the purposes of interpretation, which, if referred to only the codified part, could be limited by the inflexibility and uniqueness of the computer code.

Furthermore, given the limits just mentioned, smart contracts encourage a precise and detailed drafting, according to an approach close to that of the common law model. By virtue of the universality of the computer code and their characteristics of automation and resistance to tampering, then, smart contracts can facilitate the transnationality of exchanges.

From the point of view of the certainty of the terms, in addition to identifying the solutions that can be used to decipher the computer code, while smart contracts are suitable for the regulation of determined or determinable relationships, also through external oracles, in this context general clauses such as good faith, fairness, reasonableness, etc. are difficult to apply.

With reference to the hypotheses of programming errors, spontaneous modification, malfunctions, or errors of oracles, the peculiar attitude of the different liability profiles and the limits of the contractual remedies available were examined.

Another relevant phenomenon that emerged is the modularization of the contract, which is becoming increasingly widespread in the practice of commercial relationships. In fact, legal consultants or contracting parties use standard clauses, adapting and negotiating them with respect to the specific transaction.

This practice can represent an important alternative to the rigidity of the standardization of the contract, which otherwise could find in smart contracts further extremes, with a relative increase in the negotiation imbalance.

In relationships between professionals and weak contracting parties, smart contracts, on the one hand, make it possible to automate the protection of the latter, overcoming the problem of inertia and the costs of activating their rights. On the other hand, in cases of unilaterally drafted offers, smart contracts can accentuate the contractual imbalance and its consequences due to their rigidity, complexity, and self-execution.

These critical issues, therefore, make the protections provided in the various legal systems with respect to weak contracting parties more relevant than ever, regardless of the different purposes to which they are inspired, such as consumer protection in Europe, market integrity in the US, social control elsewhere, etc.

The characteristics of automatic execution and resistance to tampering, then, were analyzed with regard to subsequent modifications and the fulfillment of the contract.

Given the limitation of smart contracts with respect to the voluntary breach sometimes pursued by the parties in the concrete unfolding of the contractual relationships, some technological options were highlighted for the modification or cancellation of the smart contract.

Such options, in fact, appear necessary with respect to an irreversibility that would otherwise be hardly compatible with risks such as programming errors, spontaneous alterations, invalidity or contractual contingencies, and consequent judicial interventions *ex post*.

Finally, as regards the application of the remedies for withdrawal, termination and rescission of the contract, again with a view to the critical issues deriving from the automation and rigidity characteristics of the smart contracts, the programming options in the computer code and the application peculiarities of such remedies within the same were also examined.

Beyond the conclusions reported so far, a series of questions remain open. Some of them, such as the identifiability of the contracting parties, the possible rigidity of the contractual clauses, and the difficulties of modification or cancellation of the contract, seem to require techno-legal solutions which are at the same time based on technological approaches and allow compliance with the contractual regulation and the application of the relative remedies.

Other issues then, on the one hand, are emerging from the use of smart contracts in specific sectors, such as decentralized finance, art and entertainment, agriculture, etc. On the other hand, the integration of smart contracts with artificial intelligence and the Internet of Things will give rise to contractual developments or modifications deliberated by machines, possibly based on the interaction with data and other external elements.

Such further challenges, as well as those covered in this book, will require an adequate framing of the related legal questions in the system of comparative contract law.

The manufacturer's authorised representative in the EU is Springer Nature Customer Service Centre GmbH, Europaplatz 3, 69115 Heidelberg, Germany. If you have any concerns regarding our products, please contact ProductSafety@springernature.com

Printed and bound by CPI Group (UK) Ltd, Croydon, CR0 4YY
30/09/2026
02225470-0012